P9-DHB-007

CONTENTS

Preface   ix

CHAPTER 1   **Health Education and Health Promotion**   1

    Key Concepts   2
    Health, Behavior, and Health Behavior   2
    Health Education and Health Promotion   6
    Responsibilities and Competencies for Health Educators   10
    Code of Ethics for the Health Education Profession   14
    Health Education Organizations   15
    Basic Vocabulary in Health Education and Health
      Promotion   21
    Role of Theory in Health Education and Health Promotion   28
    Skill-Building Activity   30
    Summary   31
    Review Questions   32
    Website   32
    Glossary Terms   32
    References and Further Reading   33

CHAPTER 2   **Planning Models in Health Education and Health Promotion**   37

    Key Concepts   38
    Differences Between a Model and a Theory   39
    PRECEDE-PROCEED Model   41
    Planned Approach to Community Health Model   46
    The Multilevel Approach to Community Health Model   49
    Intervention Mapping   51
    Assessment Protocol for Excellence in Public Health Model   52
    Comprehensive Health Education Model   53
    Model for Health Education Planning   54
    Model for Health Education Planning and Resource
      Development   55

PEN-3 Model   55
CDCynergy   57
Other Models   58
Skill-Building Activity   58
Summary   62
Review Questions   62
Website   63
Glossary Terms   63
References and Further Reading   63

CHAPTER 3   The Health Belief Model   69

Key Concepts   70
Historical Perspectives   71
Constructs of the Health Belief Model   72
Applications of the Health Belief Model   78
Limitations of the Health Belief Model   80
Skill-Building Activity   82
Summary   83
Review Questions   85
Website   85
Glossary Terms   85
References and Further Reading   86

CHAPTER 4   The Transtheoretical Model   91

Key Concepts   92
Historical Perspectives   93
Constructs of the Transtheoretical Model   94
Phases of Interventions based on the Transtheoretical
    Model   100
Applications of the Transtheoretical Model   100
Limitations of the Transtheoretical Model (TTM)   103
Skill-Building Activity   104
Summary   108
Review Questions   109
Website   109
Glossary Terms   110
References and Further Reading   110

Theoretical Foundations of Health Education and Health Promotion

Theoretical Foundations of Health Education and Health Promotion

Manoj Sharma, MBBS, CHES, PhD
Associate Professor, Health Promotion and Education
University of Cincinnati

John A. Romas, MPH, PhD
Professor and Chair, Department of Health Science
Minnesota State University

JONES AND BARTLETT PUBLISHERS
Sudbury, Massachusetts
BOSTON   TORONTO   LONDON   SINGAPORE

World Headquarters
Jones and Bartlett Publishers
40 Tall Pine Drive
Sudbury, MA 01776
info@jbpub.com
www.jbpub.com

Jones and Bartlett
Publishers Canada
6339 Ormindale Way
Mississauga, Ontario
L5V 1J2
Canada

Jones and Bartlett
Publishers International
Barb House, Barb Mews
London W6 7PA
United Kingdom

Jones and Bartlett's books and products are available through most bookstores and online booksellers. To contact Jones and Bartlett Publishers directly, call 800-832-0034, fax 978-443-8000, or visit our website www.jbpub.com.

Substantial discounts on bulk quantities of Jones and Bartlett's publications are available to corporations, professional associations, and other qualified organizations. For details and specific discount information, contact the special sales department at Jones and Bartlett via the above contact information or send an email to specialsales@jbpub.com.

Production Credits
Acquisition Editor: Jacqueline Geraci
Senior Production Editor: Julie Champagne Bolduc
Associate Editor: Amy L. Flagg
Associate Production Editor: Jennifer M. Ryan
Associate Editor: Patrice K. Andrews
Marketing Manager: Wendy Thayer
Marketing Associate: Meagan Norlund
Manufacturing Buyer: Therese Connell

Cover Design: Anne Spencer
Cover Image: (top) © PhotoCreate/
ShutterStock, Inc., (middle) © Photo
Create/ShutterStock, Inc., (bottom) ©
Photos.com, (background) © Andreas
Guskos/ShutterStock, Inc.
Printing and Binding: Malloy, Inc.
Cover Printing: Malloy, Inc.

Library of Congress Cataloging-in-Publication Data:
Sharma, Manoj.
    Theoretical foundations of health education and health promotion / Manoj Sharma, John A. Romas.—1st ed.
        p. ; cm.
    Includes bibliographical references.
    ISBN-13: 978-0-7637-4948-4 (alk. paper)
    1. Health promotion. 2. Health education. I. Romas, John Albert. II. Title.
    [DNLM: 1. Health Education—methods. 2. Health Promotion—methods. 3. Models, Theoretical. WA 18 S531t 2007]
    RA427.8.T4548 2007
    613—dc22
                                                                                        2007005286
6048
Printed in the United States of America
12 11 10 09 08   10 9 8 7 6 5 4 3 2

CHAPTER 5 **The Theory of Reasoned Action and Theory of Planned Behavior** **115**

Key Concepts 116

Historical Perspectives 117

Constructs of the Theory of Reasoned Action and Theory
of Planned Behavior 118

Applications of the Theory of Reasoned Action and the
Theory of Planned Behavior 124

Limitations of the Theory of Reasoned Action and
Theory of Planned Behavior 126

Skill-Building Activity 128

Summary 131

Review Questions 132

Website 132

Glossary Terms 132

References and Further Reading 132

CHAPTER 6 **Theories of Stress and Coping** **137**

Key Concepts 138

Historical Perspectives 139

Constructs of the Theories of Stress and Coping 142

Applications of the Theories of Stress and Coping 148

Limitations of the Theories of Stress and Coping 152

Skill-Building Activity 152

Summary 156

Review Questions 157

Website 157

Glossary Terms 158

References and Further Reading 158

CHAPTER 7 **Social Cognitive Theory** **163**

Key Concepts 164

Historical Perspectives 165

Underpinnings of Social Cognitive Theory 167

Constructs of Social Cognitive Theory 168

Applications of Social Cognitive Theory 173

Limitations of Social Cognitive Theory 177

Skill-Building Activity   177
Summary   181
Review Questions   181
Website   182
Glossary Terms   182
References and Further Reading   182

CHAPTER 8   Social Marketing   187

Key Concepts   188
Historical Perspectives   189
Differences Between Commercial Marketing and
   Social Marketing   190
Approach and Constructs of Social Marketing   192
Applications of Social Marketing   197
Limitations of Social Marketing   199
Skill-Building Activity   200
Summary   202
Review Questions   205
Website   205
Glossary Terms   205
References and Further Reading   205

CHAPTER 9   Diffusion of Innovations   209

Key Concepts   210
Historical Perspectives   211
Constructs of the Diffusion of Innovations Theory   212
Applications of the Diffusion of Innovations Theory   220
Limitations of the Diffusion of Innovations Theory   222
Skill-Building Activity   223
Summary   225
Review Questions   226
Website   227
Glossary Terms   227
References and Further Reading   227

CHAPTER 10   Freire's Model of Adult Education   231

Key Concepts   232
Historical Perspectives   233

Approach of Freire's Model   234
Constructs of Freire's Model   236
Applications of Freire's Model in Health Education   240
Limitations of Freire's Model   242
Skill-Building Activity   243
Summary   244
Review Questions   246
Website   246
Glossary Terms   246
References and Further Reading   246

Glossary   251

Photo Credits   265

Index   267

PREFACE

We are pleased to present this text on theoretical foundations of health education and health promotion to our readers. It is well known that the field of health education and health promotion has evolved from information dissemination to knowledge-based programs to present-day theory-based, behavior change interventions. Graduate-level preparation of health educators and other public health professionals has been sufficiently influenced by these theory-based inputs.

However, for undergraduate students, "theory" still remains shrouded in mystery. The purpose of this text is to provide an introductory text for undergraduate students, entry-level graduate students, and practitioners working in the field that summarizes common theories from behavioral and social sciences that are being used in health education and health promotion. In compliance with the core competencies for entry-level practitioners described by the National Commission for Health Education Credentialing (NCHEC), this text also serves as a useful resource for those preparing to take the certification examination.

Theoretical Foundations of Health Education and Health Promotion takes an accessible, uniform approach to the theories that are commonly used in health education and health promotion. Theories are discussed in simple language with emphasis on practical application. Each theory is described in a consistent and uniform pattern to help readers grasp the new theory quickly and easily. Each chapter offers several learning tools that will aid in the understanding and application of theory-based, behavior change interventions. Some highlights include:

- Key concepts and chapter objectives begin each chapter and help readers focus their attention and retain important information.
- Chapter summaries conclude each chapter and provide an opportunity for readers to prepare for exams and master key concepts effectively by reinforcing important topics and key terms. Key terms and their definitions are also provided in the glossary at the end of the text.
- Boxed highlights from the theory include quotations from the theorists or other important aspects of the theory that provide a direct flavor of the actual theory.
- For each theory, a discussion on its historical genesis and constitutive constructs is presented. This discussion builds the foundational understanding of

the theory. A clear delineation of the constructs helps readers understand the process by which the theory is reified and used in health education and health promotion. This process of simplification of constructs helps the health education and health promotion student to apply these in designing programs.

- Each discussion of theory is accompanied by a practical skill-building activity in the context of planning and evaluation along with a set of application questions. This activity will assist the student in mastering the application of this theory to community, school, work-site or patient care settings.
- Up-to-date examples of applications from current literature are included throughout the text and serve as ideas for designing interventions and resources for initiating literature review.
- Web exercises on the text's accompanying website, http://health.jbpub.com/foundations, include reliable links to websites related to the theory discussed in the chapter. Each exercise provides interactive activities that directly relate to the chapter content and help students practically apply their new knowledge.

INSTRUCTOR AIDS

We have prepared a set of PowerPoint™ slides for each chapter that instructors can use for classroom lectures. Instructors also have access to a series of online TestBank questions for each chapter available at http://health.jbpub.com/foundations.

ACKNOWLEDGEMENTS

We want to thank all of the reviewers who read through this text and provided invaluable advice: Jeffrey S. Hallam, PhD, University of Mississippi; Randi Love, PhD, CHES, Ohio State University School of Public Health; and Liliana Rojas-Guyler, PhD, CHES, University of Cincinnati. A special appreciation is extended to Ashutosh Atri, a graduate student at University of Cincinnati for reviewing this text from a student's perspective and providing excellent suggestions. Lastly, this text could not have been published without the efforts of the Health team at Jones and Bartlett Publishers: Jacqueline Geraci, Acquisition Editor; Amy L. Flagg, Associate Editor; Julie Bolduc, Senior Production Editor; Jennifer Ryan, Associate Production Editor; Wendy Thayer, Marketing Manager; and Meagan Norlund, Marketing Associate.

ABOUT THE AUTHORS

Manoj Sharma, MBBS, CHES, PhD is a faculty member in the Department of Health Promotion and Health Education at the University of Cincinnati. He is a physician by initial training and has also completed his doctorate in Preventive Medicine/Public Health from The Ohio State University. He has worked in community health for more than 25 years at all levels: local level (Columbus Health Department, Omaha Healthy Start Program, Lead Safe Omaha Coalition); state level (Nebraska Health & Human Services, Ohio Department of Health); national level (American School Health Association, Centers for Disease Control and Prevention, United States Environmental Protection Agency); and international level (India, Italy, Mongolia, Nepal, UAE, UK, Vietnam). His research interests are in designing and evaluating theory-based health education and health promotion programs, alternative and complementary systems of health, and community-based participatory research.

John A. Romas, MPH, PhD is a professor and chair in the Department of Health Science at Minnesota State University, Mankato. Dr. Romas has been a public school teacher, public health administrator and educator, state health consultant, and small business owner. He is a well-known speaker, presenter and health consultant for educational organizations, government, healthcare, business, and industry in the areas of personal performance stress reduction, managing change, and health promotion. As a personal and career counselor, he is an associate fellow of the Albert Ellis Institute, New York City. At present Dr. Romas is working toward completion of licensure requirements as a professional counselor. He lives in Mankato, Minnesota with his wife, Judi, a kindergarten teacher. They have one grown daughter, a professional dancer, choreographer, and model.

CHAPTER 1

Health Education and Health Promotion

KEY CONCEPTS

- Behavior
- Certified health education specialist (CHES)
- Code of ethics
- Community-related terms
- Health
- Health behavior
- Health education
- Health literacy
- Health promotion
- Model
- Terms related to antecedents of behavior
- Theory

AFTER READING THIS CHAPTER YOU SHOULD BE ABLE TO

- Define health, health behavior, health education, and health promotion
- Identify the limitations of the traditional definition of health
- Differentiate between health education and health promotion
- Define terms related to antecedents of behavior
- Delineate community-related terms
- List the responsibilities of certified health education specialists
- Explain the role of theory in health education and health promotion
- Identify ten national health education organizations

HEALTH, BEHAVIOR, AND HEALTH BEHAVIOR

Health is an age-old concept. In old English the idea appeared as *haelen* ("to heal"), and in Middle English as *helthe*, meaning to be sound in body, mind, or spirit. The classical Greek definition of medicine was to "prolong life and prevent disease," or in other words to keep people healthy (Cook, 2004). Similarly, medicine in ancient India was called *Ayurveda*, or the science of life or health. By the 17th century, most medical textbooks commonly used the word *restoration*. By the end of the 19th century, the word *health* was considered colloquial and was replaced with the word *hygiene*, which was considered more scientific (Cook, 2004).

After the Second World War, interest in the word *health* resurfaced with the formation of the World Health Organization (WHO), a global entity. Around the same time, the Hygienic Laboratory in the United States was renamed the National Institutes of Health. In 1948, WHO defined health in its constitution as "a state of complete physical, mental, and social well being and not merely the absence of disease or infirmity" (WHO, 1974). This definition of health has received a lot of criticism over the years.

First, the use of the word *state* is misleading. Health is dynamic and changes from time to time. For example, a person may be healthy in the morning and then develop a headache in the afternoon and thus not be in the "state" of health. Second, the dimensions mentioned in the definition are inadequate to capture variations in health. One such dimension is the spiritual dimension (Perrin & McDermott, 1997). Bensley (1991) has identified six different perspectives related to the spiritual dimension of health: (1) sense of fulfillment, (2) values and beliefs of community and self, (3) wholeness in life, (4) well-being, (5) God or a controlling power, and (6) human-spiritual interaction. These perspectives are not mentioned in WHO's definition. Another dimension that is not mentioned is the political dimension. Do the rich get sick more often, or do the poor? Who controls greater resources to health? Do the rich or the poor have a greater burden of mortality? All these and many more such questions pertain to the politics behind health. This dimension must be explicitly mentioned in the definition for it to be meaningfully complete.

> *Health is a state of complete physical, mental, and social well being and not merely the absence of disease or infirmity.*
>
> —World Health Organization (1974)

Third, the word *well-being* is very subjective. A definition must be more objective, and subjectivity should be minimized. Fourth, the way in which health is defined makes it very difficult to measure. McDowell and Newell (1987) further point out that "just as language molds the way we think[,] our health measurements influence (and are influenced by) the way we define and think about health" (p. 14); in other words, health and measurement are inextricably linked. Fifth, WHO's definition of health presents an idealistic or utopian view. It would be impossible to find anyone who embodies all the attributes presented in the definition. Thus, the definition of health needs to be more realistic.

Sixth, in the definition health is presented as an end product, whereas most people perceive health as a means of achieving something that they value more highly.

For example, people may want to be healthy so that they can raise their families. Finally, the WHO definition of health is written from an individualistic perspective in which health is defined for one person. It lacks a community orientation, which is much needed for something that is as complex as health. These limitations of the WHO definition are summarized in Table 1.1.

Since the original statement of the WHO definition, it has been modified in subsequent discussions at the world level. In November 1986, the first International Conference on Health Promotion was held in Ottawa, Canada (WHO, 1986). The conference culminated with the drafting of the Ottawa Charter for Health Promotion. In the charter, health was defined in a broader perspective: "health has been considered less as an abstract state and more as a means to an end which can be expressed in functional terms as a resource which permits people to lead an individually, socially, and economically productive life. Health is a resource for everyday life, not the object of living. It is a positive concept emphasizing social and personal resources as well as physical capabilities" (WHO, 1986).

Another important basic concept is that of **behavior**. *Merriam-Webster's Dictionary* defines behavior as anything that an organism does involving action and response to stimulation. The key word is *action*. A behavior is any overt action, conscious or unconscious, with a measurable frequency, intensity, and duration. *Frequency* refers to how many times the behavior occurs in a given time period. For example, for the behavior of physical activity, we may classify someone as being active who participates in some sort of physical activity five days a week. *Intensity* refers to how intense or how hard the behavior is performed. For example, for physical activity behavior,

TABLE 1.1   Limitations of the World Health Organization's Definition of Health

Health is dynamic, not a state.

The dimensions are inadequate.

The definition is subjective.

Measurement is difficult.

The definition is too ideal and not realistic.

Health is not an end but a means.

The definition lacks a community orientation.

we may say that a behavior is mildly intense, moderately intense, or vigorous depending on the effect it has on the heart rate or the number of calories it burns. *Duration* refers to the amount of time spent on each session. For example, physical activity may last for so many minutes on any given day.

Any behavior is influenced by factors at five levels. The first level pertains to individual factors. For example, a person's attitude helps determine his or her behavior. A person who is partaking in physical activity behavior may believe that physical activity is refreshing. The second level pertains to interpersonal factors. For example, the person may be exercising because his or her spouse requested it. The third level pertains to institutional or organizational factors. For example, there may be a policy at the workplace that requires every person to work out for an hour, and that may be the reason the person is performing the physical activity behavior. The fourth level pertains to community factors. For example, the person may be living or working in a community where the only available parking is ten minutes away from the destination building; this may be the main reason that the person is physically active. The final level in determining one's behavior is the role of public policy factors. For example, laws and policies requiring the use of seat belts while driving may make a person perform that particular behavior.

Now let us focus our attention on defining **health behavior**. The World Health Organization (1998) defines health behavior as "any activity undertaken by an individual regardless of actual or perceived health status, for the purpose of promoting, protecting or maintaining health,

> *A behavior is any overt action, conscious or unconscious, with a measurable frequency, intensity, and duration.*

whether or not such behavior is objectively effective toward that end." David Gochman (1982, 1997) defines health behavior as "those personal attributes such as beliefs, expectations, motives, values, perceptions, and other cognitive elements; personality characteristics, including affective and emotional states and traits; and behavioral patterns, actions, and habits that relate to health maintenance, to health restoration, and to health improvement." Three key foci of health behavior are clear in these definitions: maintenance of health, restoration of health, and improvement of health.

These foci can also be seen as corresponding to the three levels of prevention, namely, primary prevention, secondary prevention, and tertiary prevention (Modeste & Tamayose, 2004; Pickett & Hanlon, 1998). **Primary prevention** refers to those preventive actions that are taken prior to the onset of a disease or injury with the intention of removing the possibility of their ever occurring. **Secondary prevention** refers to actions that block the progression of an injury or disease at its incipient stage. **Tertiary prevention** refers to those actions taken after the onset of disease or an injury with the intention of assisting diseased or disabled people. The actions for primary, secondary, and tertiary level care are taken at individual, interpersonal, organizational, community, and public policy levels. Hence health behavior can be defined as all actions with a potentially measurable frequency, intensity, and duration performed at the individual, interpersonal, organizational, community, or public policy level for primary, secondary, or tertiary prevention.

Health behaviors can be about positive attributes, such as promoting physical activity or eating five or more servings of fruits and vegetables. Health behaviors can also be about extinguishing negative attributes, such as smoking or binge drinking. A similar categorization of behaviors is as risk behaviors and protective behaviors. The World Health Organization (1998) defines risk behaviors as "specific forms of behavior which are proven to be associated with increased susceptibility to a specific disease or ill-health." For example, indiscriminate sexual behavior is a risk behavior for sexually transmitted diseases, including HIV/AIDS. Protective behaviors are those behaviors that protect a person from developing ill-health or specific disease. For example, a person may get immunized against tetanus and thus prevent the disease. Another categorization of behaviors is into what Green and Kreuter (2005) have defined as health-directed and health-related behaviors. Health-directed behaviors are those behaviors that a person consciously pursues for health improvement or health protection, such as seeking an immunization, a physical examination, a low-fat food, or a condom. *Health-related behaviors* are those actions that are performed for reasons other than health but which have health effects. An example is an individual trying to lose weight in order to improve his or her appearance.

HEALTH EDUCATION AND HEALTH PROMOTION

Health education is the profession that deals with facilitation of modifying health behaviors. Health education has been defined in several ways. Downie, Fyfe, and Tannahill (1990) defined it as "[c]ommunication activity aimed at enhancing positive health and preventing or diminishing ill-health in individuals and groups through influencing the beliefs, attitudes and behavior of those with power and of the community at large" (p. 28). The 2000 Joint Committee on Health Education and Promotion Terminology (Gold & Miner, 2002) defined health education as "any combination of planned learning experiences based on sound theories that provide individuals, groups, and communities the opportunity to acquire information and the skills needed to make quality health decisions." The World Health Organization (1998) defined health education as "compris[ing] consciously constructed opportunities for learning involving some form of communication designed to improve health literacy, including improving knowledge, and developing life skills which are conducive to individual and community health." Green and Kreuter (2005) defined it as "any planned combination of learning experiences designed to predispose, enable, and reinforce voluntary behavior conducive to health in individuals, groups or communities."

From these definitions some things are clear. First, health education is a systematic, planned application, which would qualify it as a science. Second, the delivery of health education involves a set of techniques rather than just one, such as preparing health education informational brochures, pamphlets, and videos; delivering lectures; facilitating role plays or simulations; analyzing case studies; participating and reflecting in group discussions; self reading; and interacting in computer-assisted training. In the past, *health education* was used as a term to encompass a wider range of functions, such as community mobilization, networking, advocacy, and so on. These methods are now embodied in the term *health promotion*; thus, health education is now perceived as more focused. Third, the primary purpose of health education is to influence antecedents of behavior so that healthy behaviors develop in a voluntary fashion (without any coercion). The common antecedents of behavior are awareness, information, knowledge, skills, beliefs, attitudes, and values. Finally, health education is performed at several levels. It can be done one-on-one, such as a counseling session; it can be done with a group of people, such as through a group discussion; it can be done at an organizational level, such as through an employee wellness fair; or it can be done at the community level, such as through a multiple-channel, multiple-approach campaign.

Since the publication of *Healthy People: The Surgeon General's Report on Health Promotion and Disease Prevention* (U.S. Department of Health and Human Services [USDHHS], 1979), another term that has gained popularity and continues to gain strength is the term **health promotion**. This term has been used in the *Objectives for the Nation* (U.S. DHHS, 1980), *Healthy People 2000* (U.S. DHHS, 1990), and *Healthy People 2010* (U.S. DHHS, 2000) reports. Table 1.2 summarizes the 28 focus areas in *Healthy People 2010*, and Table 1.3 summarizes the ten leading health indicators that reflect the major public health concerns in the United States. Both focus areas and leading health indicators underscore the importance of health promotion.

> *Healthy People 2010* is designed to achieve two overarching goals:
>
> - Increase quality and years of healthy life
> - Eliminate health disparities
>
> —U.S. Department of Health and Human Services (2000)

TABLE 1.2 Focus Areas in *Healthy People 2010*	
Access to quality health services	Injury and violence prevention
Arthritis, osteoporosis, and chronic back conditions	Maternal, infant, and child health
Cancer	Medical product safety
Chronic kidney disease	Mental health and mental disorders
Diabetes	Nutrition and overweight
Disability and secondary conditions	Occupational safety and health
Educational and community-based programs	Oral health
Environmental health	Physical activity and fitness
Family planning	Public health infrastructure
Food safety	Respiratory diseases
Health communication	Sexually transmitted diseases
Heart disease and stroke	Substance abuse
HIV/AIDS	Tobacco use
Immunization and infectious disease	Vision and hearing

TABLE 1.3   Leading Health Indicators in *Healthy People 2010*
Physical activity
Overweight and obesity
Tobacco use
Substance abuse
Responsible sexual behavior
Mental health
Injury and violence
Environmental quality
Immunization
Access to health care

Green and Kreuter (2005) defined health promotion as "any planned combination of educational, political, regulatory and organizational supports for actions and conditions of living conducive to the health of individuals, groups or communities." The 2000 Joint Committee on Health Education and Promotion Terminology (Gold & Miner, 2002) defined health promotion as "any planned combination of educational, political, environmental, regulatory, or organizational mechanisms that support actions and conditions of living conducive to the health of individuals, groups, and communities." The *Ottawa Charter for Health Promotion* (WHO, 1986) defined health promotion as "the process of enabling people to increase control over, and to improve their health." The Ottawa Charter identified five key action strategies for health promotion:

- Building healthy public policy
- Creating physical and social environments supportive of individual change
- Strengthening community action
- Developing personal skills such as increased self-efficacy and feelings of empowerment
- Reorienting health services to the population and partnership with patients

These action areas were confirmed in the *Jakarta Declaration on Leading Health Promotion into the 21st Century* in 1997 (WHO, 1997). In addition, the Jakarta Declaration identified five priorities for health promotion:

- Promote social responsibility for health.
- Increase investments for health development.
- Expand partnerships for health promotion.
- Increase community capacity and empower the individual.
- Secure an infrastructure for health promotion.

Once again, all these depictions of health promotion have some things in common. First, just like health education, health promotion is also a systematic, planned application that would qualify as a science. Second, it entails methods beyond mere education. Such methods could consist of community mobilization, community organization, community participation, community development, community empowerment, networking, coalition building, advocacy, lobbying, policy development, formulating legislation, developing social norms, and so on. Third, un-

> *Health for all: The attainment by all people of the world of a level of health that will permit them to lead a socially and economically productive life.*
>
> —World Health Organization (1986)

like health education, it does not endorse voluntary change in behavior and utilizes measures that compel an individual's behavior change. These measures are uniform and mandatory. Often the behavior change in health promotion comes from measures that an individual may not like, for example, an increase in insurance premium for a smoker. Finally, health promotion is done at the group or community level.

RESPONSIBILITIES AND COMPETENCIES FOR HEALTH EDUCATORS

The history of health education dates to the late 19th century, when the first academic programs emerged for developing school health educators (Allegrante et al., 2004). The 2003 *Directory of Institutions Offering Undergraduate and Graduate Degree Programs in Health Education* listed 258 institutions offering baccalaureate, master's, and doctoral degrees in health education (American Association for Health Education, 2003).

As the profession of health education has grown, greater interest has arisen in establishing standards and holding professionals accountable to those standards. In February 1978, a conference for health educators was convened in Bethesda to analyze the similarities and differences in preparation of health educators from different practice settings and discuss possibilities for developing uniform guidelines (National Commission for Health Education Credentialing [NCHEC], Society for Public Health Education [SOPHE], & American Association for Health Education [AAHE], 2006; U.S. Department of Health, Education and Welfare, 1978). Soon after, the Role Delineation Project was implemented, which looked at the role of the entry-level health education specialist and identified the desirable responsibilities, functions, skills, and knowledge for that level. These were verified by a survey of practicing health educators. The process led to the formation of a document entitled *A Framework for the Development of Competency-Based Curricula for Entry-Level Health Educators* (NCHEC, 1985).

In 1986, the second Bethesda Conference was held, which provided consensus for the certification process; in 1988, the National Commission for Health Education Credentialing was established. In 1989, a charter certification phase was introduced, during which health educators could become certified by submission of letters of support and academic records. From 1990 onward, the NCHEC has conducted competency-based national certification examinations. An individual who meets the required health education training qualifications, successfully passes the certification exam, and meets continuing education requirements is known as a **certified health education specialist (CHES)**. In 2006, there were 12,000 such certified individuals

(NCHEC, SOPHE, & AAHE, 2006). Table 1.4 summarizes the responsibilities for entry-level health educators (NCHEC, 1985).

In 1992, efforts were undertaken to determine graduate-level competencies by the AAHE and SOPHE. A Joint Committee for the Development of Graduate-Level Preparation standards was formed. *A Competency-Based Framework for Graduate Level Health Educators* was published in 1999 (AAHE, NCHEC, & SOPHE, 1999). Table 1.5 summarizes the responsibilities for graduate-level health educators (AAHE, NCHEC, & SOPHE, 1999).

TABLE 1.4   Areas of Responsibilities for Entry-Level Health Educators

I.   Assessing individual and community needs for health education

II.   Planning effective health education programs

III.   Implementing health education programs

IV.   Evaluating effectiveness of health education programs

V.   Coordinating provision of health education services

VI.   Acting as a resource person in health education

VII.   Communicating health and health education needs, concerns, and resources

TABLE 1.5   Areas of Responsibilities for Graduate-Level Health Educators

I.   Assessing individual and community needs for health education

II.   Planning effective health education programs

III.   Implementing health education programs

IV.   Evaluating effectiveness of health education programs

V.   Coordinating provision of health education services

VI.   Acting as a resource person in health education

VII.   Communicating health and health education needs, concerns, and resources

VIII.   Applying appropriate research principles and techniques in health education

IX.   Administering health education programs

X.   Advancing the profession of health education

In 1998 the profession launched the National Health Educator Competencies Update Project (CUP), a six-year project to reverify the entry-level health education responsibilities, competencies, and subcompetencies and to verify the advanced-level competencies and subcompetencies (Airhihenbuwa et al., 2005; Gilmore, Olsen, Taub, & Connell, 2005). The CUP model identifies three levels of practice: (1) entry (competencies and subcompetencies performed by health educators with a baccalaureate or master's degree and less than 5 years of experience), (2) advanced 1 (competencies and subcompetencies performed by health educators with a baccalaureate or master's degree and more than 5 years of experience), and (3) advanced 2 (competencies and subcompetencies performed by health educators with a doctoral degree and 5 years or more of experience). The CUP model contains seven areas of responsibility, 35 competencies, and 163 subcompetencies, many of which are similar to previous models. Table 1.6 summarizes the responsibilities. Research and advocacy have been combined to form Area IV, and communication and advocacy have been combined in Area VII. The CUP model also identifies six settings for health education (Table 1.7).

TABLE 1.6   Areas of Responsibilities for Health Educators in the CUP Model

I.   Assess individual and community needs for health education

II. Plan health education strategies, interventions, and programs

III. Implement health education strategies, interventions, and programs

IV. Conduct evaluation and research related to health education

V.   Administer health education strategies, interventions, and programs

VI. Serve as a health education resource person

VII. Communicate and advocate for health and health education

---

TABLE 1.7   Settings for Health Education Identified in the CUP Model

Community

School (K–12)

Health care

Business/industry

College/university

University health services

Health education is an important and integral function of public health. The Institute of Medicine defined three core functions of public health in its *Future of Public Health* report (1988):

1. *Assessment:* Every public health agency should regularly and systematically collect, assemble, analyze, and make available information on the health of the community.
2. *Policy development:* Every public health agency should assist in the development of comprehensive public health policies.
3. *Assurance:* Every public health agency should ensure that services necessary to achieve agreed-upon goals in communities are provided either directly or by regulations or by other agencies.

Building on these identified functions, the Public Health Functions Steering Committee (1994) identified six public health goals and ten essential public health services. The six goals are to (1) prevent epidemics and the spread of disease, (2) protect against environmental hazards, (3) prevent injuries, (4) promote and encourage healthy behaviors, (5) respond to disasters and assist communities in recovery, and (6) assure the quality and accessibility of health services. The ten essential public health services are to (1) monitor health status to identify community health problems; (2) diagnose and investigate health problems and health hazards in the community; (3) inform, educate, and empower people about health issues; (4) mobilize community partnerships to identify and solve health problems; (5) develop policies and plans that support individual and community health efforts; (6) enforce laws and regulations that protect health and ensure safety; (7) link people to needed personal health services and ensure the provision of health care when it is otherwise unavailable; (8) ensure the availability of a competent public health and personal health care workforce; (9) evaluate the effectiveness, accessibility, and quality of personal and population-based health services; and (10) research new insights and innovative solutions to health problems. It can be seen from both these lists that health education is a core and integral function of public health and that health educators are key public health functionaries.

The Institute of Medicine published another report, *The Future of the Public's Health in the 21st Century*, in 2002 that echoed the vision articulated in *Healthy People 2010* (U.S. DHHS, 2000): healthy people in healthy communities. It emphasized the following key areas of actions:

- Adopting a focus on population health that includes multiple determinants of health
- Strengthening the public health infrastructure

- Building partnerships
- Developing systems of accountability
- Emphasizing evidence
- Improving communication

Once again, all these functions underscore the inextricable linkage between public health and health education. Health education is an important subset of public health.

CODE OF ETHICS FOR THE HEALTH EDUCATION PROFESSION

In recent years, there has been an increasing interest regarding ethics in all walks of life. Ethics is a major area of philosophy that deals with the study of morality. Practicing ethical behavior provides a standard for performance in any profession. In the profession of health education, the earliest effort to develop a code of ethics appears to be the 1976 code of ethics developed by the Society for Public Health Education (Taub, Kreuter, Parcel, & Vitello, 1987). A coalition of national health education organizations, composed of the American Academy of Health Behavior (AAHB), the American Association for Health Education (AAHE), the American College Health Association (ACHA), the American Public Health Association's (APHA) Public Health Education and Health Promotion (PHEHP) Section, APHA's School Health Education and Services (SHES) Section, the American School Health Association (ASHA), the Directors of Health Promotion and Education (DHPE), Eta Sigma Gamma, the Society for Public Health Education (SOPHE), and the Society of State

---

TABLE 1.8   Articles in the Code of Ethics for the Health Education Profession

Responsibility to the public: Supports principles of self-determination and freedom of choice for the individual

Responsibility to the profession: Exhibits professional behavior

Responsibility to employers: Accountable for professional activities and actions

Responsibility in the delivery of health education: Respects the rights, dignity, confidentiality, and worth of people

Responsibility in research and evaluation: Conducts oneself in accordance with federal and state laws, organizational and institutional policies, and professional standards

Responsibility in professional preparation: Provides quality education that benefits the profession and the public

Directors of Health, Physical Education and Recreation (SSDHPER), has developed a unified **code of ethics for health educators** (Coalition of National Health Education Organizations, 2004). The code of ethics has six areas, which are summarized in Table 1.8.

HEALTH EDUCATION ORGANIZATIONS

Ten health education organizations exist at the national level. The following subsections provide a brief description of each of these organizations.

American Academy of Health Behavior (AAHB)

The American Academy of Health Behavior was established in 1998. The mission of this organization is to advance the practice of health education and health promotion through health behavior research. Its specific objectives are to

- Foster and disseminate findings of health behavior, health education, and health promotion research through sponsorship of scientific meetings, symposia, and publications
- Recognize outstanding achievements in the areas of health behavior, health education, and health promotion research
- Facilitate collaborative research efforts by bringing its members in contact with each other through a membership directory, professional meetings, professional publications, and electronic media
- Advance health education and health promotion by influencing health policy and allocation of resources (government agencies, private foundations, universities, etc.) by developing and disseminating a cohesive body of knowledge in the area of health behavior research

Its website is www.aahb.org.

American Association for Health Education (AAHE)

The American Association for Health Education was established in 1937, but its parent organization, the Association of the American Alliance for Health, Physical Education, Recreation, and Dance (AAHPERD), was established in 1885. The AAHE is a membership organization representing 7,500 health educators and health promotion specialists and is the oldest and largest health education association. It advances the profession by serving health educators and other professionals who strive to promote the health of all people. Its specific objectives are to

- Develop and promulgate standards, resources, and services regarding health education to professionals and nonprofessionals
- Foster the development of national research priorities in health education and promotion
- Provide mechanisms for the translation of theory and research into practice and the translation of practice into theory and research
- Facilitate communication among members of the profession, the lay public and other national and international organizations with respect to the philosophic basis and current application of health education principles and practices
- Provide technical assistance to legislative and professional bodies engaged in drafting pertinent legislation and related guidelines
- Provide leadership in promoting policies and evaluative procedures that will result in effective health education programs
- Assist in the development and mobilization of resources for effective health education and promotion

Its website is www.aahperd.org/aahe.

American College Health Association (ACHA)

The American College Health Association was established in 1920. The mission of the organization is to be the principal advocate and leadership organization for college and university health. The association provides advocacy, education, communications, products, and services, as well as promotes research and culturally competent practices to enhance its members' ability to advance the health of all students and the campus community. Its main objectives are

- To support and promote systems and programs that produce optimum health outcomes for college students and campus communities
- To be the primary source of information, education, and consultation on health and health promotion issues affecting college and university students within the campus community
- To be the leading source of evidence-based knowledge about the field of college health

- To be the principal advocate for national public policy affecting the health of all college students and campus communities
- To develop and maximize the use of human, financial, and technological resources to ensure and sustain growth

Its website is www.acha.org.

American Public Health Association's (APHA) Public Health Education and Health Promotion (PHEHP) Section

The Public Health Education and Health Promotion section was established in 1920, whereas the parent organization, the American Public Health Association, was formed in 1872. The section has over 3,000 members. Its specific objectives are

- To be a strong advocate for health education, disease prevention, and health promotion directed to individuals, groups, and communities in all activities of the association
- To encourage the inclusion of health education, disease prevention, and health promotion activities in all of the nation's health programs
- To stimulate thought, discussion, research, and programmatic applications aimed at improving the public's health
- To improve the quality of research and practice in all public health programs of health education, disease prevention, and health promotion
- To provide networking opportunities for persons whose professional interests and training include, but are not limited to, the disciplines of health education, health communication, health promotion, social marketing, behavioral and social sciences, and public relations
- To provide section members with opportunities to become informed and engaged in all of the activities and matters of concern to the association
- To facilitate collaboration with all of the association's boards, committees, the special primary interest groups, caucuses, sections, and affiliates
- To provide section members with such benefits as the annual meeting program, continuing education opportunities, newsletters, and a structure for exercising association leadership
- To identify and recognize individuals who make outstanding and substantial contributions to health education, disease prevention, and health promotion

Its website is www.jhsph.edu/hao/phehp/.

American Public Health Association's School Health Education and Services (SHES) Section

The School Health Education and Services section was established in 1942 and has over 300 members. Its specific objectives are

- To provide a section within the association which works independently, with other association substructures, and with external organizations toward the improvement of early childhood, school, and college health programs
- To interpret the functions and responsibilities of health agencies to daycare, preschool, school, and college personnel
- To interpret early childhood, school, and college health education and service objectives to other public health personnel and assist them in integrating the objectives in their community
- To provide a forum for discussion of practices and research in early childhood, school, and college health
- To encourage the provision of health promotion programs within the school and college settings which address the needs of children and school personnel
- To encourage among interested association members the study and discussion of procedures and problems in early childhood, school, and college health services, health education, and environmental health programs

Its website is www.hsc.usf.edu/CFH/cnheo/apha-shes.htm.

American School Health Association (ASHA)

The American School Health Association was established in 1927 and has a membership of over 3,000. The mission of the ASHA is to protect and promote the health of children and youth by supporting coordinated school health programs as a foundation for school success. Its specific objectives are

- To promote interdisciplinary collaboration among all who work to protect and improve the health, safety, well-being, and school success of children, youth, families, and communities
- To provide professional development opportunities for all those associated with school health programs
- To provide advocacy for building and strengthening effective school health programs

- To advance a research agenda that promotes quality school health programs
- To fulfill these initiatives by acquiring human, fiscal, and material resources

Its website is www.ashaweb.org.

Directors of Health Promotion and Education (DHPE)

The Directors of Health Promotion and Education was established in 1946 and has over 200 members. Its specific objectives are

- To serve as a channel through which directors of public health education programs of states and territories of the United States may exchange and share methods, techniques, and information for the enrichment and improvement of public health education programs
- To establish position statements and make recommendations on legislation and public policy related to and having implications for public health education
- To participate with the Association of State and Territorial Health Officials (ASTHO) in promoting health and preventing disease
- To identify methods of improving the quality and practice of education, public health education, and health promotion
- To elicit the cooperation and coordination with those national, public, private, and voluntary agencies related to public health programs
- To provide a forum for continuing education opportunities in public health education and health promotion

Its website is www.dhpe.org/.

Eta Sigma Gamma

Eta Sigma Gamma was established in 1967. It is the national professional health education honorary society. The specific objectives of this organization are

- To support the planning, implementation, and evaluation of health education programs and resources
- To stimulate and disseminate scientific research
- To motivate and provide health education services
- To recognize academic achievement
- To support health education advocacy initiatives

- To promote professional standards and ethics
- To promote networking activities among health educators and related professionals

Its website is www.etasigmagamma.org.

Society for Public Health Education (SOPHE)

The Society for Public Health Education was established in 1950 and has over 4,000 members. The primary mission of SOPHE is to provide leadership to the profession of health education and to contribute to the health of all people through advances in health education theory and research, excellence in health education practice, and the promotion of public policies conducive to health. The specific objectives of this organization are

- To expand the reach and effectiveness of advocacy efforts beyond SOPHE membership

- To promote the use of health education to eliminate health disparities

- To review, expand, and promote a dynamic research agenda for health education and behavioral sciences

- To support and enhance the professional preparation and training of health educators and public health professionals

- To proactively market health education

- To continually elevate SOPHE's performance in operations, governance, and resource development to achieve the strategic plan

Its website is www.sophe.org.

Society of State Directors of Health, Physical Education and Recreation (SSDHPER)

The Society of State Directors of Health, Physical Education and Recreation was established in 1926. The mission of the SSDHPER is to provide leadership in facilitating and promoting initiatives to achieve national health and education goals and objectives. Its members supervise and coordinate programs in health, physical education, and related fields within state departments of education. Associate members are those who are interested in the goals and programs of the society who do not work within a state education agency. Its specific objectives are

- To help shape national and state policy defining and supporting comprehensive school health and physical education programs
- To link state health, physical education, and recreation leaders with their counterparts in other states
- To work to forge school/family/community linkages in support of school health, physical education, and recreation programs
- To foster professional growth and the development of leadership and advocacy skills
- To help resolve complex issues in education and health reform
- To provide leadership in the effort to link postsecondary institutions to school districts for improvement in curriculum, instruction, and assessment
- To provide a supportive network of professional and social relationships among members
- To provide training and workshops for members to help them increase capacity to improve comprehensive school health education and programs within their states

Its website is www.thesociety.org.

BASIC VOCABULARY IN HEALTH EDUCATION AND HEALTH PROMOTION

Health education and health promotion have their roots in several disciplines: biological science, behavioral science, economics, political science, and other social sciences. As in any other field, there are certain terms and jargon that health promotion and education professionals use. Some of these terms are presented in this section. These terms are used when we talk of antecedents of health behavior change.

Awareness

A concept commonly used by health educators is developing awareness of health topics. To undergo any behavior change, the person first needs to become aware of what he or she is going to change. *American Heritage Dictionary* defines being *aware* as being mindful or heedful. The word *aware* implies knowledge gained through one's own perceptions or other means of information. **Awareness** refers to becoming conscious about an action, idea, object, person, or situation. An example of building awareness is a health educator screening a film about avian flu (bird flu) in a community in which there have been no cases of avian flu and no one knows about this disease. However, if people are already aware of an issue—for example, that smoking is harmful to health—there is no need to build awareness regarding that issue.

Information

After becoming aware of the need to make a behavior change, the person starts to gather facts about the change. The collection of facts related to an action, idea, object, person, or situation is called **information**. Health educators spend time providing information on various health topics. In the process they make pamphlets, brochures, flyers, compact discs, videos, and so forth.

Knowledge

After gathering information for making a behavior change, the person needs to learn facts and gain insights related to the action, idea, object, person, or situation. This learning of facts and gaining of insights is called **knowledge**. Bloom (1956) identified knowledge as part of the cognitive domain and identified six categories of cognitive learning. The first of these categories is *knowledge*, which entails recalling data or information—for example, reciting the symptoms of a disease or knowing safety procedures. The second level is *comprehension*, or understanding the meaning, translation, interpolation, and interpretation of instructions and problems. An example is the ability to state a problem in one's own words. The third level is *application*, which entails using a concept in a new situation. It also means applying what was learned in the classroom setting to novel situations in the workplace. The fourth level is *analysis*, in which the person is able to separate concepts into component parts so that their organizational structure may be understood. For example, a health educator collects information about a community and then prioritizes the needs to decide what program to offer in the community. The fifth level is *synthesis*, in which the parts are put together to form a whole, with emphasis on creating a new meaning or structure. The sixth and final level is *evaluation*, where one makes judgments about the value of ideas or materials. Knowledge can be tested as being correct or incorrect. The usual methods by which knowledge is tested are true/false questions or multiple choice questions.

Science is organized knowledge.

—Herbert Spencer

Skills

In performing any action, a set of psychomotor **skills** is required. Performance of these skills entails physical movement, coordination, and use of the motor skill. Development of these skills requires practice and is measured in terms of speed, precision, distance, procedures, or techniques in execution (Simpson, 1972). Seven categories, ranging from the simplest skill to the most complex skill, have been identified:

1. *Perception.* The ability to use sensory cues to guide motor activity.
2. *Set.* The readiness to act. It includes mind-set, which predetermines a person's response to different situations.
3. *Guided response.* Early stages in learning a complex skill, which include imitation and trial and error.
4. *Mechanism.* Learned responses have become habitual and the movements can be performed with some confidence and proficiency.
5. *Complex overt response.* Performance without hesitation; automatic performance.
6. *Adaptation.* Skills are well developed, and the individual can modify movement patterns to fit special requirements.
7. *Origination.* The person creates new movement patterns to fit a particular situation or specific problem.

Psychomotor skills are required in almost all health education programs. These are tested by demonstration and re-demonstration. For example, in a cardiopulmonary resuscitation program, the instructor first shows the correct technique and then checks whether the participants have learned the technique correctly.

Health Literacy

The 2000 Joint Committee on Health Education and Promotion Terminology (Gold & Miner, 2002) has defined **health literacy** as "the capacity of an individual to obtain, interpret, and understand basic health information and services and the competence to use such information and services in ways that are health enhancing." Zarcadoolas, Pleasant, and Green (2003) have suggested a four-part model to understand health literacy. The four domains of this model are as follows:

1. *Fundamental literacy/numeracy:* Competence in understanding and using printed language, spoken language, numerals, and basic mathematical symbols or terms. This domain is involved in a wide range of cognitive, behavioral, and social skills and abilities.

2. *Literacy pertaining to science and technology:* Understanding of the basic scientific and technological concepts, technical complexity, the phenomenon of scientific uncertainty, and the phenomenon of rapid change.
3. *Community/civic literacy:* Understanding about sources of information, agendas, and methods of interpreting those agendas. It enables people to engage in dialogue and decision making. It includes media interpretation skills and understanding of civic and legislative functions.
4. *Cultural literacy:* Understanding of collective beliefs, customs, worldviews, and social identity relationships to interpret and produce health information.

Beliefs

Beliefs are convictions that a phenomenon is true or real (Rokeach, 1970). In other words, beliefs are statements of perceived fact or impressions about the world. These are neither correct nor incorrect. For example, a student may enter a classroom and say that the classroom is big. She may be used to smaller classrooms, and thus from her perspective the current classroom seems big. Another student may enter the same classroom and say that it is small. He may be used to bigger classrooms and thus his perspective finds the classroom smaller.

Attitudes

Attitudes are relatively constant feelings, predispositions, or sets of beliefs directed toward an idea, object, person, or situation (Mucchielli, 1970). Put another way, attitudes can be considered as beliefs with an evaluative component. Attitudes have an affective component and demonstrate what one likes and what one does not like. For example, building on the example presented earlier about beliefs, a student might find a room small and may qualify that belief by saying that it is an ugly, small room. Since an evaluation has been done that the student dislikes the room, it becomes an attitude. Likewise, another student might find the same room to be a small, cozy room and thus demonstrate an attitude of liking the object.

Attitudes are usually measured by self-reporting scales, such as Likert scales. Likert scales list several sentences about an object and then ask respondents whether they strongly agree, agree, disagree, or strongly disagree with each statement. The scores are then summed to measure the respondent's attitude toward that object.

Values

A collection of beliefs and attitudes comprises a value system. **Values** are enduring beliefs or systems of beliefs regarding whether a specific mode of conduct or end state of behavior is personally or socially preferable (Rokeach, 1970). Let us take the example of the student who likes small, cozy classrooms. He also likes the students and the instructor in the classroom, and likes the textbook that has been assigned by his instructor. He likes to read and to complete his assignments on time. Such a student can be said to have a value system that values education.

Community Mobilization

A **community** is a collection of people identified by a set of shared values. Working with communities is fundamental to the practice of health education. The first step in working with a community is **community mobilization**, which involves persuading community members to attend or participate in any activity planned by the health educator. The purpose of community mobilization is to enhance awareness on a given issue at the community level. Activities such as organizing a talk in the community, arranging a health fair, and bringing together key leaders of the community for a panel discussion are all methods used in community mobilization.

Community Organization

The second step for action at a community level is **community organization**. The term *community organization* was coined by American social workers in the late 1800s to describe their efforts with immigrants and indigent people (Minkler & Wallerstein, 1997). In community organization, community members identify needs, set objectives, prioritize issues, develop plans, and implement projects for community improvement in health and related matters. Green and Kreuter (2005) define community organization as "the set of procedures and processes by which a population and its institutions mobilize and coordinate resources to solve a mutual problem or to pursue mutual goals." Activities such as group discussions and committee meetings are commonly done in this stage.

Community Participation

When community members actively participate in planning or implementing projects, it is called **community participation**. Community participation can take place on health-related matters or other civic matters. Community members must be in leadership roles in true community participation. Arnstein (1971) has identified eight different types of participation in a ladder of participation. At the bottom of the ladder there is no participation—only manipulation. Token participation entails the levels of information, consultation, and placation. Development of partnerships, delegation of power, and citizen control are levels of participation that are desirable.

Community Development

Community development is the stage at which local initiative and leadership in a community has been organized and stimulated to a level at which change in health or other matters is occurring. The key word in the concept of community development is the term *change* at the community level. Change can be measured by assessing changes in services or the provision of new services or by replacement of existing policies or by incorporation of new policies.

Community Empowerment

The concept of **community empowerment** is closely related to the Ottawa Charter definition of community action for health. The World Health Organization (1998) defines it as "a process through which people gain greater control over decisions and actions affecting their health." In essence, empowerment is a process whereby individuals gain mastery over their lives in the context of changing their social and political environments. Empowerment can be a social, cultural, psychological, or political process. Individual empowerment is different from community empowerment. Individual empowerment is mainly about an individual gaining control over his or her personal life. Community empowerment entails individuals collectively gaining greater influence and control over the determinants of health and the quality of life in their community.

Networking

An important function of health promotion is to establish a network. Creating interdependent relationships with individuals, groups, and organizations to accomplish mutually set objectives in health or other matters is called **networking.**

Coalition Building

No single organization is able to effectively achieve changes in the health status of a community. Hence, collaboration between agencies, groups, and organizations is needed. A grouping of separate organizations in a community united to pursue a common goal related to health or other matters affecting a large number of people is called a **coalition**. It takes time and concerted effort to develop such coalitions; this art is called *coalition building*, and it is a vital function for achieving health promotion goals.

Advocacy

Advocacy is active support of an idea or cause that entails especially the act of pleading or arguing for something. Green and Kreuter (2005) define advocacy as "working for political, regulatory, or organizational change on behalf of a particular interest group or population." Advocacy in health is about creating a shift in public opinion and mobilizing the essential resources to support any issue or policy that affects the health of a community or constituency. It is a vital function for achieving health promotion goals.

Lobbying

Lobbying is working with and influencing policy makers to develop an issue or a policy affecting the health of a community. It is an important activity in health promotion. Oftentimes health lobbyists have to compete with more powerful and resource-rich lobbyists from business or industry.

Policy Development

Policies are made by institutions or government (local, state, or federal). Health promotion professionals work with institutional heads or other lawmakers so that healthy policies are developed. The process of developing a policy with ramifications for affecting the health of communities is called **policy development**.

Legislation

Legislation is laws passed by elected officials at the local, state, or federal level. Legislation has ramifications for affecting the health of a large number of people. Health promotion professionals work at every step of the way to influence laws that foster healthy behaviors and help in extinguishing negative and unhealthy behaviors.

Development of Social Norms

Creating social acceptance for a practice, behavior, condition, policy, law, or environment that may affect the health in a community is called **development of social norms**. Health promotion professionals aim at developing social norms so that healthy behaviors become acceptable and normative.

ROLE OF THEORY IN HEALTH EDUCATION AND HEALTH PROMOTION

We have seen that health education and health promotion have multiple influences from several disciplines. But the primary influence on health education is derived from behavioral sciences, and health promotion is deeply embedded in social sciences. It is from these behavioral and social sciences that the practice of health education and health promotion borrows the strategic planning of its methods.

The core concepts in behavioral and social sciences are organized in the form of theories. Kerlinger and Lee (2000) have defined *theory* as "a set of interrelated, concepts, definitions, and predispositions that present a systematic view of events or situations by specifying relations among variables in order to explain and predict the events or situations." In health education and health promotion, we are primarily interested in predicting or explaining changes in behaviors or environments. Use of theory is becoming almost mandatory for practitioners of health education and health promotion. These days, even for entry-level health educators, competency for developing a logical scope and sequence plan for health education is a requirement (NCHEC, SOPHE, & AAHE, 2006). Theories help us articulate assumptions and hypotheses regarding the strategies and targets of interventions (National Cancer Institute, 2005).

Polit and Hungler (1999) have classified theories into three types. The first are the *macro theories* or *grand theories* that purport to explain and describe large segments of the environment or human experience, for example, Talcott Parsons's (1951) theory on social functioning. Second are *middle-range theories* that describe or explain phenomena such as specific behaviors, for example, Albert Bandura's (1986, 2004) social cognitive theory. Finally there are *descriptive theories* that describe or explain a single discrete phenomenon, for example, Hans Selye's (1974) general adaptation syndrome.

Glanz, Rimer, and Lewis (2002) have classified theories as *explanatory theories*, or *theories of the problem*, and *change theories*, or *theories of action*. Explanatory theories help describe and identify why a problem exists and search for modifiable constructs. Change theories guide the development of interventions and form the basis of evaluation.

Theories start from discussing concepts or ideas that are abstract entities. These are not measurable or observable. The concepts are adopted into theories and become known as *constructs*. For example, in social cognitive theory (Bandura, 1986, 2004), self-efficacy is a construct. When specific properties are assigned to the construct, then it becomes an *indicator*. For example, ten items may be written in the form of a questionnaire for the construct of self-efficacy for physical activity, constituting what the construct means. From the indicator is derived the *variable* or quantitative score, which varies from one individual to other. For example, in the ten-item questionnaire each item may be ranked from 1 to 5 and the summation may yield a score of 10 to 50. The constructs of a theory are constantly refined from empirical testing. Ideally, a theory must be able to demonstrate predictive power. Behavioral theories must be able to make significant changes on affect (feelings or conation), thought (cognition), and action (volition). Ideally a theory must be able to provide practical guidance on what, why, and how. An ideal theory must be testable and must be generalizable. The constructs of the theory must be able to explain phenomena, which for health education and health promotion are behaviors or environmental conditions.

Use of theory derived from behavioral or social science helps the practice of health education and health promotion in several ways. First, it helps in developing program objectives that are measurable. For example, if the health education program uses social cognitive theory

> *There is nothing so practical as a good theory.*
>
> —Kurt Lewin

(Bandura, 1986, 2004) to change physical activity behavior in elementary school students, then the objectives can be based on three constructs derived from the theory. The objectives could be as follows: (1) At the end of the program 80% of the participants are able to demonstrate positive change in physical activity expectations score from before to after the intervention, (2) at the end of the program 80% of the participants are able to demonstrate positive change in their physical activity self-efficacy score from before to after the intervention, and (3) at the end of the program 80% of the participants are able to demonstrate positive change in physical activity self-control score from before to after the intervention.

Second, the theory helps in identifying the method to use in health education or health promotion. For example, continuing with the previous example, the theory prescribes that in order to change self-efficacy the behavior must be taught in small steps, so demonstration could be used as a method. Third, the theory helps in deciding the timing of the intervention. For example, theoretically it would make sense to design more interventions that prevent use of tobacco at the middle

TABLE 1.9   Benefits of Theory in Health Education and Health Promotion
Helps in discerning measurable program outcomes
Specifies methods for behavior change
Identifies the timing for interventions
Helps in choosing the right mix of strategies
Enhances communication between professionals
Improves replication
Improves program efficiency and effectiveness

school level because the behavior is beginning to get started at that point. Fourth, the theory helps in choosing the right mix of strategies and methods. In the earlier example, we were able to choose three constructs of the social cognitive theory because the theory suggests that those three are important for early-stage adolescents.

Fifth, theory aids communication between professionals. The constructs of each theory remain the same in different applications, and thus readers can understand across the studies what was done. Sixth, the use of theory helps in replication of the program because the same constructs can be used from one intervention to the other. Finally, behavioral and social science theories help in making programs more effective (greater impact) and efficient (less time). These benefits are summarized in Table 1.9.

SKILL-BUILDING ACTIVITY

Think of either a positive behavior or a negative behavior amenable to modification by health education. Choose a target population for whom this behavior would be most relevant. Now, using the SMART way of writing objectives that is shown in Table 1.10, write at least three program objectives that would help bring about positive change in this behavior in the chosen target population.

TABLE 1.10   The SMART Way to Write Objectives
S = Specific (e.g., what exactly is being changed and in whom)
M = Measurable (e.g., percentage of participants who will change)
A = Action verb (e.g., *list, describe, identify, explain*)
R = Realistic (i.e., must be achievable)
T = Time frame (e.g., end of the session, end of one year)

SUMMARY

Health can be defined as a means to achieve desirable goals in life while maintaining a multidimensional (physical, mental, social, political, economic, and spiritual) equilibrium that is operationalized for individuals as well as for communities. *Health behavior* can be defined as actions with potentially measurable frequency, intensity, and duration performed at the individual, interpersonal, organizational, community, or public policy level for primary, secondary, or tertiary prevention. *Health education* can be defined as systematic application of a set of techniques to voluntarily and positively influence health through changing the antecedents of behavior (awareness, information, knowledge, skills, beliefs, attitudes, and values) in individuals, groups, or communities. *Health promotion* can be defined as a process of empowering people to improve their health by providing educational, political, legislative, organizational, social, and community supports.

Health education and health promotion professionals have to perform responsibilities that include assessing individual and community needs; planning health education strategies, interventions, and programs; implementing health education strategies, interventions, and programs; conducting evaluation and research related to health education; administering health education strategies, interventions, and programs; serving as health education resources; and communicating and advocating for health and health education. All these functions can be aided by the use of theories from the behavioral and social sciences. Use of a theory helps in discerning measurable program outcomes, specifies methods for behavior change, identifies the timing for interventions, helps in choosing the right mix of strategies, enhances communication between professionals, improves replication, and improves program efficiency and effectiveness.

REVIEW QUESTIONS

1. How has the World Health Organization defined health? Discuss the limitations of this definition of health.
2. Differentiate between health education and health promotion.
3. Differentiate among primary, secondary, and tertiary prevention.
4. What are the areas of responsibilities for entry-level health educators?
5. What are the differences in responsibilities for entry-level health educators and graduate-level health educators?
6. Identify at least five settings for health education.
7. Discuss at least five areas in the code of ethics for the health education profession.
8. Discuss the objectives of any one national-level health education organization.
9. Differentiate between attitudes and beliefs.
10. Differentiate between community mobilization and community empowerment.

WEBSITE

Go to the Web component of *Theoretical Foundations of Health Education and Health Promotion* at http://health.jbpub.com/foundations for Web exercises, additional resources related to this chapter, and student review tools.

GLOSSARY TERMS

advocacy

attitudes

awareness

behavior

beliefs

certified health education specialist (CHES)

coalition

code of ethics for health educators

community

community development

community empowerment

community mobilization

community organization

community participation

development of social norms

health

health behavior

health education

health literacy

health promotion

information

knowledge

legislation

lobbying

networking

policy development

primary prevention

secondary prevention

skills

tertiary prevention

values

REFERENCES AND FURTHER READING

Airhihenbuwa, C. O., Cottrell, R. R., Adeyanju, M., Auld, M. E., Lysoby, L., & Smith, B. J. (2005). The National Health Educator Competencies Update Project: Celebrating a milestone and recommending next steps to the profession. *American Journal of Health Education, 36*, 361–370.

Allegrante, J. P., Airhihenbuwa, C. O., Auld, M. E., Birch, D. A., Roe, K. M., & Smith, B. J. (2004). Toward a unified system of accreditation for professional preparation in health education: Final report of the National Task Force on Accreditation in Health Education. *Health Education and Behavior, 31*, 668–683.

American Association for Health Education. (2003). Directory of institutions offering undergraduate and graduate degree programs in health education. 2003 edition. *American Journal of Health Education, 34*(4), 219–235.

American Association for Health Education, National Commission for Health Education Credentialing, & Society for Public Health Education. (1999). *A competency-based framework for graduate-level health educators.* Allentown, PA: National Commission for Health Education Credentialing.

Arnstein, S. R. (1971). Eight rungs on the ladder of citizen participation. In E. S. Cahn & B. A. Passett (Eds.), *Citizen participation: Effecting community change* (p. 70). New York: Praeger.

Bandura, A. (1986). *Social foundations of thought and action.* Englewood Cliffs, NJ: Prentice Hall.

Bandura, A. (2004). Health promotion by social cognitive means. *Health Education and Behavior, 31*, 143–164.

Bensley, R. J. (1991). Defining spiritual health: A review of the literature. *Journal of Health Education, 22*(5), 287–290.

Bloom, B. S. (1956). *Taxonomy of educational objectives. Handbook I: The cognitive domain.* New York: David McKay.

Coalition of National Health Education Organizations. (2004). Code of ethics. Retrieved November 12, 2006, from http://www.hsc.usf.edu/CFH/cnheo/ethics.htm.

Cook, H. (2004). Historical keywords. Health. *Lancet, 364*, 1481.

Downie, R., Fyfe, C., & Tannahill, A. (1990). *Health promotion: Models and values.* Oxford, UK: Oxford University Press.

Gilmore, G. D., Olsen, L. K., Taub, A., & Connell, D. (2005). Overview of the National Health Educator Competencies Update Project, 1998–2004. *Health Education and Behavior, 32*, 725–737.

Glanz, K., Rimer, B. K., & Lewis, F. M. (2002). *Health behavior and health education. Theory, research, and practice* (3rd ed.). San Francisco: Jossey-Bass.

Gochman, D. S. (1982). Labels, systems, and motives: Some perspectives on future research. *Health Education Quarterly, 9*, 167–174.

Gochman, D. S. (1997). Health behavior research: Definitions and diversity. In D. S. Gochman (Ed.), *Handbook of health behavior research: Vol. 1. Personal and social determinants.* New York: Plenum Press.

Gold, R. S., & Miner, K. R., for the 2000 Joint Committee on Health Education and Promotion Terminology. (2002). Report of the 2000 Joint Committee on Health Education and Promotion Terminology. *Journal of School Health, 72*, 3–7.

Green, L. W., & Kreuter, M. W. (2005). *Health program planning: An educational and ecological approach* (4th ed.). Boston: McGraw Hill.

Institute of Medicine. (1988). *Future of public health.* Washington, DC: National Academy Press.

Institute of Medicine. (2002). *The future of the public's health in the 21st century.* Washington, DC: National Academy Press.

Kerlinger, F. N., & Lee, H. B. (2000). *Foundations of behavioral research* (4th ed.). Fort Worth, TX: Harcourt College Publishers.

McDowell, I., & Newell, C. (1987). The theoretical and technical foundations of health measurement. In I. McDowell & C. Newell (Eds.), *Measuring health: A guide to rating scales and questionnaires* (pp. 10–42). New York: Oxford University Press.

Minkler, M., & Wallerstein, N. (1997). Improving health through community organization and community building. A health education perspective. In M. Minkler (Ed.), *Community organizing and community building for health.* New Brunswick, NJ: Rutgers University Press.

Modeste, N. M., & Tamayose, T. (Eds.). (2004). *Dictionary of public health promotion and education. Terms and concepts* (2nd ed.). San Francisco: Jossey Bass.

Mucchielli, R. (1970). *Introduction to structural psychology.* New York: Funk and Wagnalls.

National Cancer Institute. (2005). *Theory at a glance: A guide for health promotion practice* (2nd ed.). Washington, DC: U.S. Department of Health and Human Services. Retrieved May 20, 2006, from http://www.nci.nih.gov/theory/pdf.

National Commission for Health Education Credentialing. (1985). *A framework for the development of competency based curricula for entry-level health educators.* New York: Author.

National Commission for Health Education Credentialing, Society for Public Health Education, & American Association for Health Education. (2006). *Competency-based framework for health educators—2006.* Whitehall, PA: Author.

Parsons, T. (1951). *The social system.* New York: Free Press.

Perrin, K. M., & McDermott, R. J. (1997). The spiritual dimension of health: A review. *American Journal of Health Studies, 13*(2), 90–99.

Pickett, G., & Hanlon, J. J. (1998). *Public health: Administration and practice* (10th ed.). St. Louis, MO: Mosby.

Polit, D. F., & Hungler, B. P. (1999). *Nursing research: Principles and methods* (6th ed.). Philadelphia: Lippincott.

Public Health Functions Steering Committee. (1994). *Public health in America.* Retrieved May 18, 2006, from http://www.health.gov/phfunctions/public.htm.

Rokeach, M. (1970). *Beliefs, attitudes and values.* San Francisco: Jossey Bass.

Selye, H. (1974). *The stress of life.* New York: McGraw Hill.

Simpson, E. J. (1972). *The classification of educational objectives in the psychomotor domain.* Washington, DC: Gryphon House.

Taub, A., Kreuter, M., Parcel, G., & Vitello, E. (1987). Report from the AAHE/SOPHE Joint Committee on Ethics. *Health Education Quarterly, 14*(1), 79–90.

U.S. Department of Health, Education and Welfare. (1978). *Preparation and practice of community, patient, and school health educators: Proceedings of the workshop on commonalities and differences.* Washington, DC: Division of Allied Health Professions.

U.S. Department of Health and Human Services. (1979). *Healthy People: The surgeon general's report on health promotion and disease prevention.* Washington, DC: Author.

U.S. Department of Health and Human Services. (1980). *Promoting health—preventing disease. Objectives for the nation*. Washington, DC: Author.

U.S. Department of Health and Human Services. (1990). *Healthy People 2000. National health promotion and disease prevention objectives*. Washington, DC: Author.

U.S. Department of Health and Human Services. (2000). *Healthy People 2010* (Vols. 1–2). Washington, DC: Author.

World Health Organization. (1974). Constitution of the World Health Organization. *Chronicle of the World Health Organization, 1,* 29–43.

World Health Organization. (1986). *Ottawa Charter for Health Promotion, 1986*. Geneva, Switzerland: Author.

World Health Organization. (1997). *The Jakarta Declaration on leading health promotion into the 21st century*. Geneva, Switzerland: Author.

World Health Organization. (1998). *Health promotion glossary*. Available from http://www.who.int/hpr/NPH/docs/hp_glossary_en.pdf.

Zarcadoolas, C., Pleasant A., & Greer, D. S. (2003). Elaborating a definition of health literacy: A commentary. *Journal of Health Communication, 8,* 119–120.

CHAPTER 2

Planning Models in Health Education and Health Promotion

KEY CONCEPTS

- Assessment Protocol for Excellence in Public Health (APEXPH)
- CDCynergy
- Comprehensive Health Education Model (CHEM)
- Intervention mapping model
- Model
- Model for Health Education Planning (MHEP)
- Model for Health Education Planning and Resource Development (MHEPRD)
- Multilevel Approach to Community Health (MATCH)
- PEN-3 model
- Planned Approach to Community Health (PATCH)
- PRECEDE-PROCEED model

AFTER READING THIS CHAPTER YOU SHOULD BE ABLE TO

- Differentiate between a theory and model
- Apply the PRECEDE-PROCEED model of planning in health education and health promotion
- Identify the main components of the Planned Approach to Community Health (PATCH) model
- Describe the Multilevel Approach to Community Health (MATCH) model
- Narrate the steps and processes in the intervention mapping model
- Explain the Assessment Protocol for Excellence in Public Health (APEXPH) model
- Explicate the Comprehensive Health Education Model (CHEM)
- Describe the Model for Health Education Planning (MHEP)
- Elaborate on the Model for Health Education Planning and Resource Development (MHEPRD)
- Explain the PEN-3 model
- Summarize the CDCynergy model

DIFFERENCES BETWEEN A MODEL AND A THEORY _____

The previous chapter discussed how a theory helps health education and health promotion programs by helping identify program objectives, specifying methods for facilitating behavior change, providing guidance about the timing of the methods, and helping select the methods. These are all very specific functions in the broad area of planning. Chapter 1 also stated that planning skills are one of the seven essential responsibilities of health educators. When planning, various other functions are needed besides setting objectives and selecting methods. These functions could include assessing needs, prioritizing needs, allocating resources, matching human resources to tasks, and so on. Hence, models are used for planning in health promotion and health education.

A less refined form of a theory is called a **model**. Models are eclectic, creative, simplified, miniaturized applications of concepts for addressing problems. Models are used for planning interventions and can be seen as theories in their early stages. The term *model* connotes that there may not be enough empirical evidence to call it a theory. Model makers present their ideas but do not necessarily test these through experimentation. Sometimes the model makers may start with the term *model* and then test the model thoroughly, yet the word *model* sticks as part of its name. Models do not provide guidance for micro-level management, unlike theories, which do. An example of a model is the PRECEDE-PROCEED model (Green & Kreuter, 2005), which is used in planning health promotion and health education programs. Table 2.1 summarizes the differences between a model and a theory.

TABLE 2.1 Comparison Between a Model and a Theory	
Theory	**Model**
Explains or predicts phenomena	Simplified, miniaturized application of concepts for addressing problems
Micro-level guidance	Macro-level guidance
Empirically tested	Not enough empirical evidence
Based in previous literature	Creative
Usually parsimonious	Usually tries to cover a lot
Does not contain any model	May embody one or more theories
Example: Social cognitive theory	Example: PRECEDE-PROCEED model

Planning is bringing the future into the present so that you can do something about it now.

—Alan Lakein

The essential competencies identified by the Competencies Update Project (CUP) for health educators who are planning health education strategies, interventions, and programs are summarized in Table 2.2. To fulfill these competencies at the macro level, planning models are needed; for accomplishing these functions at the micro level, theories are needed.

This chapter focuses on planning models, that is, models that are used in planning health promotion and health education programs at the macro level. However, in the remainder of the book the emphasis is on micro-level planning by use of behavioral and social science theories. This chapter provides an overview of the various planning models and the process of planning. The models discussed in this chapter are the PRECEDE-PROCEED model (Green & Kreuter, 2005); Planned Approach to Community Health (PATCH) model (U.S. Department of Health and Human Services [DHHS], 2005); Multilevel Approach to Community Health (MATCH) model (Simons-Morton, Greene, & Gottlieb, 1995); intervention mapping model (Bartholomew, Parcel, Kok, & Gottlieb, 2006); Assessment Protocol for Excellence in Public Health (APEXPH) model (National Association of County and City Health Officials, 1991); Comprehensive Health Education Model (CHEM) (Sullivan, 1973); Model for Health Education Planning (MHEP) (Ross & Mico, 1980); Model for Health Education Planning and Resource Development (MHEPRD) (Bates &

TABLE 2.2	Competencies Identified by the Competencies Update Project for Health Educators Who Are Planning Health Education Strategies, Interventions, and Programs
A. Involve people and organizations in program planning
B. Incorporate data analysis and principles of community organization
C. Formulate appropriate and measurable program objectives
D. Develop a logical scope and sequence plan for health education practice
E. Design strategies, interventions, and programs consistent with specified objectives
F. Select appropriate strategies to meet objectives
G. Assess factors that affect implementation

Winder, 1984); PEN-3 model (Airhihenbuwa, 1993); and the CDCynergy model (Centers for Disease Control and Prevention [CDC], 2004). These models are presented in the order of their popularity, as identified in a study by Linnan and colleagues (2005).

PRECEDE-PROCEED MODEL

One of the most popular models (Linnan et al., 2005) in health education is the PRECEDE-PROCEED model (Green & Kreuter, 2005). As of the mid-2000s, there were close to 1,000 published applications of the **PRECEDE-PROCEED model** in the health field (Green & Kreuter, 2005). The acronym PRECEDE stands for predisposing, reinforcing, and enabling constructs in educational/environmental diagnosis and evaluation. The acronym PROCEED stands for policy, regulatory, and organizational constructs in educational and environmental development.

The model originated in the 1970s from applications in hypertension trials (Green, Levine, & Deeds, 1975; Green, Levine, Wolle, & Deeds, 1979), cost-benefit evaluations (the ratio of benefits accrued in dollar amounts to the dollars spent on the program) of health education (Green, 1974), family planning studies (Green, 1970), and immunization campaigns (Rosenstock, Derryberry, & Carriger, 1959). The model was initially called PRECEDE (predisposing, reinforcing, and enabling constructs in educational diagnosis and evaluation) and remained popular under that name throughout the 1980s (Green, Kreuter, Deeds, & Partridge, 1980). In the 1980s the movement for health promotion grew very strong; in response, the model evolved and came to be known in its present-day form as PRECEDE-PROCEED, in which a number of health promotion functions were added. In the 1990s the role of socioenvironmental approaches was strengthened even further, and the model emphasized the ecological approach. The latest edition of this model was published in 2005 (Green & Kreuter, 2005). For detailed discussion of this model, see *Health Program Planning: An Educational and Ecological Approach* (Green & Kreuter, 2005). Figure 2.1 depicts the model.

The PRECEDE-PROCEED model has eight phases that provide guidance in planning any health program. The first phase is the *social assessment and situational analysis phase*. In this phase an assessment of community perceptions is done as a starting point for identifying quality of life concerns, using such methods as asset mapping, social reconnaissance, nominal group process, the Delphi method, focus groups, central location intercept interviews, and surveys. Asset mapping is an assessment of the strengths, capacities, and skills of individuals and the existing resources in

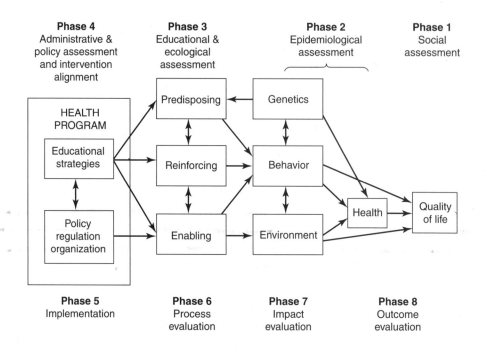

FIGURE 2.1   Generic representation of the PRECEDE-PROCEED model for health program planning and evaluation that shows the main lines of causation from program inputs and determinants of health to outcomes by the direction of the arrows
Note. From Green, L. W., & Kreuter, M. W. (2005). *Health program planning: An educational and ecological approach* (4th ed., p. 10). Boston: McGraw Hill. Reproduced with permission.

a community. In social reconnaissance, a point of entry into the community is chosen and local players are identified; this is followed by preparation of research and briefing materials and identification of leaders and representatives, followed in turn by field interviews and then analysis, reporting, and follow-up. In the nominal group process, community participants are recruited and are given a single question on which to reflect. The responses are collected and then ranked in importance by the participants to establish a priority list. In the Delphi method, a panel of experts is recruited and sent a questionnaire. Subsequent mailings of the questionnaire aim at deriving consensus and narrow the choices at each iteration. Focus group discussions are small group discussions on a given topic that are moderated by a facilitator. Central location intercept interviews are conducted at shopping malls, churches, and other such places where target population members can be found. These interviews typically include structured, close-ended questions. Surveys also consist of asking questions of the target population and can be done by mail, e-mail, online, or other means.

The second phase is *epidemiological assessment* and includes identifying what specific health problems are contributing to or interacting with the quality of life concerns identified in the social assessment. This phase also identifies the causative factors in the three categories of genetics, behaviors, and environments. Epidemiology consists of two parts: descriptive and analytical. This phase attempts to gather information on both these aspects. In **descriptive epidemiology**, facts regarding the time, place, and population attributes of the health problem are collected through mortality (death), morbidity (illness), and disability rates. **Analytical epidemiology** examines the determinants of health. In this model analytical work translates into identifying behaviors and environments. Behaviors are of three types: proximal, or direct, actions affecting health; actions influencing the health of others; and distal actions affecting the organizational or policy environment. To diagnose behaviors that need targeting, a listing of all behavioral factors is made and the factors are rated in terms of importance and changeability, focusing on those behaviors that are more changeable and more important; behavioral objectives are then developed for those selected. To diagnose environments, the environmental factors are listed and then rated in terms of importance and changeability, again focusing on the more changeable and more important ones; environmental objectives are then determined.

The third phase is *educational and ecological assessment.* In this phase, factors are classified into the hallmark categories of this model as predisposing, enabling, or reinforcing factors. **Predisposing factors** are those factors that are antecedents to behavioral change and that provide motivation for the behavior (for example, knowledge, beliefs, attitudes, values, perceptions). **Enabling factors** are antecedents to behavioral or environmental change that allow a motivation or environmental policy to be realized (for example, availability of resources, accessibility, laws, legislations, skills). **Reinforcing factors** are those factors that follow a behavior and provide continuing reward for sustenance of the behavior (for example, family, peers, teachers, employers, health providers, community leaders, decision makers). In this phase the factors are identified and sorted, priorities are determined, and once again priorities within categories are identified using the criteria of changeability and importance.

The fourth phase is the *administrative and policy assessment and intervention alignment* phase. In this phase the program components are aligned with priorities, the resources needed to run the program are identified, the barriers that can influence the program are identified, and the policies needed to run the program are developed. In aligning priority determinants with program components, first matching of ecological levels with program components is done, followed by mapping of specific interventions, and finally pooling of previous interventions to patch any gaps. This phase assesses aspects such as time, personnel, and budget.

The fifth phase is the *implementation phase*. In this phase several factors play a role that may hinder or augment the impact of the program. These pertain to the program (such as resources and goals), implementing organization (such as employee attributes, organizational goals, and organizational climate), political milieu, and environment (such as timing and other organizations).

The sixth phase is the *process evaluation*. In this phase, it is first determined whether the intervention is being done in the manner in which it has been planned. For example, if ten activities were planned, have all of these been implemented, and to what extent have they been implemented? Second, the reception of the program at the site where it has been implemented is determined. Third, the attitudes of the recipients of the program are considered. How satisfied have they been with the program? What are things they liked and what are things they disliked about the program? Fourth, the response of the person implementing the program is determined. What difficulties did he or she face while implementing the program? What things were easy to do? Finally, the competencies of the personnel involved are assessed. For example, if health education work was done, was it done by a certified health education specialist or someone else?

The seventh phase is the *impact evaluation*. Impact evaluation assesses the immediate effect of the program on its target behaviors or environments and their predisposing, enabling, and reinforcing antecedents. For example, a program designed to combat obesity in a community would measure physical activity behavior and consumption of fruits and vegetables.

The final phase is *outcome evaluation*. In this phase, changes in health status (such as mortality, morbidity, and disability indicators) and quality of life concerns (such as perceived quality of life and unemployment) are measured.

The PRECEDE-PROCEED model has been used in a variety of applications within health promotion and health education programming. Some of the areas in which this model has been used are for coalition building (Fisher et al., 1996), enhancing community participation (Watson, Horowitz, Garcia, & Canto, 2001), planning multiple-channel interventions (Hall & Best, 1997), developing health instruments (Chang, Brown, Nitzke, & Baumann, 2004), conducting needs assessments (Brouse, Basch, Wolf, & Shmukler, 2004), implementing health risk appraisals at worksites (Bailey, Rukholm, Vanderlee, & Hyland, 1994), planning disease prevention programs at worksites (Wilkens, 2003), planning employee assistance programs at worksites (Dille, 1999), planning health programs in school settings (MacDonald & Green, 2001), training health care staff (Macrina, Macrina, Horvath, Gallaspy, & Fine, 1996), improving self-care (Chiang, Huang, Yeh, & Lu, 2004), and ensuring compliance behaviors (Kang, Han, Kim, & Kim, 2006). Table 2.3 summarizes these applications.

The developers of this model, Larry Green and Marshall Kreuter, teamed up with Robert Gold to develop a computerized software program designed to help health educators in academia who teach community health courses and assist practitioners in the field to plan and implement community health programs. The software is called *EMPOWER (Enabling Methods of Planning and Organizing Within Everyone's Reach)* (Gold, Green, & Kreuter, 1998). The program provides a specific example in the area of breast cancer prevention and control and walks the user through the various steps of the PRECEDE-PROCEED model.

The PRECEDE-PROCEED model is by far the most popular and most researched model in the field of health promotion and health education. It has been in existence for four decades, and professionally trained health educators are familiar with this model. It is very comprehensive and covers all areas of planning. The initiation of

---

TABLE 2.3   Applications of the PRECEDE-PROCEED Model

Coalition building

Enhancing community participation

Planning multiple-channel interventions

Developing health instruments

Conducting needs assessments

Implementing health risk appraisals at worksites

Planning disease prevention programs at worksites

Planning employee assistance programs (EAPs) at worksites

Planning health programs in school settings

Improving self-care

Ensuring compliance behaviors

> *The hallmarks of the PRECEDE-PROCEED model are: (1) flexibility and scalability, (2) evidence-based process and evaluability, (3) its commitment to the principle of participation, and (4) its provision of a process for appropriate adaptation of evidence-based "best practices."*
>
> —Green and Kreuter
> (2005, p. 18)

the model utilizes community inputs and participation, which is a big plus. The phase-wise evaluation is also a strong feature of the model.

However, the model does have a few limitations. First, it is too comprehensive to be implemented in its totality in all situations. Often, health promotion and education funding is allocated for working in a specific area, and there is no provision for social assessment or epidemiological assessment. In such cases the model is implemented in a piecemeal fashion. Second, health promotion and education programs are often implemented on a limited basis. These programs often do not account for changes in health outcomes, and thus outcome evaluation is often not possible. Third, the model is a mixture of several theories, and thus it is not possible to discern which component of the model is working and to what extent. Finally, comparative studies of this model in comparison with other models have not been done. Therefore, the relative utility of this model in relation to other models cannot be commented upon.

PLANNED APPROACH TO COMMUNITY HEALTH MODEL

The **Planned Approach to Community Health (PATCH) model** is a community health planning model developed in the mid-1980s by the Centers for Disease Control and Prevention in partnership with state and local health departments and several

> *PATCH was built on the same philosophy as the World Health Organization's Health for All and the Ottawa Charter for Health Promotion which specifies that health promotion is the process of enabling people to increase control over their health and to improve their health.*
>
> —U.S. Department of Health and Human Services
> (2005, p. I-H-I)

community groups (U.S. DHHS, 2005). It is an effective community health planning model that is used by many states and communities and several countries. PATCH aims at increasing the capacity of communities to plan, implement, and evaluate community-based health promotion programs. Thus, capacity building is a very important part of the model. The PATCH model builds on the PRECEDE model (Kreuter, 1992) but is more user friendly and does not use heavy academic terminology. A key strategy of the PATCH model is that it builds linkages within the community and between the community and the state health department, universities, and other regional and national organizations.

After its initial development in 1984–1985, the PATCH model was pilot tested in 6 states by the CDC. Based on the feedback received, it was revised and then delivered in 11 additional states. In 1988, three evaluation studies were performed by the University of North Carolina, the Research Triangle Institute, and the PATCH National Working Group to assess the effects of PATCH, which found it to be effective. Since 1991, the CDC has not directly delivered the PATCH program in communities but rather provides training and consultation to state health departments. At present, most state health departments have staff trained in the PATCH model and also have a state coordinator for the PATCH model. Table 2.4 summarizes the five key elements of the PATCH model.

Active participation of community members is vital in the PATCH model. People participate in analyzing community data, setting priorities, planning intervention activities, and making decisions on the health priorities of their communities. Using qualitative and quantitative data to identify a community's health status and needs is also important in the PATCH model. Community members are engaged in analyzing the factors that are responsible for contributing to a health problem, linking with Healthy People 2010 objectives, and designing health promotion interventions. Examples of these interventions could be educational programs, mass media campaigns, policy advocacy, and so on. These interventions are conducted in various settings, such as schools, health care facilities, community sites, and workplaces. Community members then conduct timely evaluations. Finally, the community becomes empowered and can replicate the process for more than one health condition.

The PATCH model has five distinct phases for planning a health program. The first phase is *mobilizing the community*. In this phase the target community is defined, participants are actively recruited from the community, partnerships are formed, and a demographic profile of the community is completed. Efforts are made to ensure

TABLE 2.4   Key Elements of the PATCH Model

Community members participate in the process.

Data guides the development of programs.

Participants develop a comprehensive health promotion strategy.

Evaluation emphasizes feedback and program improvement.

Community capacity for health promotion is increased.

that the participants who have been recruited are representative of the demographic profile of the community. In this phase a steering committee is also formed and community leaders are involved.

The second phase is *collecting and organizing data*. In this phase, community members obtain data on mortality, morbidity, community opinion, and behaviors. The quantitative data is collected from sources such as vital statistics and surveys, whereas qualitative data is collected from sources such as the opinions of community leaders. The data is analyzed and shared with the community.

The third phase is *choosing health priorities*. In this phase the community group analyzes the social, economic, political, and environmental factors that affect the behaviors that are detrimental for health. As a result of this analysis they identify priorities and develop objectives for those priorities.

The fourth phase is *developing a comprehensive intervention plan*. In this phase the community group identifies resources, assesses existing programs, reviews existing policies, and appraises conditions. Then the group develops intervention objectives and an intervention plan. The intervention plan includes details of strategies, a time line, and an activity plan for things such as recruiting volunteers, publicizing activities, evaluating activities, and informing the community about results.

The fifth phase is the *evaluation phase*. The purpose of the evaluation is to monitor and assess progress achieved during the phases of PATCH and to evaluate interventions. The unique feature here is that the community determines the end points of evaluation, and feedback is provided to the community.

Goodman and colleagues (1993) studied PATCH projects to see how communities traversed the various stages of PATCH. They found the approach to be effective, but suggested the following recommendations for enhancing the effectiveness of the PATCH model:

1. Conduct a community capacity assessment prior to initiating a community needs assessment.
2. Do not rely solely on Behavioral Risk Factor Surveys.
3. Analyze needs assessment data quickly and share it with the community as soon as possible.
4. Allow for flexibility and modifications by the community when determining priority health objectives.
5. Provide technical assistance throughout the project and not just in the beginning.
6. Fund at least one full-time local coordinator and allow extensive capacity building.
7. Emphasize multiple interventions around one chronic condition at a time.
8. Emphasize program institutionalization.

Suen and colleagues (1995) studied the performance of 2,888 local health departments regarding core public health functions. They categorized the core functions of local health departments as follows: (1) health-related data collection, surveillance, and outcomes monitoring; (2) protection of environment, housing, food, and water; (3) investigation and control of diseases and injuries; (4) public information and education; (5) accountability and quality assurance; (6) laboratory services; (7) training and education; and (8) leadership, policy development, and administration. They found that the performance index was greater for all eight functions in those local health departments using health planning models such as the PATCH model. PATCH is indeed a very user-friendly model at the local health department level. For more specific details of this model, see the *Guide for the Local Coordinator* (U.S. DHHS, 2005).

THE MULTILEVEL APPROACH TO COMMUNITY HEALTH MODEL

In the late 1980s, Simons-Morton, Greene, and Gottlieb (1995) introduced the **Multilevel Approach to Community Health (MATCH) model**. It is a very practical and yet comprehensive model. It places the health educator at the center of planning and allows for the lack of an extensive local needs assessment. However, in terms of its popularity, not many publications of this model are available other than those by the authors. Table 2.5 summarizes the five phases in the MATCH model.

The first phase is that of *goals selection* and includes four steps: (1) selecting health status goals by looking at prevalence, perceived and actual importance, changeability, and availability of programmatic resources; (2) selecting the target population by looking at health problem prevalence, accessibility, and programmatic interests; (3) identifying health behavior goals by looking at prevalence, association,

TABLE 2.5   Phases of the MATCH Model
Phase 1. Goals selection
Phase 2. Intervention planning
Phase 3. Program development
Phase 4. Implementation preparations
Phase 5. Evaluation

and changeability; and (4) identifying environmental goals by looking at access to services, availability of programs and resources, enabling policies, practices, and regulations, and barriers.

The second phase is that of *intervention planning*, which includes the following four steps: (1) identifying the targets of intervention at the community level, (2) selecting intervention objectives, (3) identifying mediators of the intervention objectives (such as knowledge, skills, attitudes, and practices), and (4) selecting intervention approaches by applying theories.

The third phase is that of *program development* and also includes four steps: (1) creating program units or components that include paying attention to the target population, intervention targets, intervention objectives, structural units, and channels; (2) selecting or developing curricula and creating intervention guides that include learning objectives, content, teaching/learning methods, and materials; (3) developing session plans in which educational objectives are delineated with teaching/learning activities, materials, and specific instructions; (4) creating or acquiring instructional materials in which existing materials are reviewed and selected and new materials developed after pilot testing.

The fourth phase is *implementation preparation* and comprises two steps. The first step includes facilitating, adopting, implementing, and maintaining a health behavior by developing a specific proposal; developing the need, readiness, and environmental supports for change; providing evidence of the efficacy of the intervention; identifying change agents and opinion leaders; and establishing constructive working relationships with decision makers. The second step in this phase concerns selecting and training implementers.

> *W*hereas PRECEDE-PROCEED emphasizes formal needs assessment, MATCH as formulated by Simons-Morton and associates (1988) is a framework that gives more attention to implementation.
>
> —Simons-Morton, Greene, and Gottlieb (1995, p. 132.)

The fifth and final phase is *evaluation*. There are three levels of evaluation: (1) process evaluation, which assesses recruitment, session, and program implementation, quality of learning activities, and immediate outcomes; (2) impact evaluation, which examines antecedents of behaviors and environments, changes in behaviors and environments, and any side effects of the program; and (3) outcome evaluation, which assesses health outcomes, cost effectiveness, and policy recommendations. For more details on this model, see *Introduction to Health Education and Health Promotion* (Simons-Morton, Greene, & Gottlieb, 1995).

INTERVENTION MAPPING _____

In the 1990s, Bartholomew and colleagues (2006) proposed a model for health education and health promotion planning called **intervention mapping**. The model advocates a socioecological approach that looks at individual behaviors in an environmental context. Intervention mapping has been used for several types of programs in health promotion and education. Some examples of such programs are breast and cervical cancer screening (Fernandez, Gonzales, Tortolero-Luna, Partida, & Bartholomew, 2005), diet and physical activity promotion (Brug, Oenema, & Ferreira, 2005), fruit and vegetable promotion (Perez-Rodrigo et al., 2005), HIV and sexually transmitted disease (STD) prevention (Tortolero et al., 2005), healthy lifestyles for leg ulcer patients (Heinen, Bartholomew, Wensing, Kerkhof, & Achterberg, 2006), sexual and reproductive health (Aaro et al., 2006), socioeconomic health inequities (Abbema, Van Assema, Kok, De Leeuw, & De Vries, 2004), promoting exercise therapy for urinary incontinence patients (Alewijnse, Mesters, Metsemakers, & van den Borne, 2002), violence prevention (Murray, Kelder, Parcel, Frankowski, & Orpinas, 1999), and weight gain prevention (Kremers et al., 2005). These applications are summarized in Table 2.6.

> *In Intervention Mapping we argue for a social ecological approach in which health is viewed as a function of individuals and of the environments in which individuals live, including family, social networks, organizations, communities, and societies.*
>
> —Bartholomew, Parcel, Kok, and Gottlieb (2006, p. 9)

TABLE 2.6 Applications of Intervention Mapping
Breast and cervical cancer screening
Diet and physical activity promotion
Fruit and vegetable promotion
HIV and STD prevention
Supporting healthy lifestyles in leg ulcer patients
Sexual and reproductive health
Socioeconomic health inequities
Promoting exercise therapy for urinary incontinence patients
Violence prevention
Weight gain prevention

Intervention mapping is a six-step process.

1. *Performing needs assessment or problem analysis.* Assessment of health, quality of life, behavior, and environment is done, along with assessment of community capacity. In this step program outcomes are established.
2. *Creating matrices of change objectives based on the determinants of behavioral and environmental conditions.* In this step performance objectives are established.
3. *Selecting theory-based intervention methods and practical strategies.* In this step the program is reviewed with interested participants, theoretical methods are identified, program methods are chosen, and design strategies that match change objectives are chosen.
4. *Translating methods and strategies into an organized program.* In this step consultation with program participants and implementers is done; program scope, sequence, theme, and materials are listed; protocols are designed; and program materials are prepared and pretested with the target audience.
5. *Planning for the adoption, implementation, and sustainability of the program.* In this step adopters and users are identified; adoption, implementation, and sustainability performance objectives are decided; and interventions are designed to affect program use.
6. *Generating an evaluation plan.* In this step the program is described, along with program outcomes, effect questions, and process questions. Then indicators and measures are developed and evaluation designs are specified.

For complete details on this model, see *Planning Health Promotion Programs: An Intervention Mapping Approach* (Bartholomew, Parcel, Kok, & Gottlieb, 2006).

ASSESSMENT PROTOCOL FOR EXCELLENCE IN PUBLIC HEALTH MODEL

The **Assessment Protocol for Excellence in Public Health (APEXPH) model** was developed by the National Association of County and City Health Officials (NACCHO) with funding from the CDC in the late 1980s (NACCHO, 1991). The users for this planning model are intended to be local health departments. The model helps in building organizational capacity and establishes a leadership role for the local health departments. The unique features of this model are as follows:

- It is a form of self-assessment tool.
- It leads to development of a practical plan of action.

- It focuses on the local health department's capacity and the community's actual and perceived needs.
- It helps the local health department to build its relationships with other local governmental agencies and community, state, and federal agencies.
- It provides a protocol through which a health department can assess health needs, set priorities, develop policy, and assure that health needs are met.
- It fits local situations and resources.

APEXPH is a three-part process. The first part is *organizational capacity assessment.* In this part an internal review of the local health department is done to determine the administrative capacity of the department, and a plan of action is created. The second part is the *community process*, in which key members of the community are involved to assess the health of the community. In this part a community advisory committee to identify and prioritize key health problems is established. Then health data is collected and analyzed, followed by the setting of goals and objectives and the identification of local resources. The third part is *completing the cycle*. Monitoring and evaluating of the organizational action plan and community health plan are done in this part, as is institutionalization of the three core functions of assessment, policy development, and assurance.

> *APEXPH is a voluntary process for organizational and community self-assessment, planned improvements, and continuing evaluation and reassessment.*
>
> —National Association of County and City Health Officials (1991)

COMPREHENSIVE HEALTH EDUCATION MODEL

One of the earliest planning models was the **Comprehensive Health Education Model (CHEM),** developed in the early 1970s by Sullivan (1973). The chief advantage of this model lies in its simplicity. This model is hardly ever used in practice these days and is included in this discussion mainly for historical reasons. The model comprises six steps.

1. *Involving people.* In this step, the target population and the personnel required to carry out the program are identified and a working relationship between the two is established.
2. *Setting goals.* In this step, programmatic goals and objectives are established that mirror health education practices and resources in the target population.
3. *Defining problems.* The planners determine the gaps between what is and what ought to be. Prioritization is also done in this step.

4. *Designing plans.* The most appropriate approach is identified, program objectives are set, a time line is defined, activities and resources are selected, and a pretest is conducted.
5. *Conducting activities.* In this step the program is implemented.
6. *Evaluating results.* The evaluation results are used for continuing or changing the program.

As the planners move through each of these steps, they must consider the interaction of the health problem with the chosen behaviors, reflect on the available best practices, contemplate the limitations of health education, and identify resources needed to conduct the program.

MODEL FOR HEALTH EDUCATION PLANNING

Another one of the earliest models in health education planning, developed in the 1960s, was the **Model for Health Education Planning (MHEP)** (Ross & Mico, 1980). This model is also not used much in current practice. There are six phases in the model, each of which has three dimensions: the content dimension (subject matter), the method dimension (steps and techniques), and the process dimension (interactions).

1. *Program initiation.* Planners develop an understanding of the target population's problem, develop a relationship with the population, and create awareness of the problem.
2. *Needs assessment.* Planners identify past assessment efforts, collect new data, analyze data, and describe the problem.
3. *Goal setting.* Goals are based on the problems identified in the needs assessment. Goals must be appropriate and realistic. In addition, input from those who will be affected is gathered, and strategies are developed for implementing the identified goals.
4. *Planning/programming.* Planners translate the strategies into a rational implementation plan or program, design systems and tools for managing the activities, and arrange for commitments among all the involved parties.
5. *Implementation.* The activities are initiated, any training and technical assistance consultations are obtained, problem solving is carried out, and reporting is done.
6. *Evaluation.* Clarification of evaluation measures is done, data is collected and analyzed, and refinements to the program and process are made.

MODEL FOR HEALTH EDUCATION PLANNING AND RESOURCE DEVELOPMENT (MHEPRD)

The **Model for Health Education Planning and Resource Development (MHEPRD)** was proposed by Bates and Winder (1984) in the early 1980s but is not among the popular models. It is not commonly used in health education practice these days. The hallmarks of this model are that it considers planning a cyclical process, it separates processes from the end products, and it considers evaluation not as a separate step but as an integrated element throughout the model. There are five phases in the model:

1. *Health education plans.* An end result of the needs assessment (which in this model is called a *policy analysis process*) and an ongoing evaluation process.
2. *Demonstration programs.* Developed through a development process and an ongoing evaluation process.
3. *Operational programs.* The validation process determines which programs should be continued and thus made operational and which ones must be dropped. The ongoing evaluation process continues in this phase. This phase also entails development of an implementation plan.
4. *Research programs.* Implementation of those programs that are based on sound research continues in the implementation process.
5. *Information and statistics.* The data generated once again goes through the policy analysis process in phase 1 and guides further planning.

PEN-3 MODEL

The **PEN-3 model** originated for child survival programs in African countries (Airhihenbuwa, 1993, 1995). Later its use was extended to several other applications with minority populations, such as breast and cervical cancer screening in Latina women (Erwin, Johnson, Feliciano-Libid, Zamora, & Jandorf, 2005), cancer screening in African American men (Abernethy et al., 2005), dietary behaviors in African Americans (James, 2004), health factors in Latino immigrants (Garces, Scarinci, & Harrison, 2006), and smoking practices in African Americans (Beech & Scarinci, 2003). Table 2.7 summarizes these applications.

TABLE 2.7   Applications of the PEN-3 Model
Breast and cervical cancer screening in Latina women
Cancer screening in African American men
Child survival in African countries
Dietary behavior in African Americans
Health factors in Latino immigrants
Smoking practices in African Americans

The model consists of three dimensions, each of which contains the acronym PEN. The three dimensions are interrelated and interdependent. The first dimension, *health education*, has the following PEN:

P   *Person*. Health education should be committed to improving the health of every person.

E   *Extended family*. Health education should be directed toward not just the immediate family but also the extended family or kinships of the person.

N   *Neighborhood*. Health education should be directed toward improving health in neighborhoods and communities. Involvement of community leaders is vital for culturally appropriate health programming.

The second dimension of the PEN-3 model is *educational diagnosis of health behavior*. This dimension evolved from the health belief model (Hochbaum, 1958), the theory of reasoned action (Fishbein & Ajzen, 1975), and the PRECEDE-PROCEED model (Green & Kreuter, 2005). In this dimension the PEN acronym is as follows:

P   *Perceptions*. These pertain to knowledge, beliefs, attitudes, and values that may facilitate or hinder motivation for changing a given behavior. Here the health programs must start with the perceived perceptions of the person rather than the real needs identified by the planners for the latter to be meaningful and acceptable.

E   *Enablers*. These are societal or systemic forces that may augment the health behavior or hinder it by creating barriers. These include available resources, accessibility, referrals, and types of service.

N   *Nurturers*. These are reinforcing factors that an individual may receive from significant others. These significant others could be members of the extended family, peers, employers, health personnel, religious leaders, or government officials.

The third dimension of the PEN-3 model is the *cultural appropriateness of health beliefs*. Thus this model is particularly useful for work with minority populations and yields a culturally appropriate program. The PEN acronym in this dimension is as follows:

P   *Positive*. These are the positive perceptions, enablers, and nurturers that help the person, family, or community to engage in positive healthy practices. These positive health practices lead to empowerment at the individual level, family level, and community level.

E   *Exotic*. These consist of practices that are neither good nor bad and thus do not need to be changed.

N   *Negative*. These are the negative perceptions, enablers, and nurturers that help the person, family, or community to engage in negative practices that impair health.

In planning, this model goes through several phases. The first phase is health education, in which the planners must decide whether the health education effort is directed toward individuals, extended families, or communities. In the second phase, the planners collect data by surveys and/or interviews and identify the beliefs and practices related to perceptions, enablers, and nurturers. The third phase entails classifying these beliefs into three categories: positive, exotic, or negative. In the final phase, the planners classify beliefs into those which are rooted in cultural patterns and those which are newly formed and select culturally appropriate health education strategies.

CDCYNERGY

CDCynergy, created in the 1990s by the Centers for Disease Control and Prevention, is a multimedia CD-ROM used for planning, managing, and evaluating public health communication programs (CDC, 2004). It originated as a planning model for communication programs but has now been expanded and its usage tailored to a variety of public health planning applications. Systematic training for its usage and application is conducted by the Society of Public Health Education (SOPHE). The training curriculum includes a template for creating a health communication plan, examples of real-world public health interventions, a glossary of health communication terminology, and resources useful for developing and evaluating health intervention and communication plans (SOPHE, 2002).

The CDCynergy process is basically a six-phase process:

1. *Problem definition and description.* The problem is defined and resources are considered.
2. *Problem analysis.* Goals are set.
3. *Communication program planning.* The primary and secondary target audiences are chosen and communication objectives are set.
4. *Program and evaluation development.*
5. *Program implementation and management.*
6. *Feedback.* Feedback is given and used to refine the program.

OTHER MODELS

Some less commonly used models in health promotion and education are the effectiveness-based model from social work (Kettner, Moroney, & Martin, 1999), the evidence-based/risk factor analysis model (Dever, 1997), the Social Marketing Assessment and Response Tool (SMART) (Neiger, Thackeray, Barnes, & McKenzie, 2003), and total quality improvement (TQI) (Batten, 1992). These models are not frequently used in health promotion and health education and thus have not been discussed in this chapter.

SKILL-BUILDING ACTIVITY

Let us take the most popular model for planning health education and health promotion programs, the PRECEDE-PROCEED model, and see how we can apply it to a practical situation. Let us assume we are interested in developing a physical activity promotion program for African American women in a midwestern city. Figure 2.2 depicts each phase of the model and how it can be applied.

In the first phase, you could choose focus group discussion with the target audience for social assessment. The focus group discussion would identify the target audience's quality of life concerns, common leisure time physical activities, and program expectations. In the first part of the second phase, epidemiological assessment, you could collect local data from the county health department, statewide health data, and national health data about overweight and obesity and a sedentary lifestyle and compile mortality and morbidity (incidence and prevalence) statistics of diseases associated with a sedentary lifestyle. In the second part of the second phase, only a behavioral factor of moderate-intensity leisure time physical activity can be chosen from the genetic, behavioral, and environmental factors.

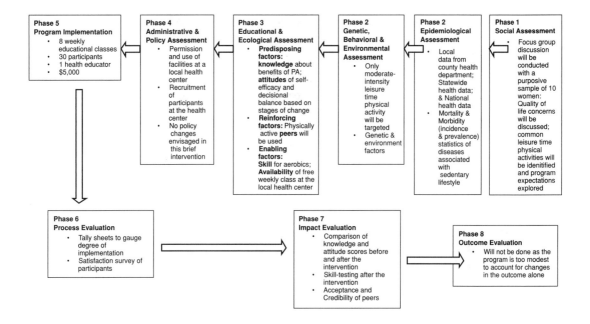

FIGURE 2.2 Application of the PRECEDE-PROCEED model for changing moderate-intensity leisure time physical activity in a small group of African American women in a midwestern city through a brief first-time educational intervention

In the third phase, educational and ecological assessment, you can select predisposing factors of knowledge about benefits of physical activity, attitudes of self-efficacy, and decisional balance based on the stages of change model (Prochaska & DiClemente, 1983). Physically active peers can be used as reinforcing factors. In the enabling factors category, the program can build skills for aerobics and make a free class available.

In the fourth phase of administrative and policy assessment, permission and use of facilities at a local health center can be obtained, participants can be recruited at the health center, and policy changes would be planned. In the fifth phase, program implementation, one health educator could conduct eight weekly educational sessions with 30 participants at a total cost of $5,000.

In the sixth phase, process evaluation, you could use tally sheets to gauge the degree of implementation, and perform a satisfaction survey of participants. In the seventh phase, impact evaluation, you could compare participants' knowledge and attitude scores before and after the intervention, test their skills after the intervention, and assess the acceptance and credibility of peers after the intervention. Since the program is modest and short in duration, the eighth phase of outcome evaluation cannot be done.

Using this approach, you can also plan to work on a health issue of your choice with a target population of your choice. You can apply the PRECEDE-PROCEED model or another model of your choice to plan your program. Table 2.8 provides a set of questions to assist you in choosing different activities that correspond to different phases of the PRECEDE-PROCEED model.

TABLE 2.8 Choosing Activities for Health Education Program Planning Using the PRECEDE-PROCEED Model

1. What will be the best activity to facilitate social assessment?
   - Asset mapping
   - Social reconnaissance
   - Focus group discussion
   - Delphi method
   - Nominal group process
   - Central location intercept interviews
   - Surveys
   - Public service data
   - Other

2. What data will be needed to conduct epidemiological assessment?
   - Mortality data
   - Morbidity data
   - Disability data
   - Behavioral data
   - Environmental data
   - Genetic data
   - Other

3. What factors should be considered in educational and ecological assessment?
   - Predisposing
     - Knowledge
     - Beliefs
     - Attitudes
     - Values
     - Others

TABLE 2.8 *(Continued)*

- Reinforcing
  - Peers
  - Parents
  - Decision makers
  - Employers
  - Others
- Enabling
  - Availability
  - Accessibility
  - Legislation
  - Skills
  - Others

4. What should be considered in administrative and policy assessment?
   - Alignment with priorities
   - Assessment of resources
   - Identification of barriers
   - Assessment of policies
   - Other

5. What should be considered in implementation?
   - Time
   - Personnel
   - Budget
   - Other

6. What should be considered in process evaluation?
   - Degree of fidelity
   - Reception at the site
   - Recipient response
   - Implementer's response
   - Competencies of personnel

7. What should be considered in impact evaluation?
   - Predisposing antecedents
   - Reinforcing antecedents
   - Enabling antecedents
   - Behaviors
   - Environments

8. What should be considered in outcome evaluation?
   - Health status
   - Quality of life

SUMMARY

Planning is an essential responsibility for health educators. Theories from behavioral and social sciences help in micro-level planning (setting of objectives and identification of methods), but the macro-level, or overall, planning is done by models. Models are miniaturized and simplified applications of concepts for addressing problems and usually contain inputs from several theories. This chapter discussed several planning models: the PRECEDE-PROCEED model, the Planned Approach to Community Health (PATCH) model, the Multilevel Approach to Community Health (MATCH) model, the intervention mapping model, the Assessment Protocol for Excellence in Public Health (APEXPH) model, the Comprehensive Health Education Model (CHEM), the Model for Health Education Planning (MHEP), the Model for Health Education Planning and Resource Development (MHEPRD), the PEN-3 model, and CDCynergy.

The most popular model is the PRECEDE-PROCEED model, which has been applied in a variety of settings for purposes such as coalition building, enhancing community participation, planning multiple-channel interventions, developing health instruments, conducting needs assessments, implementing health risk appraisals at worksites, planning disease prevention programs at worksites, planning employee assistance programs at worksites, planning health programs in school settings, training health care staff, and improving self-care and compliance behaviors.

PATCH is a community health planning model that works equally well at state and local levels and builds capacity. MATCH is a model that emphasizes implementation and is feasible in situations where extensive needs assessment cannot be done. Intervention mapping builds on a socioecological approach that looks at individual behaviors in an environmental context. APEXPH is the model that is used at the local level. CHEM, MHEP, and MHEPRD are not commonly used and have been discussed mainly from a historical perspective. The PEN-3 model is culturally sensitive and helps in culturally appropriate planning. CDCynergy is a health communication model that has been tailored to a variety of other applications.

REVIEW QUESTIONS

1. Differentiate between a model and a theory.
2. Define the PRECEDE-PROCEED model. How would you design a program to prevent smoking in adolescents using the PRECEDE-PROCEED model?
3. What are the competencies for health educators who are planning health education strategies, interventions, and programs?

4. Describe the essential features of the PATCH model.
5. Discuss the five phases of the MATCH model.
6. Identify the six steps of intervention mapping.
7. What does the acronym APEXPH mean? Briefly discuss this model.
8. Differentiate between the Comprehensive Health Education Model and the Model for Health Education Planning.
9. Describe the PEN-3 model.
10. Summarize the main features of CDCynergy.

WEBSITE

Go to the Web component of *Theoretical Foundations of Health Education and Health Promotion* at http://health.jbpub.com/foundations for Web exercises, additional resources related to this chapter, and student review tools.

GLOSSARY TERMS

analytical epidemiology
Assessment Protocol for Excellence in Public Health (APEXPH) model
CDCynergy
Comprehensive Health Education Model (CHEM)
descriptive epidemiology
enabling factors
intervention mapping
model
Model for Health Education Planning (MHEP)

Model for Health Education Planning and Resource Development (MHEPRD)
Multilevel Approach to Community Health (MATCH) model
PEN-3 model
Planned Approach to Community Health (PATCH) model
PRECEDE-PROCEED model
predisposing factors
reinforcing factors

REFERENCES AND FURTHER READING

Aaro, L. E., Flisher, A. J., Kaaya, S., Onya, H., Fuglesang, M., Klepp, K. I., et al. (2006). Promoting sexual and reproductive health in early adolescence in South Africa and Tanzania: Development of a theory- and evidence-based intervention programme. *Scandinavian Journal of Public Health, 34*(2), 150–158.

Abbema, E. A., Van Assema, P., Kok, G. J., De Leeuw, E., & De Vries, N. K. (2004). Effect evaluation of a comprehensive community intervention aimed at reducing socioeconomic health inequalities in The Netherlands. *Health Promotion International, 19*(2), 141–156.

Abernethy, A. D., Magat, M. M., Houston, T. R., Arnold, H. L., Jr., Bjorck, J. P., & Gorsuch, R. L. (2005). Recruiting African American men for cancer screening studies: Applying a culturally based model. *Health Education and Behavior, 32*(4), 441–451.

Airhihenbuwa, C. O. (1993). Health promotion for child survival in Africa: Implications for cultural appropriateness. *Hygie, 12*(3), 10–15.

Airhihenbuwa, C. O. (1995). *Health and culture: Beyond the Western paradigm.* Thousand Oaks, CA: Sage Publications.

Alewijnse, D., Mesters, I. E., Metsemakers, J. F., & van den Borne, B. H. (2002). Program development for promoting adherence during and after exercise therapy for urinary incontinence. *Patient Education and Counseling, 48*(2), 147–160.

Bailey, P. H., Rukholm, E. E., Vanderlee, R., & Hyland, J. (1994). A heart health survey at the worksite: The first step to effective programming. *AAOHN Journal, 42,* 9–14.

Bartholomew, L. K., Parcel, G. S., Kok, G., & Gottlieb, N. H. (2006). *Planning health promotion programs: An intervention mapping approach.* San Francisco: Jossey Bass.

Bates, I. J., & Winder, A.E. (1984). *Introduction to health education.* Mountain View, CA: Mayfield.

Batten, J.D. (1992). *Building a total quality culture.* Menlo Park, CA: Crisp Publications.

Beech, B. M., & Scarinci, I. C. (2003). Smoking attitudes and practices among low-income African-Americans: Qualitative assessment of contributing factors. *American Journal of Health Promotion, 17*(4), 240–248.

Brouse, C. H., Basch, C. E., Wolf, R. L., & Shmukler, C. (2004). Barriers to colorectal cancer screening: An educational diagnosis. *Journal of Cancer Education, 19*(3), 170–173.

Brug, J., Oenema, A., & Ferreira, I. (2005). Theory, evidence and intervention mapping to improve behavior nutrition and physical activity interventions. *International Journal of Behavioral and Nutrition and Physical Activity, 2*(1), 2.

Centers for Disease Control and Prevention. (2004). CDCynergy overview. Retrieved May 31, 2006, from http://www.cdc.gov/communication/cdcynergy.htm.

Chang, M. W., Brown, R. L., Nitzke, S., & Baumann, L. C. (2004). Development of an instrument to assess predisposing, enabling, and reinforcing constructs associated with fat intake behaviors of low-income mothers. *Journal of Nutrition, Education and Behavior, 36,* 27–34.

Chiang, L. C., Huang, J. L., Yeh, K. W., & Lu, C. M. (2004). Effects of a self management asthma educational program in Taiwan based on PRECEDE PROCEED model for parents with asthmatic children. *Journal of Asthma, 41*(2), 205–215.

Dever, G. E. (1997). *Improving outcomes in public health practice: Strategy and methods.* Gaithersburg, MD: Aspen.

Dille, J. H. (1999). Worksite influenza immunization. Successful program. *AAOHN Journal, 47*(7), 292–300.

Erwin, D. O, Johnson, V. A., Feliciano-Libid, L., Zamora, D., & Jandorf, L. (2005). Incorporating cultural constructs and demographic diversity in the research and development of a Latina breast and cervical cancer education program. *Journal of Cancer Education, 20*(1), 39–44.

Fernandez, M. E., Gonzales, A., Tortolero-Luna, G., Partida, S., & Bartholomew, L. K. (2005). Using intervention mapping to develop a breast and cervical cancer screening program for Hispanic farmworkers: Cultivando La Salud. *Health Promotion Practice, 6*(4), 394–404.

Fishbein, M., & Ajzen, I. (1975). *Belief, attitude, intention, and behavior: An introduction to theory and research*. Reading, MA: Addison Wesley.

Fisher, E. B., Jr., Strunk, R. C., Sussman, L. K., Arfken, C., Sykes, R. K., Munro, J. M., et al. (1996). Acceptability and feasibility of a community approach to asthma management: The Neighborhood Asthma Coalition (NAC). *Journal of Asthma, 33*(6), 367–383.

Garces, I. C., Scarinci, I. C., & Harrison, L. (2006). An examination of sociocultural factors associated with health and health care seeking among Latina immigrants. *Journal of Immigrant and Minority Health, 8*(4), 377–385.

Gold, R. S., Green, L. W., & Kreuter, M. W. (1998). *EMPOWER: Enabling methods of planning and organizing within everyone's reach*. Sudbury, MA: Jones and Bartlett.

Goodman, R. M., Steckler, A., Hoover, S., & Schwartz, R. (1993). A critique of contemporary community health promotion approaches: Based on a qualitative review of six programs in Maine. *American Journal of Health Promotion, 7*(3), 208–220.

Green, L. W. (1970). Identifying and overcoming barriers to the diffusion of knowledge about family planning. *Advances in Fertility Control, 5*, 21–29.

Green, L. W. (1974). Toward cost-benefit evaluations of health education: Some concepts, methods and examples. *Health Education Monographs, 2*(Suppl. 1) 34–64.

Green, L. W., & Kreuter, M. W. (2005). *Health program planning: An educational and ecological approach* (4th ed.). Boston: McGraw Hill.

Green, L. W., Kreuter, M. W., Deeds, S. G., & Partridge, K. B. (1980). *Health education planning: A diagnostic approach*. Palo Alto, CA: Mayfield.

Green, L. W., Levine, D. M., & Deeds, S. G. (1975). Clinical trials of health education for hypertensive outpatients: Design and baseline data. *Preventive Medicine, 4*, 417–425.

Green, L. W., Levine, D. M., Wolle, J., & Deeds, S. G. (1979). Development of randomized patient education experiments with urban poor hypertensives. *Patient Counseling and Health Education, 1*, 106–111.

Hall, N., & Best, J. A. (1997). Health promotion practice and public health: Challenge for the 1990s. Heart Health Think Tank Group. *Canadian Journal of Public Health, 88*, 409–415.

Heinen, M. M., Bartholomew, L. K., Wensing, M., Kerkhof, P., & Achterberg, T. (2006). Supporting adherence and healthy lifestyles in leg ulcer patients: Systematic development of the Lively Legs program for dermatology outpatient clinics. *Patient Education and Counseling, 61*(2), 279–291.

Hochbaum, G. M. (1958). *Public participation in medical screening programs: A sociopsychological study* (PHS Publication No. 572). Washington, DC: U.S. Government Printing Office.

James, D. C. (2004). Factors influencing food choices, dietary intake, and nutrition-related attitudes among African Americans: Application of a culturally sensitive model. *Ethnicity and Health, 9*(4), 349–367.

Kang, J. H., Han, H. R., Kim, K. B., & Kim, M. T. (2006). Barriers to care and control of high blood pressure in Korean-American elderly. *Ethnicity and Disease, 16*(1), 145–151.

Kettner, P., Moroney, R., & Martin, L. (1999). *Designing and managing programs: An effectiveness based approach* (2nd ed.). Thousand Oaks, CA: Sage Publishers.

Kremers, S. P., Visscher, T. L., Brug, J., Chin, A. P. M. J., Schouten, E. G., Schuit, A. J., et al. (2005). Netherlands research programme weight gain prevention (NHF-NRG): Rationale, objectives and strategies. *European Journal of Clinical Nutrition, 59*(4), 498–507.

Kreuter, M. W. (1992). PATCH: Its origin, basic concepts, and links to contemporary public health policy. *Journal of Health Education, 23*(3), 135–139.

Linnan, L. A., Sterba, K. R., Lee, A. M., Bontempi, J. B., Yang, J., & Crump, C. (2005). Planning and the professional preparation of health educators: Implications for teaching, research, and practice. *Health Promotion Practice, 6,* 308–319.

MacDonald, M. A., & Green, L. W. (2001). Reconciling concept and context: The dilemma of implementation in school-based health promotion. *Health Education and Behavior, 28*(6), 749–768.

Macrina, D., Macrina, N., Horvath, C., Gallaspy, J., & Fine, P. R. (1996). An educational intervention to increase use of the Glasgow Coma Scale by emergency department personnel. *International Journal of Trauma Nursing, 2*(1), 7–12.

Murray, N. G., Kelder, S. H., Parcel, G. S., Frankowski, R., & Orpinas, P. (1999). Padres Trabajando por la Paz: A randomized trial of a parent education intervention to prevent violence among middle school children. *Health Education Research, 14*(3), 421–426.

National Association of County and City Health Officials. (1991). *Assessment Protocol for Excellence in Public Health (APEXPH) workbook.* Washington, DC: Author.

Neiger, B. L., Thackeray, R., Barnes, M. D., & McKenzie J. F. (2003). Positioning social marketing as a planning process for health education. *American Journal of Health Studies, 18*(2/3), 75–81.

Perez-Rodrigo, C., Wind, M., Hildonen, C., Bjelland, M., Aranceta, J., Klepp, K. I., et al. (2005). The pro children intervention: Applying the intervention mapping protocol to develop a school-based fruit and vegetable promotion programme. *Annals of Nutrition and Metabolism, 49*(4), 267–277.

Prochaska, J. O., & DiClemente, C. C. (1983). Stages and processes of self change of smoking: Toward an integrative model of change. *Journal of Consulting and Clinical Psychology, 51,* 390–395.

Rosenstock, I. M., Derryberry, M., & Carriger, B. (1959). Why people fail to seek poliomyelitis vaccination. *Public Health Reports, 74,* 98–103.

Ross, H., & Mico, P. (1980). *Theory and practice in health education.* Palo Alto, CA: Mayfield Publishing.

Simons-Morton, B. G., Greene, W. H., & Gottlieb, N. H. (1995). *Introduction to health education and health promotion* (2nd ed.). Prospect Heights, IL: Waveland.

Society for Public Health Education. (2002). CDCynergy training. Retrieved May 30, 2006, from http://www.sophe.org/public/cdcynergy/cdc_description.html.

Suen, J., Christenson, G. M., Cooper, A., & Taylor, M. (1995). Analysis of the current status of public health practice in local health departments. *American Journal of Preventive Medicine, 11*(6 Suppl.), 51–54.

Sullivan, D. (1973). Model for comprehensive, systematic program development in health education. *Health Education Report, 1*(1), 4–5.

Tortolero, S. R., Markham, C. M., Parcel, G. S., Peters, R. J., Jr., Escobar-Chaves, S. L., Basen-Engquist, K., et al. (2005). Using intervention mapping to adapt an effective HIV, sexually transmitted disease, and pregnancy prevention program for high-risk minority youth. *Health Promotion Practice, 6*(3), 286–298.

U.S. Department of Health and Human Services. (2005). *Planned Approach to Community Health: Guide for the local coordinator*. Atlanta, GA: U.S. Department of Health and Human Services, Centers for Disease Control and Prevention, National Center for Chronic Disease Prevention and Health Promotion. Retrieved May 23, 2006, from http://www.cdc.gov/nccdphp/publications/PATCH/index.htm.

Watson, M. R., Horowitz, A. M., Garcia, I., & Canto, M. T. (2001). A community participatory oral health promotion program in an inner-city Latino community. *Journal of Public Health Dentistry*, *61*, 34–41.

Wilkens, P. M. (2003). Preventing work-related musculoskeletal disorders in VDT users: A comprehensive health promotion program. *Work*, *20*(3), 171–178.

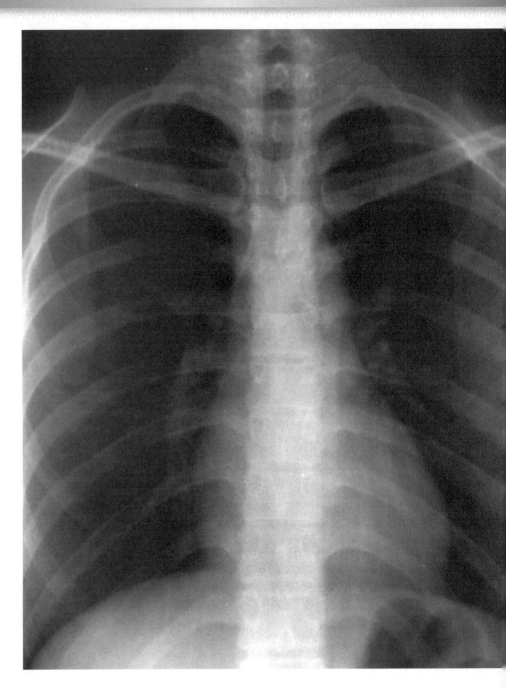

CHAPTER 3

The Health Belief Model

KEY CONCEPTS

- Cues to action
- Health belief model (HBM)
- Illness behaviors
- Perceived barriers
- Perceived benefits
- Perceived severity

- Perceived susceptibility
- Perceived threat
- Preventive or health behaviors
- Self-efficacy
- Sick role behaviors
- Value expectancy theories

AFTER READING THIS CHAPTER YOU SHOULD BE ABLE TO

- Describe the historical genesis of the health belief model (HBM)
- List six constructs of the HBM
- Summarize the applications of the HBM in health education and health promotion
- Identify educational methods and match these to modify each construct from the HBM
- Apply the HBM in changing a health behavior of your choice

The **health belief model (HBM)** is one of the first theories developed exclusively for health-related behaviors. The previous chapter talked about the differences between a model and a theory. The HBM is labeled a model, which is a misnomer because it meets all the criteria for a theory. It originated in the 1950s and has been thoroughly tested in a variety of situations since that time. Even in contemporary literature it is among the most popular models. The constructs of the model provide specific guidance at the micro level for planning the "how to" part of interventions. Based on experimentation over the years, the model has expanded and borrowed from other theories to strengthen its predictive and explanatory potential.

This chapter begins by describing the historical aspects of the genesis of this model. Next it describes the various constructs that make up this model. It then discusses the applications of the HBM in behavioral research, primary prevention, and secondary prevention. Next it notes the limitations of the model and presents a skill-building application using the HBM.

HISTORICAL PERSPECTIVES

The HBM originated from the work of a group of social psychologists in the U.S. Public Health Service in the 1950s: Godfrey Hochbaum, Stephen Kegels, and Irwin Rosenstock (Rosenstock, 1974a). These social psychologists were confronted with the problem that very few people were participating in preventive and disease detection programs. The Public Health Service was sending out chest x-ray units to neighborhoods to conduct free screening for tuberculosis, yet very few people were taking advantage of those services. To explain this phenomenon and help recruit more participation from people, the group looked at the then-existing theories and developed the HBM.

The model was influenced by the theory of Kurt Lewin (Lewin, 1935; Lewin, Dembo, Festinger, & Sears, 1944). Lewin and colleagues' theory is that behavior depends on two variables: (1) the value placed by an individual on an outcome (value) and (2) the individual's estimate of the likelihood that a given action will result in that outcome (expectancy). It is a goal-setting theory based on level of aspiration, in which the individual sets the target of future performance based on past performance (Maiman & Becker, 1974). Such theories are called **value expectancy theories**; the HBM falls into this category. Maiman and Becker (1974) note that the HBM was similar in its conceptualization to five other theories of decision making that were prominent in the 1950s: Atkinson's (1957) risk-taking model, Edwards's (1954) subjective expected utility model, Feathers's (1959) decision making under uncertainty model, Rotter's (1954) reinforcement model, and Tolman's (1955) performance behavior theory.

According to Atkinson's (1957) risk-taking model, behavior is a multiplicative relationship among expectancy, incentive, and motive. *Expectancy* means the person's anticipation of outcomes from an action. These can be positive or negative. *Incentives* are rewards that will accrue when one performs the behavior. *Motives* are characteristics that foster an individual to pursue positive incentives and avoid negative incentives. Edwards's (1954) subjective expected utility model purports that action is based on the subjective value or utility of attaining the goal and the subjective probability or likelihood of attaining that goal.

Feathers's (1959) decision making under uncertainty model utilizes three constructs: attainment attractiveness, which is the individual's preference to pursue a goal; success probability, which is the likelihood that a given goal is attainable; and choice potential, which is the behavior to be done. Rotter's (1954) reinforcement model purports that behavior is based on the expectancy that a certain action will lead to a certain outcome and on reinforcement from previous learning. Tolman's (1955) theory advocates use of six variables (three positive and three negative) for the performance of any behavior. These are as follows: (1) need-push for food, (2) positive valence of expected food, (3) expectation of food, (4) need-push against work, (5) negative valence of expected work, and (6) expectation of work.

> *The Health Belief Model relates psychological theories of decision making (which attempt to explain action in a choice situation) to an individual's decision about alternative health behaviors.*
>
> —Maiman and Becker (1974, p. 9)

Maiman and Becker (1974) note that all these models predict behavior on two basic variables, namely, the value placed by an individual on a particular goal (attractiveness of the goal) and the individual's estimation regarding the likelihood of attainability of that goal (subjective probability). All these theories are thus value expectancy theories.

Kasl and Cobb (1966) classified three kinds of behaviors regarding health. The first are **preventive (or health) behaviors**, which consist of actions taken for the purpose of preventing disease or detecting disease in an asymptomatic phase by a person who believes himself or herself to be healthy. The second are **illness behaviors**, which consist of actions taken by a person who feels sick and indulges in the behavior for the purpose of defining the state of his or her health and for discovering suitable remedies. The third are **sick role behaviors**, which consist of actions taken by people who are sick for the purpose of getting well. Initially, the HBM was developed mainly to cater to preventive or health behaviors (Rosenstock, 1974b), but later it was applied to illness behaviors (Kirscht, 1974), sick role behaviors (Becker, 1974), and behaviors related to chronic illness (Kasl, 1974).

In the 1970s a review was published regarding measuring various dimensions of the HBM on standardized scales (Maiman, Becker, Kirscht, Haefner, & Drachman, 1977). In the 1980s the model was strengthened further, mostly by the work of Marshall Becker and colleagues (Janz & Becker, 1984). In the late 1980s the model was expanded to include self-efficacy (Rosenstock, Strecher, & Becker, 1988). Since then the model has continued to be applied to a variety of health behaviors; it is currently among the most popular models.

CONSTRUCTS OF THE HEALTH BELIEF MODEL

Theories from behavioral and social sciences have what are known as *constructs*, or building blocks, that can be distinctly identified. The HBM has six constructs, the first of which is **perceived susceptibility**. This refers to the subjective belief that a person has with regard to acquiring a disease or reaching a harmful state as a result of indulging in a particular behavior. Individuals vary considerably with regard to their perception of susceptibility to any given illness or harmful condition. On one extreme are individuals who completely deny any possibility of their acquiring the disease. In the middle are the people who may admit to the possibility of acquiring the disease but believe that it is not likely to happen to them. At the other extreme are people who are so fearful of acquiring the disease that they believe that they will in all probability acquire it. The more susceptible a person feels, the greater the likelihood of his or her taking preventive measures.

Perceived susceptibility has a strong cognitive component and is partly dependent on knowledge (Rosenstock, 1974a). According to the HBM, health educators need to build perceived susceptibility by elaborating on the possibility of negative consequences and personalizing those risks for their participants. For example, in a smoking prevention program, health educators might mention that smoking causes lung cancer and, based on the relative risk calculated from epidemiological studies, mention that this risk is 22 times higher for a smoker than for a nonsmoker. A word of caution needs to be kept in mind: in building perceived susceptibility, one should not create unrealistic or exaggerated fear about the condition.

The second construct of HBM is **perceived severity**, which refers to a person's subjective belief in the extent of harm that can result from the acquired disease or harmful state as a result of a particular behavior. This perception also varies from person to person. One person might perceive the disease from a purely medical perspective and thus be concerned with signs, symptoms, any limitations arising out of the condition, the temporary or permanent nature of the condition, its potential for causing death, and so on, whereas another individual might look at the disease from a broader perspective, such as having adverse effects on his or her family, job, and relationships.

Similar to perceived susceptibility, perceived severity has a strong cognitive component dependent on knowledge (Rosenstock, 1974a). According to the HBM, health educators need to build perceived severity by mentioning serious negative consequences and personalizing those for the participants. For example, in a nutrition education class, health educators might mention that consuming large amounts of saturated fats may lead to development of heart disease and might share a story about a member of the community who suffered a heart attack. Besides the clinical consequences, the effects on family, job, and relationships would also be shared.

The constructs of perceived severity and perceived susceptibility are often grouped together and called **perceived threat**.

The third construct of the HBM is **perceived benefits**, which refers to belief in the advantages of the methods suggested for reducing the risk or seriousness of the disease or harmful state resulting from a particular behavior. The relative effectiveness of known available alternatives plays a role in shaping actions. An alternative is likely to be seen as beneficial if it reduces the perceived susceptibility or perceived severity of the disease (Rosenstock, 1974a). In facilitating the construct of perceived benefits, health educators need to specify the exact action to be taken and specify the advantages or benefits that would result from that course of action. For example, health educators teaching about breast self-examination would need to specify the exact technique and the benefits, namely, ability to detect cancer or other diseases early, feeling good about oneself, feeling in control of one's health, and feeling more responsible toward oneself and one's family.

The fourth construct, which goes hand in hand with the construct of perceived benefits, is **perceived barriers**. Perceived barriers refer to beliefs concerning the actual and imagined costs of following the new behavior. An individual may believe that a new action is effective in reducing perceived susceptibility or perceived severity of the disease but may consider the action to be expensive, inconvenient, unpleasant, painful, or upsetting (Rosenstock, 1974a). Health educators need to reduce such barriers to keep them from hindering the person from taking recommended actions. They may do so by giving reassurance, correcting misperceptions, and/or providing incentives. For example, in a smoking cessation class, health educators might continually reassure the participants that they can overcome the habit of smoking, they might correct the misperception that tobacco addiction is impossible to break by giving examples of persons who have broken the habit, and they might provide monetary incentives for participants to continue in the smoking cessation class.

The fifth construct in the HBM is **cues to action**, which are the precipitating forces that make a person feel the need to take action. Such cues may be internal (e.g., perception of a bodily state) or external (e.g., interpersonal interactions, media communication, or receiving a postcard from the doctor for a follow-up examination) (Rosenstock, 1974a). If the perceived susceptibility or perceived severity is low, then a very intense stimulus is needed as a cue to action. When the perceived susceptibility or perceived severity is high, then even a slight stimulus is adequate.

The final construct is called **self-efficacy** and was added to the model in the 1980s (Rosenstock, Strecher, & Becker, 1988). We will learn more about this construct in Chapter 7 on the social cognitive theory, from which it was borrowed. Self-efficacy is the confidence that a person has in his or her ability to pursue a behavior. It is behavior specific and is in the present. It is not about the past or future. Four strategies can be used to build self-efficacy:

1. *Breaking down the complex behavior into practical and doable small steps*. For example, instead of telling women to perform breast self-examination, the women could be taught the entire procedure in small steps.
2. *Using a demonstration from a credible role model*. For example, in facilitating an educational program about quitting alcohol, a popular movie star (with whom the participants identify) who has himself or herself successfully gone through the rehabilitation process could share his or her story to help in enhancing the self-efficacy of the participants.
3. *Using persuasion and reassurance*. If a person has failed in the past to make a behavior change, those failures can be attributed to external reasons. For example, in a smoking cessation program, a health educator could ask participants to identify their past failures with smoking cessation and then mention that they could have failed because of bad timing, having too many tasks at hand at that time, the season in which they were attempting the change, and so on.
4. *Reducing stress*. Any behavior change is associated with some amount of stress, which hinders the change process. When this stress is negative, or distress, it hinders the learning process. Thus, reducing distress is an effective means of building self-efficacy. For example, if the participants find breast self-examination to be stressful, then they must be instructed to relax either by taking a shower or listening to music or practicing progressive muscle relaxation before performing the behavior.

Table 3.1 summarizes the key constructs of the health belief model.

> *T*he Health Belief Model (HBM) hypothesizes that health related action depends upon the simultaneous occurrence of three classes of factors:
>
> 1. The existence of sufficient motivation (or health concern) to make health issues salient or relevant.
> 2. The belief that one is susceptible (vulnerable) to a serious health problem or to the sequelae of that illness or condition. This is often termed perceived threat.
> 3. The belief that following a particular health recommendation would be beneficial in reducing the perceived threat, and at a subjectively-acceptable cost.
>
> —Rosenstock, Strecher, and Becker (1988, p. 177)

TABLE 3.1	Key Constructs of the Health Belief Model	
Construct	**Definition**	**How to Modify?**
Perceived susceptibility	Subjective belief that a person may acquire a disease or enter a harmful state as a result of a particular behavior	• Mention negative consequences (e.g., smoking causes lung cancer) • Personalize the risks for the education participants (e.g., the chances of your developing lung cancer if you are a smoker are 22 times more than a nonsmoker, based on a relative risk computed by epidemiological studies)
Perceived severity	Belief in the extent of harm that can result from the acquired disease or harmful state as a result of a particular behavior	• Mention serious negative consequences (e.g., eating saturated fats causes heart disease) • Personalize the seriousness for the education participants (e.g., sharing a story about a person who died of heart attack in the community)
Perceived benefits	Belief in the advantages of the methods suggested for reducing the risk or seriousness of the disease or harmful state resulting from a particular behavior	• Specify the exact action to be taken (e.g., the individual will carry out breast self-examination in every quadrant every month after taking a shower) • Specify the positive benefits that will accrue from the behavior (e.g., doing breast self-examination monthly will allow you to be able to detect cancer or other diseases early, to feel good about yourself, to feel in control of your health, and to feel more responsible toward yourself and your family)
Perceived barriers	Belief concerning actual and imagined costs of following the new behavior	• Reassure the education recipients that the behavior they will be doing will have minimal costs (e.g., for breast self-examination, state that it would only mean spending another 15 minutes while taking a shower)

TABLE 3.1   *(Continued)*

Construct	Definition	How to Modify?
		• Correct any misperceptions that education participants may have (e.g., a person may think a gall bladder ultrasound is an invasive procedure; correcting that misperception may increase the likelihood of the person getting that test) • Provide incentives for indulging in the behavior (e.g., free cholesterol testing may be offered to increase the chances that more people will get tested)
Cues to action	Precipitating force that makes a person feel the need to take action	• Ensuring a reminder system for indulging in behaviors (e.g., posting Post-it Notes, giving a phone call)
Self-efficacy	Confidence in one's ability to pursue a behavior	• Practicing in small steps (e.g., breaking down the complex behavior of breast self-examination into doable small steps) • Having a role model demonstrate the behavior (e.g., having a video of a well-known movie star with whom the target audience can identify performing the same behaviors) • Using persuasion and reinforcement (e.g., telling the participants that they have what it takes to perform the behavior, and attributing failures to outside reasons) • Reducing stress associated with implementing a new behavior (e.g., having the participants take a relaxing shower before doing a breast self-examination)

APPLICATIONS OF THE HEALTH BELIEF MODEL

> *The Health Belief Model was originally formulated to explain (preventive) health behavior.*
>
> —Rosenstock (1974b, p. 27)

Applications of the HBM began in the 1950s, and it continues to be a popular model. It is not possible to summarize all the applications of the HBM in this chapter because so many practitioners and researchers have used it. However, the applications can be divided into three categories:

1. Behavioral research model building and instrument development
2. Primary prevention, where HBM has been used for health education regarding prevention of diseases or for specific protection against diseases, such as immunization
3. Screening for diseases, compliance with treatment, and other secondary prevention tasks

Some examples of behavioral research in which the HBM was used are as follows: developing an AIDS health belief scale (Zagumny & Brady, 1998), identifying factors associated with infant mortality (Eshleman, Poole, & Davidhizar, 2005), refining an instrument for breast cancer screening (Champion, 1993), involvement of dental practitioners in the prevention of eating disorders (DiGioacchino, Keenan, & Sargent, 2000), modeling for physical activity behavior (Juniper, Oman, Hamm, & Kerby, 2004), predictive modeling to prevent severe acute respiratory syndrome (SARS) (Wong & Tang, 2005), predictors of health behaviors in college students (Von Ah, Ebert, Ngamvitroj, Park, & Kang, 2004), modeling of sexual behavior (Lin, Simoni, & Zemon, 2005), smoking in college students (Kofahi & Haddad, 2005), sociopsychological modeling for diabetes (Gillibrand & Stevenson, 2006), and using a sodium adherence dietary scale (Welch, Bennett, Delp, & Agarwal, 2006). Table 3.2 summarizes these applications.

Some examples in which the HBM has been used for primary prevention are for promoting bicycle helmet use (Lajunen & Rasanen, 2004), promoting condom use in female sex workers (Buckingham, Moraros, Bird, Meister, & Webb, 2005), decreasing tanning bed use (Greene & Brinn, 2003), promoting healthy dietary behavior (Chew, Palmer, & Kim, 1998), genetic testing (Raz, Atar, Rodnay, Shoham-Vardi, & Carmi, 2003), promoting hepatitis B vaccination (Bigham et al., 2006), promoting influenza vaccination (Lau, Yang, Tsui, & Kim, 2006), measles immunization (Pielak & Hilton, 2003), pesticide safety (Martinez, Gratton, Coggin, Rene, & Waller, 2004), prevention

TABLE 3.2	Examples of Applications of the Health Belief Model in Behavioral Research

AIDS health belief scale

Factors associated with infant mortality

Instrument for breast cancer screening

Involvement of dental practitioners in the prevention of eating disorders

Modeling for physical activity behavior

Predictive modeling to prevent severe acute respiratory syndrome (SARS)

Predictors of health behaviors in college students

Modeling of sexual behavior

Smoking in college students

Sociopsychological modeling for diabetes

Sodium adherence dietary scale

of periodontal disease (Ndiokwelu, 2004), solar disinfection of drinking water (Rainey & Harding, 2005), and tuberculosis prevention (Rodriguez-Reimann, Nicassio, Reimann, Gallegos, & Olmedo, 2004). Table 3.3 summarizes these applications.

Some examples in which the HBM has been used for secondary prevention are for adherence to malaria chemoprophylaxis (Farquharson, Noble, Barker, & Behrens, 2004), breast self-examination and mammography (Dundar et al., 2006), cervical cancer screening (Park, Chang, & Chung, 2005), cognitive status examination for Alzheimer's disease (Werner, 2003), colorectal cancer screening (Greenwald, 2006), compliance with anticoagulant warfarin therapy (Orensky & Holdford, 2005), compliance with antiviral therapy in hepatitis B patients (Wai et al., 2005), HIV testing (de Paoli, Manongi, & Klepp, 2004), medication compliance in schizophrenia (Seo & Min, 2005), medication use in osteoporosis (Unson, Fortinsky, Prestwood, & Reisine, 2005), patient acceptance of continuous positive airway pressure (CPAP) therapy in sleep apnea (Tyrrell, Poulet, Pe Pin, & Veale, 2006), prostate cancer screening (Doukas, Localio, & Li, 2004), recurrent injury prevention in trauma patients (Van

TABLE 3.3   Examples of Applications of the Health Belief Model in Primary Prevention
Bicycle helmet use
Condom use in female sex workers
Decreasing tanning bed use
Dietary behavior
Genetic testing
Hepatitis B vaccination
Influenza vaccination
Measles immunization
Pesticide safety
Prevention of periodontal disease
Solar disinfection of drinking water
Tuberculosis prevention

Horn, 2005), screening for bone loss in epileptic patients (Elliott & Jacobson, 2006), and tuberculosis screening (Poss, 1999). Table 3.4 summarizes these applications.

LIMITATIONS OF THE HEALTH BELIEF MODEL

The health belief model is particularly useful for planning programs for disease avoidance and injury avoidance, but it does not lend itself very well to promotion of behaviors, particularly long-term behavior change. Harrison, Mullen, and Green (1992) conducted a meta-analysis of the relationships among four HBM dimensions (perceived susceptibility, perceived severity, perceived benefits, and perceived costs) and health behaviors in 16 studies. They computed mean effect sizes for all studies and found weak effect sizes and lack of homogeneity in a majority of the studies. They concluded that the model lacked consistent predictive power mainly because it focuses on a limited number of factors. Factors other than health beliefs (such as cultural factors, socioeconomic status, and previous experiences) also shape health behaviors, and those factors are not accounted for in the model. A study by Mullen and colleagues (1987) also found that the predictive power of the HBM was less when

TABLE 3.4	Examples of Applications of the Health Belief Model in Secondary Prevention

Adherence to malaria chemoprophylaxis

Breast self-examination and mammography

Cervical cancer screening

Cognitive status examination for Alzheimer's disease

Colorectal cancer screening

Compliance with anticoagulant warfarin therapy

Compliance with antiviral therapy in hepatitis B patients

HIV testing

Medication compliance in schizophrenia

Medication use in osteoporosis

Patient acceptance of continuous positive airway pressure (CPAP) therapy in sleep apnea

Prostate cancer screening

Recurrent injury prevention in trauma patients

Screening for bone loss in epileptic patients

Tuberculosis screening

compared with the theory of reasoned action, the theory of planned behavior, and the PRECEDE-PROCEED model. This conclusion once again underscores the need for the HBM to expand its predictors. To some extent, that has been done by adding the construct of self-efficacy.

Another problem with the HBM (which is also true for other models) is that different questions are used in different studies to determine the same beliefs, thereby making it difficult to compare studies. Janz, Champion, and Strecher (2002) note that different constructs of the HBM have different contributions. For example, perceived barriers are the single most important predictors of behaviors in the HBM. Often it is not possible to easily influence the barriers, and thus the model would not work.

Ogden (2003) noted that the HBM is a pragmatic model, but has criticized its conceptual basis. First, she notes that some studies of the HBM have found no role of perceived susceptibility, indicating that its constructs are unspecific and thus making it difficult to be tested. Second, she talks about two types of truth in the philosophy of science: synthetic truth, which can be known through exploration and testing; and analytic truth, which is known by definition. She contends that the HBM focuses on analytic truth; thus, its conclusions are not supported by observation. Finally, she notes that completing questions about an individual's cognition in the operationalization of the HBM may change and create that person's thinking rather than tap into how the individual was originally thinking. In a rejoinder to Ogden's article, Ajzen and Fishbein (2004) refuted all these assertions.

SKILL-BUILDING ACTIVITY

Let us see how we can apply the HBM to the issue of safer sex practices among youth. Let us assume we are working with college students. Figure 3.1 depicts each of the

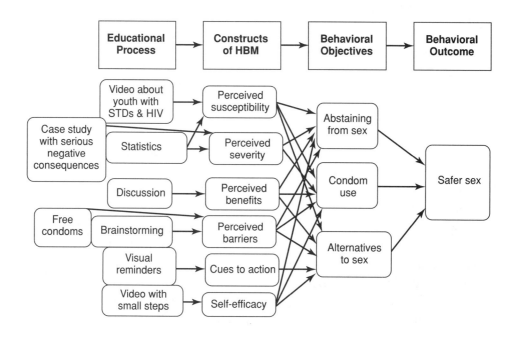

FIGURE 3.1   How the health belief model can be used to modify sexual behavior in youth to promote safer sex

constructs from the HBM and links these with the educational processes and behavior objectives in this example.

The health education intervention would start with modifying the construct of perceived susceptibility, which can be done by showing a video about college students suffering from HIV/AIDS and STDs. The video must show characters who are similar to the target audience in their characteristics. The construct of perceived severity can be built by making a presentation using statistics and a case study that underscores the serious negative consequences. These consequences can be medical as well as involving school, work, family, and relationships. To influence perceived benefits, make sure that students have all the information they need to take the action, for example, where to get condoms, how to choose them, how to store them, when to use them, how to put them on, how to remove them, and how to dispose of them. To modify perceived barriers, have the students brainstorm all real and imagined barriers. Then discuss in a large group how each of these barriers can be overcome to either abstain from sex, use condoms, or use alternatives to sex. In addition, as an incentive, the students could be provided with a small supply of free condoms. To influence cues to action, visual reminders would be used. Youth would be provided key chains with the messages so that they could remember to perform the chosen healthy behaviors. To build self-efficacy, a video with a credible role model would be shown that depicts the behaviors in small steps; reinforces the messages about abstinence, condom use, and alternatives to sex; and provides practical advice to reduce stress and anxiety in times of making love.

Using this approach, you can plan to apply the HBM to a health behavior issue for a target group of your choice. Table 3.5 provides a set of questions to assist you in choosing an appropriate educational method that corresponds to different constructs of the HBM.

SUMMARY

The health belief model is the first theory that was developed exclusively for health-related behaviors. It had its start in an exploration of the reasons people were not accessing free screening for tuberculosis. The HBM predicts behavior based on the constructs of perceived susceptibility, perceived severity, perceived benefits, perceived costs, cues to action, and self-efficacy. *Perceived susceptibility* refers to the subjective belief a person has regarding the likelihood of acquiring a disease or harmful

TABLE 3.5   Choosing the Educational Methods for Health Education Program Planning Using the Health Belief Model

1. What will be the best educational method to facilitate perceived susceptibility?
   - Lecture underscoring negative consequences
   - Presenting statistics
   - Case study with negative consequences
   - Video film highlighting negative consequences
   - Other

2. What will be the best educational method to facilitate perceived severity?
   - Lecture
   - Presenting statistics
   - Case study
   - Video film
   - Other

3. What will be the best educational method to facilitate perceived benefits?
   - Lecture
   - Small group discussion
   - Large group discussion
   - Other

4. What will be the best educational method to facilitate perceived barriers?
   - Brainstorming
   - Small group discussion
   - Large group discussion
   - Incentives
   - Other

5. What will be the best educational method to facilitate cues to action?
   - Visual reminders
   - Phone call
   - Personal reminder
   - Other

6. What will be the best educational method to facilitate self-efficacy?
   - Demonstration
   - Role play
   - Video with a credible role model
   - Stress reduction techniques
     - Progressive muscle relaxation
     - Visual imagery
     - Autogenic training
     - Yoga
     - Other
   - Other

state as a result of indulging in a particular behavior. *Perceived severity* refers to the subjective belief in the extent of harm that can result from the acquired disease or harmful state as a result of a particular behavior. Perceived susceptibility and perceived severity are together called *perceived threat*. *Perceived benefits* are beliefs in the advantages of the methods suggested for reducing the risk or seriousness of the disease or harmful state resulting from a particular behavior. *Perceived barriers* are beliefs concerning the actual and imagined costs of following the new behavior. *Cues to action* are the precipitating forces that make a person feel the need to take action. *Self-efficacy* is the confidence that a person has in his or her ability to pursue a behavior. The HBM has been widely used in behavioral research, primary prevention, and secondary prevention.

REVIEW QUESTIONS

1. Discuss the historical genesis of the health belief model.
2. Describe the constructs of the health belief model.
3. Define self-efficacy. How is self-efficacy built?
4. Differentiate between perceived severity and perceived susceptibility.
5. How can the construct of perceived barriers be modified?
6. Discuss the limitations of the health belief model.

WEBSITE

Go to the Web component of *Theoretical Foundations of Health Education and Health Promotion* at http://health.jbpub.com/foundations for Web exercises, additional resources related to this chapter, and student review tools.

GLOSSARY TERMS

cues to action

health belief model (HBM)

illness behaviors

perceived barriers

perceived benefits

perceived severity

perceived susceptibility

perceived threat

preventive (or health) behaviors

self-efficacy

sick role behaviors

value expectancy theories

REFERENCES AND FURTHER READING

Ajzen, I., & Fishbein, M. (2004). Questions raised by a reasoned action approach: Comment on Ogden (2003). *Health Psychology*, *23*, 431–434.

Atkinson, J. W. (1957). Motivational determinants of risk taking behavior. *Psychological Review*, *64*, 359–372.

Becker, M. H. (1974). The health belief model and sick role behavior. In M. H. Becker (Ed.), *The health belief model and personal health behavior* (pp. 82–92). Thorofare, NJ: Charles B. Slack.

Bigham, M., Remple, V. P., Pielak, K., McIntyre, C., White, R., & Wu, W. (2006). Uptake and behavioural and attitudinal determinants of immunization in an expanded routine infant hepatitis B vaccination program in British Columbia. *Canadian Journal of Public Health*, *97*(2), 90–95.

Buckingham, R. W., Moraros, J., Bird, Y., Meister, E., & Webb, N. C. (2005). Factors associated with condom use among brothel-based female sex workers in Thailand. *AIDS Care*, *17*(5), 640–647.

Butraporn, P., Pach, A., Pack, R. P., Masngarmmeung, R., Maton, T., Sri-aroon, P., et al. (2004). The health belief model and factors relating to potential use of a vaccine for shigellosis in Kaeng Koi district, Saraburi province, Thailand. *Journal of Health, Population, and Nutrition*, *22*, 170–181.

Champion, V. L. (1993). Instrument refinement for breast cancer screening behaviors. *Nursing Research*, *42*,139–143.

Chew, F., Palmer, S., & Kim, S. (1998). Testing the influence of the health belief model and a television program on nutrition behavior. *Health Communication*, *10*(3), 227–245.

de Paoli, M. M., Manongi, R., & Klepp, K. I. (2004). Factors influencing acceptability of voluntary counselling and HIV-testing among pregnant women in northern Tanzania. *AIDS Care*, *16*(4), 411–425.

DiGioacchino, R. F., Keenan, M. F., & Sargent, R. (2000). Assessment of dental practitioners in the secondary and tertiary prevention of eating disorders. *Eating Behaviors*, *1*(1), 79–91.

Doukas, D. J., Localio, A. R., & Li, Y. (2004). Attitudes and beliefs concerning prostate cancer genetic screening. *Clinical Genetics*, *66*(5), 445–451.

Dundar, P. E, Ozmen, D., Ozturk, B., Haspolat, G., Akyildiz, F., Coban, S., et al. (2006). The knowledge and attitudes of breast self-examination and mammography in a group of women in a rural area in western Turkey. *BMC Cancer*, *6*, 43.

Edwards, W. (1954). The theory of decision making. *Psychological Bulletin*, *51*, 380–417.

Elliott, J. O., & Jacobson, M. P. (2006). Bone loss in epilepsy: Barriers to prevention, diagnosis, and treatment. *Epilepsy and Behavior*, *8*(1), 169–175.

Eshleman, M. J., Poole, V., & Davidhizar, R. (2005). An investigation of factors associated with infant mortality in two midwest counties. *Journal of Practical Nursing*, *55*(3), 5–10.

Farquharson, L., Noble, L. M., Barker, C., & Behrens, R. H. (2004). Health beliefs and communication in the travel clinic consultation as predictors of adherence to malaria chemoprophylaxis. *British Journal of Health Psychology*, *9*(Pt. 2), 201–217.

Feather, N. T. (1959). Subjective probability and decision under uncertainty. *Psychological Review*, *66*, 150–164.

Gillibrand, R., & Stevenson, J. (2006). The extended health belief model applied to the experience of diabetes in young people. *British Journal of Health Psychology*, *11*, 155–169.

Greene, K., & Brinn, L. S. (2003). Messages influencing college women's tanning bed use: Statistical versus narrative evidence format and a self-assessment to increase perceived susceptibility. *Journal of Health Communication, 8*(5), 443–461.

Greenwald, B. (2006). Promoting community awareness of the need for colorectal cancer screening: A pilot study. *Cancer Nursing, 29*(2),134–141.

Harrison, J. A., Mullen, P. D., & Green, L. W. (1992). A meta-analysis of studies of the health belief model with adults. *Health Education Research, 7*(1), 107–116.

Janz, N. K., & Becker, M. H. (1984). The health belief model: A decade later. *Health Education Quarterly, 11*, 1–47.

Janz, N. K., Champion, V. L., & Strecher, V. J. (2002). The health belief model. In K. Glanz, B. K. Rimer, & F. M. Lewis (Eds.), *Health behavior and health education: Theory, research, and practice* (3rd ed., pp. 45–66). San Francisco: Jossey Bass.

Juniper, K. C., Oman, R. F., Hamm, R. M., & Kerby, D. S. (2004). The relationships among constructs in the health belief model and the transtheoretical model among African-American college women for physical activity. *American Journal of Health Promotion, 18*(5), 354–357.

Kasl, S. V. (1974). The health belief model and behavior related to chronic illness. In M. H. Becker (Ed.), *The health belief model and personal health behavior* (pp. 106–127). Thorofare, NJ: Charles B. Slack.

Kasl, S. V., & Cobb, S. (1966). Health behavior, illness behavior, and sick role behavior. I. Health and illness behavior. *Archives of Environmental Health, 12*(2), 246–266.

Kirscht, J. P. (1974). The health belief model and illness behavior. In M. H. Becker (Ed.), *The health belief model and personal health behavior* (pp. 60–81). Thorofare, NJ: Charles B. Slack.

Kofahi, M. M., & Haddad, L. G. (2005). Perceptions of lung cancer and smoking among college students in Jordan. *Journal of Transcultural Nursing, 16*(3), 245–254.

Lajunen, T., & Rasanen, M. (2004). Can social psychological models be used to promote bicycle helmet use among teenagers? A comparison of the health belief model, theory of planned behavior and the locus of control. *Journal of Safety Research, 35*(1), 115–123.

Lau, J. T., Yang, X., Tsui, H. Y., & Kim, J. H. (2006). Prevalence of influenza vaccination and associated factors among community-dwelling Hong Kong residents of age 65 or above. *Vaccine, 24*(26), 5526–5534.

Lewin, K. (1935). *A dynamic theory of personality: Selected papers.* New York: McGraw Hill.

Lewin, K., Dembo, T., Festinger, L., & Sears, P. S. (1944). Level of aspiration. In J. M. Hunt (Ed.), *Personality and the behavior disorders: A handbook based on experimental and clinical research* (pp. 333–378). New York: The Ronald Press.

Lin, P., Simoni, J. M., & Zemon, V. (2005). The health belief model, sexual behaviors, and HIV risk among Taiwanese immigrants. *AIDS Education & Prevention, 17*(5), 469–483.

Maiman, L. A., & Becker, M. H. (1974). The health belief model: Origins and correlates in psychological theory. In M. H. Becker (Ed.), *The health belief model and personal health behavior* (pp. 9–26). Thorofare, NJ: Charles B. Slack.

Maiman, L. A., Becker, M. H., Kirscht, J. P., Haefner, D. P., & Drachman, R. H. (1977). Scales for measuring health belief model dimensions: A test of predictive value, internal consistency, and relationships among beliefs. *Health Education Monographs, 5*, 215–230.

Martinez, R., Gratton, T. B., Coggin, C., Rene, A., & Waller, W. (2004). A study of pesticide safety and health perceptions among pesticide applicators in Tarrant County, Texas. *Journal of Environmental Health*, *66*(6), 34–37, 43.

Mullen, P. D., Hersey, J. C., & Iverson, D. C. (1987). Health behavior models compared. *Social Science and Medicine*, *24*, 973-981.

Ndiokwelu, E. (2004). Applicability of Rosenstock-Hochbaum health behaviour model to prevention of periodontal disease in Enugu students. *Odontostomatologie Tropicale*, *27*(106), 4–8.

Ogden, J. (2003). Some problems with social cognition models: A pragmatic and conceptual analysis. *Health Psychology*, *22*, 424–428.

Orensky, I. A., & Holdford, D. A. (2005). Predictors of noncompliance with warfarin therapy in an outpatient anticoagulation clinic. *Pharmacotherapy*, *25*(12), 1801–1808.

Park, S., Chang, S., & Chung, C. (2005). Effects of a cognition-emotion focused program to increase public participation in Papanicolaou smear screening. *Public Health Nursing*, *22*(4), 289–298.

Pielak, K. L., & Hilton, A. (2003). University students immunized and not immunized for measles: A comparison of beliefs, attitudes, and perceived barriers and benefits. *Canadian Journal of Public Health*, *94*(3), 193–196.

Poss, J. E. (1999). Developing an instrument to study the tuberculosis screening behaviors of Mexican migrant farmworkers. *Journal of Transcultural Nursing*, *10*(4), 306–319.

Rainey, R. C., & Harding, A. K. (2005). Acceptability of solar disinfection of drinking water treatment in Kathmandu Valley, Nepal. *International Journal of Environmental Health Research*, *15*(5), 361–372.

Raz, A. E., Atar, M., Rodnay, M., Shoham-Vardi, I., & Carmi, R. (2003). Between acculturation and ambivalence: Knowledge of genetics and attitudes towards genetic testing in a consanguineous Bedouin community. *Community Genetics*, *6*(2), 88–95.

Rodriguez-Reimann, D. I., Nicassio, P., Reimann, J. O., Gallegos, P. I., & Olmedo, E. L. (2004). Acculturation and health beliefs of Mexican Americans regarding tuberculosis prevention. *Journal of Immigrant Health*, *6*(2), 51–62.

Rosenstock, I. M. (1974a). Historical origins of the health belief model. In M. H. Becker (Ed.), *The health belief model and personal health behavior* (pp. 1–8). Thorofare, NJ: Charles B. Slack.

Rosenstock, I. M. (1974b). The health belief model and preventive health behavior. In M. H. Becker (Ed.), *The health belief model and personal health behavior* (pp. 27–59). Thorofare, NJ: Charles B. Slack.

Rosenstock, I. M., Strecher, V. J., & Becker, M. H. (1988). Social learning theory and the health belief model. *Health Education Quarterly*, *15*, 175–183.

Rotter, J. B. (1954). *Social learning and clinical psychology*. New York: Prentice Hall.

Seo, M. A., & Min, S. K. (2005). Development of a structural model explaining medication compliance of persons with schizophrenia. *Yonsei Medical Journal*, *46*(3), 331–340.

Toepell, A. R. (2003) The health belief model and safer sex: Implications for women's health. *Women's Health and Urban Life*, *2*(1), 22–41.

Tolman, E. C. (1955). Principles of performance. *Psychological Review*, *62*, 315–326.

Tyrrell, J., Poulet, C., Pe Pin, J. L., & Veale, D. (2006). A preliminary study of psychological factors affecting patients' acceptance of CPAP therapy for sleep apnoea syndrome. *Sleep Medicine*, 7(4), 375–379.

Unson, C. G., Fortinsky, R., Prestwood, K., & Reisine, S. (2005). Osteoporosis medications used by older African-American women: Effects of socioeconomic status and psychosocial factors. *Journal of Community Health*, 30(4), 281–297.

Van Horn, E. (2005). An exploration of recurrent injury prevention in patients with trauma. *Orthopaedic Nursing*, 24(4), 249–258.

Von Ah, D., Ebert, S., Ngamvitroj, A., Park, N., & Kang, D. H. (2004). Predictors of health behaviours in college students. *Journal of Advanced Nursing*, 48(5), 463–474.

Wai, C. T., Wong, M. L., Ng, S., Cheok, A., Tan, M. H., Chua, W., et al. (2005). Utility of the health belief model in predicting compliance of screening in patients with chronic hepatitis B. *Alimentary Pharmacology and Therapeutics*, 21(10), 1255–1262.

Welch, J. L., Bennett, S. J., Delp, R. L., & Agarwal, R. (2006). Benefits of and barriers to dietary sodium adherence. *Western Journal of Nursing Research* 28(2), 162–180.

Werner, P. (2003). Factors influencing intentions to seek a cognitive status examination: A study based on the health belief model. *International Journal of Geriatric Psychiatry*, 18(9), 787–794.

Wong, C. Y., & Tang, C. S. (2005). Practice of habitual and volitional health behaviors to prevent severe acute respiratory syndrome among Chinese adolescents in Hong Kong. *Journal of Adolescent Health*, 36(3), 193–200.

Zagumny, M. J., & Brady, D. B. (1998). Development of the AIDS Health Belief Scale (AHBS). *AIDS Education and Prevention*, 10(2), 173–179.

CHAPTER 4

The Transtheoretical Model

KEY CONCEPTS

- Action stage
- Consciousness raising
- Contemplation stage
- Counterconditioning
- Decisional balance
- Dramatic relief
- Environmental reevaluation
- Helping relationships
- Levels of change
- Maintenance stage
- Precontemplation stage

- Preparation stage
- Reinforcement management
- Self-efficacy
- Self-liberation
- Self-reevaluation
- Social liberation
- Stages of change
- Stimulus control
- Temptation
- Transtheoretical model

AFTER READING THIS CHAPTER YOU SHOULD BE ABLE TO

- Describe the historical genesis of the transtheoretical model
- List ten processes of the transtheoretical model
- Summarize the applications of the transtheoretical model in health education and health promotion
- Identify educational methods for modifying each process from the transtheoretical model
- Apply the transtheoretical model in changing a health behavior of your choice

This chapter discusses the **transtheoretical model (TTM)**. Over the years this model has been tested and expanded and called by various names, yet it is known as a *model* because it has essentially evolved from reviewing a number of theories. That is why one of its names is the transtheoretical model, which is the name that this chapter uses. This model focuses on explaining behavior change, whereas many other models focus just on the behavior. This model is also unique in that it specifies a time dimension in behavior change. It proposes that people move through various stages while making a behavior change and that the whole process can take as long as six months to five years. With this emphasis on stages, the model is also known as the stages of change (SOC) model. It is one of the most popular models used in the field of behavior change. More than 1,000 publications have cited this model since its origin in the late 1970s.

This chapter begins by describing the historical aspects of the genesis of this model. Next it describes the various constructs or processes that make up this model. It then discusses the applications of the TTM in behavioral research, primary prevention, and secondary prevention. Finally, it discusses the limitations of the model and presents a skill-building application using the TTM.

HISTORICAL PERSPECTIVES

In the late 1970s James Prochaska from the University of Rhode Island undertook to review various theories behind psychotherapy. In the process he laid the foundations of the transtheoretical model (Prochaska, 1979). James Prochaska is currently the director of the Cancer Prevention Research Consortium and professor of clinical and health psychology at the University of Rhode Island. He completed his doctorate in clinical psychology in 1969 from Wayne State University. He has won several awards, including the Top Five Most Cited Authors in Psychology award from the American Psychology Society. In his book *Systems of Psychotherapy: A Transtheoretical Analysis*, published in 1979, he reviewed 18 theories of psychotherapy, among them Adlerian therapy (Adler, 1929), behavior therapy (Wolpe, 1973), emotional flooding therapies (Olsen, 1976), existential analysis (Binswanger, 1958), Freud's psychoanalysis (1959), gestalt therapy (Perls, 1969), rational emotive therapy (Ellis, 1973), Rogers's client-centered therapy (1951), and transactional analysis (Berne, 1966). He found that despite the multifarious psychotherapies, there are certain commonalities, not necessarily in the therapy but in the process of change (Prochaska, 1999). During the same time he teamed with Carlo DiClemente, who did his doctoral work at the University of Rhode Island and is now a professor of psychology at the University of Maryland, to develop and refine the TTM (Prochaska & DiClemente, 1983).

In the 1980s, the University of Rhode Island Change Assessment (URICA) scale was developed for problems leading individuals to psychotherapy (McConnaughy, DiClemente, Prochaska, & Velicer, 1989). This is a 32-item self-report using the TTM that measures attitudes toward behavior change for different problems. A version of URICA for alcohol use has also been developed called URICA-A (Migneault, Velicer, Prochaska, & Stevenson, 1999).

TTM has been a major force in helping the field progress to more inclusive approaches to research and practice that complement old paradigms with new ones. It does not put old paradigms to rest, but rather complements these with more comprehensive approaches.

James O. Prochaska
(2006, p. 772)

In the 1990s two scales were developed using the TTM. The first is the Readiness to Change Questionnaire (RCQ), developed by Rollnick and colleagues (1992). The RCQ consists of three 4-item scales, namely, precontemplation, contemplation, and action. Items pertaining to maintenance were included in the original scale, but empirically the factor was not found to be valid and was thus excluded. The second scale is the Stages of Change Readiness and Treatment Eagerness Scale (SOCRATES), which was developed by Miller and Tonigan (1996). Originally this was a 40-item instrument, but it has now been reduced to 19 items. The transtheoretical model at present enjoys the status of being the most popular model. Several studies continue to be published on this model every year.

CONSTRUCTS OF THE TRANSTHEORETICAL MODEL

The first construct of the TTM is **stages of change**. The construct of stages provides a temporal or time dimension and implies that change occurs over time (Prochaska, 2000). The construct also offers a middle level of abstraction between psychological states and personality traits. Stages are dynamic like psychological states and yet have stable characteristics like personality traits. This enables a person to move from one stage to another while making a behavior change. A person transits through five stages when considering changing a behavior (Table 4.1).

TABLE 4.1 Stages of Behavior Change in the Transtheoretical Model	
Precontemplation	One is not considering change in the foreseeable future, usually defined as the next six months.
Contemplation	One is considering change in the foreseeable future but not immediately, usually defined as between one and six months.
Preparation	One is planning for change in the immediate future, usually defined as in the next month.
Action	One has made meaningful change in the past six months.
Maintenance	One has maintained change for a period of time, usually considered as six or more months.

The first stage is the **precontemplation stage**, when a person is not considering change in the foreseeable future, usually defined as the next six months. There are two categories of people in this stage. First are uninformed or less informed people who are unaware of the consequences of their behavior. Second are people who have experimented with change but have failed in the past so that they are no longer seeking to change. Usually this second category is resistant or unmotivated to change.

The second stage is the **contemplation stage**, when one is considering change in the foreseeable future but not immediately, usually defined as between one and six months. These people have considered the benefits (or pros) and costs (or cons) of changing their behavior. The third stage is the **preparation stage**, when one is planning for change in the immediate future, usually defined as in the next month. The people in this stage have taken some significant steps, such as going to a recovery group, buying some exercise equipment, consulting a counselor, buying self-help materials, and so on.

The fourth stage is the **action stage**, in which the person has made meaningful change in the past six months. Behaviors are actions, and the new actions can be observed clearly in this stage. The person is making conscious efforts to perform the new actions. The fifth stage is the **maintenance stage**, in which the person has maintained the change for a period of time, usually considered as six or more months. Prochaska (2000) estimates that the maintenance stage can range in duration from six months to up to five years. When changing negative habits, the term **termination** is used when the person has completely quit the habit, has no temptation to relapse, and is fully self-efficacious to continue with the change.

The progression through these stages is not linear but cyclical or spiral; one might progress from precontemplation to action and then regress to contemplation, and then again progress to action, and so on (Prochaska, DiClemente, & Norcross, 1992).

The second construct of the TTM pertains to the ten processes of change, summarized in Table 4.2. The first process of change, which is borrowed from the Freudian school of psychotherapy (Freud, 1960) is the process of **consciousness raising**. Consciousness raising is an experiential process that entails raising awareness about the causes, consequences, and cures for a particular problem. This can be achieved by arranging for observation sessions, by confronting the participants on the issue, providing interpretations from the literature, providing feedback to the participants, and giving an informational lecture or talk. This process is important in the precontemplation and contemplation stages in helping people move forward.

TABLE 4.2   Key Processes of the Transtheoretical Model

Construct	Definition	How to Modify?
Consciousness raising	Experiential process that entails raising awareness about causes, consequences, and cures for a particular problem	• Discussion sharing observations • Discussion with confrontations • Discussion sharing interpretations • Discussion with feedback • Lecture
Dramatic relief	Experiential process that enhances emotional arousal about one's behavior and the relief that can come from changing it	• Psychodrama • Role playing • Personal testimony • Grieving
Environmental reevaluation	Experiential process that involves both affective and cognitive components on how the behavior affects one's environment and how changing the behavior would influence the environment	• Empathy training • Discussion with value clarification • Family or network interventions
Self-reevaluation	Experiential process that involves both affective and cognitive components and includes one's assessment of self-image with the new behavior	• Imagery • Healthier role models • Discussion with values clarification
Self-liberation	Behavioral process that entails belief that one can change and a commitment and recommitment to act on that change	• Making public commitments • Making resolutions • Providing multiple alternatives to choose from
Counterconditioning	Behavioral process that requires learning of new, healthier behavior instead of old, unhealthy behavior	• Desensitization • Assertion • Practicing relaxation • Cognitive counters to irrational self-statements
Reinforcement management	Behavioral process that utilizes reinforcements and punishments for taking steps in a particular direction	• Self-reinforcements • Contracting • Group recognition

TABLE 4.2 *(Continued)*		
Construct	**Definition**	**How to Modify?**
Stimulus control	Behavioral process that involves modifying the environment to increase cues for healthy behavior and decrease cues for unhealthy behavior	• Avoidance • Environmental reengineering by removing cues for unhealthy behavior • Self-help groups that provide cues for healthier behavior
Helping relationships	Behavioral process that entails developing caring, open, trusting, and accepting relationships to adhere to the healthy behavior	• Rapport building • Health educator calls • Buddy systems • Self-help groups
Social liberation	Experiential process that refers to an increase in social opportunities or alternatives	• Advocacy • Empowerment methods • Policies

The second process of change is **dramatic relief**, which is an experiential process that enhances emotional arousal about one's behavior and emphasizes the relief that can come from changing it. This can be facilitated through methods such as enacting a psychodrama, having the participants partake in a role play, sharing personal testimony from people in similar situations, or allowing the participants to grieve over their situation so that their emotions are brought forward. This process is important in the precontemplation and contemplation stages in helping people move forward.

The third process of change is **environmental reevaluation**, which is the experiential process that involves both affective and cognitive components regarding how the behavior affects one's environment and how changing the behavior would influence the environment. It can be influenced by empathy training, values clarification, or family or network interventions. It is also important in the precontemplation and contemplation stages.

The fourth process of change is **self-reevaluation**, an experiential process that involves both affective and cognitive components and includes a person's assessment of his or her self-image with the new behavior. The self-image can be changed by us-ing imagery, healthier role models, and values clarification. Self-reevaluation is im-portant in the contemplation and preparation stages.

The fifth process of change is **self-liberation**, a behavioral process that entails belief that one can change and a commitment and recommitment to act on that change. It can be facilitated by making public commitments as opposed to private commitments, making resolutions, or having multiple alternatives to choose from. Prochaska (2000) notes that whenever possible we should try to provide people with three of the best possible choices. Having fewer than or more than three choices is usually not very effective. This process is important in the preparation stage and helps to confirm one's commitment toward behavior change.

The sixth process of change is **counterconditioning**. Counterconditioning refers to a behavioral process that requires learning of new, healthier behavior to replace the unhealthy behavior. Methods such as desensitization, assertion, practicing relaxation, or using cognitive counters to irrational self-statements can be utilized to facilitate this process. This process is important in the action stage.

The seventh process of change is borrowed from the Skinnerian tradition (Skin-ner, 1953) and is called **contingency management** or **reinforcement management**. These terms refer to a behavioral process that utilizes reinforcements and punish-ments for taking steps in a particular direction. The process can be fostered by devel-oping self-reinforcements, using contracts, and providing group recognition for achievements with regard to behavior acquisition. This process is important in the ac-tion stage.

The eighth process of change is **stimulus control**, a behavioral process that in-volves modifying the environment to increase cues for healthy behavior and decrease cues for unhealthy behavior. Behavior can be modified by avoidance of the cues for unhealthy behavior, environmental reengineering that removes cues for unhealthy behaviors, and participation in self-help groups that provide cues for healthy behav-iors. This process is important in the action stage.

The ninth process of change is borrowed from the Rogerian school of psy-chotherapy (Rogers, 1961) and is called **helping relationships**. Helping relation-ships is a behavioral process that entails developing caring, open, trusting, and ac-cepting relationships to adhere to the healthy behavior. These can be developed through rapport building, health educator calls, formation of buddy systems, and participation in self-help groups. This process is important in the action and mainte-nance stages.

The tenth process of change is **social liberation**, which refers to an experiential process that increases social opportunities or alternatives. Social liberation can be enhanced through advocacy, empowerment-building methods, and having policies that increase social opportunities. This process is important in the preparation and action stages.

The third construct of the TTM is **decisional balance**, or pros and cons. This construct has been taken from the work of Janis and Mann (1977) with decision making. It addresses the relative importance placed by an individual on the advantages (pros) of behavior change as opposed to the disadvantages (cons). According to this model, behavior change occurs when the pros of the behavior change are viewed as more important than the cons of change. Hence, educators must make an attempt to enhance the pros while reducing the cons. This construct is especially important in the precontemplation and contemplation stages of change.

The fourth construct of the TTM is **self-efficacy**. This construct, taken from Bandura's social cognitive theory (1986), was discussed in Chapter 3 in connection with the health belief model and will be discussed in detail in Chapter 7. Self-efficacy is the confidence that a person has in his or her ability to pursue a given behavior. It is specific to the behavior and is in the present. It is not about the past or future.

The fifth construct of the TTM, which goes hand in hand with self-efficacy, is **temptation**. Temptation refers to the urge to engage in unhealthy behavior when confronted with a difficult situation (Prochaska, Redding, & Evers, 2002). It is, in essence, the converse of self-efficacy. In research, the same set of items using different response formats is used to measure both self-efficacy and temptation. Temptation is represented by three factors that denote the most common types of tempting situations: negative affect or emotional distress, positive social situations, and craving.

The sixth construct of TTM that is usually considered in psychotherapy is **levels of change** (Prochaska, 1995). Levels of change represent five distinct but interrelated levels of psychological problems that can be addressed in psychotherapy: symptom/situational problems, maladaptive cognitions, current interpersonal conflicts, family/system conflicts, and intrapersonal conflicts. These levels have limited utility for designing

> *While research results to date are encouraging, much still needs to be done to advance the Transtheoretical Model. Basic research should explore relationships of TTM variables with constructs from other established health behavior theories including perceived risk, subjective norms, and problem severity.*
>
> —Prochaska, Redding, and Evers (2002, p. 115)

health behavior change interventions and have been included in this chapter mainly to give a sense of completeness.

PHASES OF INTERVENTIONS BASED ON THE TRANSTHEORETICAL MODEL

Prochaska (1999) has identified five phases for planning interventions based on the TTM:

1. Recruitment phase
2. Retention phase
3. Progress phase
4. Process phase
5. Outcomes phase

In the *recruitment phase*, measures are taken to persuade a large number of people to join the program. In this phase professionals must proactively reach out to the target population. With regard to the stage of change people are in for any given behavior to be changed, DiClemente and Prochaska (1998) suggest a thumb rule of 40, 40, 20, that is, 40% in the precontemplation stage, 40% in the contemplation stage, and 20% in the preparation stage.

> *The strong principle of progress holds that to progress from precontemplation to effective action, the pros of changing must increase 1 standard deviation.*
>
> *The weak principle of progress holds that to progress from contemplation to effective action, the cons of changing must decrease $1/2$ standard deviation.*
>
> —Prochaska (2000, p. 117)

In the *retention phase*, efforts must be taken to retain people who join the program. This can be done by matching the processes of change with the stage of change a person is in. In the *progress phase*, efforts must be taken to make people progress during and after the intervention. In the process phase, efforts must be made to help the participants move from one stage to another, and processes of change must be applied. The pros for changing must be underscored in precontemplation. The cons must be decreased during contemplation to progress to action. Processes of change must be matched with the stage. In the *outcomes phase*, the end results are measured.

APPLICATIONS OF THE TRANSTHEORETICAL MODEL

Some examples of behavioral research in which the TTM has been used are studying gender differences in intimate partner violence (Babcock, Canady, Senior, & Eckhardt, 2005), modeling to remedy alcohol abuse among patients with mental illness (Zhang, Harmon, Werkner, & McCormick, 2006), studying patients' participation in medical decision making (Arora, Ayanian, & Guadagnoli, 2005), predicting physician behavior to recommend colonoscopy (Honda & Gorin, 2006), predictive modeling for bicycle helmet use (Weiss, Okun, & Quay, 2004), predictive modeling for chlamydia and gonorrhea (Chacko et al., 2006), predictive modeling for physical activity (Rhodes & Plotnikoff, 2006), predictive modeling in ethnically diverse women at risk for HIV (Gazabon, Morokoff, Harlow, Ward, & Quina, 2006), evaluating a processes of change scale for alcohol misuse (Freyer et al., 2006), profiling youth who do not use drugs (J. L. Johnson et al., 2006), and developing a scale for osteoporosis prevention behaviors in older adults (Popa, 2005). Table 4.3 summarizes these applications.

Some examples in which the transtheoretical model has been used for primary prevention are for increasing acceptance of contraceptives in men (Ha, Jayasuriya, & Owen, 2005); changing sun protection behaviors (Kristjansson, Ullen, & Helgason, 2004); HIV, STD, and pregnancy prevention in adolescents (Hacker, Brown, Cabral, & Dodds, 2005); increasing fruit and vegetable consumption (Henry,

TABLE 4.3   Examples of Applications of the Transtheoretical Model in Behavioral Research
Gender differences in intimate partner violence
Modeling to remedy alcohol abuse among patients with mental illness
Patients' participation in medical decision making
Predicting physician behavior to recommend colonoscopy
Predictive modeling for bicycle helmet use
Predictive modeling for chlamydia and gonorrhea
Predictive modeling for physical activity
Predictive modeling in ethnically diverse women at risk for HIV
Processes of change scale for alcohol misuse
Profiling youth who do not use drugs
Scale for osteoporosis prevention behaviors in older adults

Reimer, Smith, & Reicks, 2006); overweight and obesity reduction in primary care (Logue et al., 2005); promoting physical activity (Fahrenwald & Shangreaux, 2006); training of lay health advisors (Kobetz, Vatalaro, Moore, & Earp, 2005); tobacco cessation counseling by dental hygienists (Monson & Engeswick, 2005); promoting use of a food thermometer when cooking meat (Takeuchi, Edlefsen, McCurdy, & Hillers, 2006); and promoting use of hearing protection devices in workers (Raymond & Lusk, 2006). Table 4.4 summarizes these applications.

Some examples in which the TTM has been used for secondary and tertiary prevention are adherence to activity recommendations in chronic low back pain (Basler, Bertalanffy, Quint, Wilke, & Wolf, 2007), adherence to antiretroviral therapy in AIDS (Highstein, Willey, & Mundy, 2006), adherence to lipid-lowering drugs (S. S. Johnson et al., 2006), adherence to medication for treatment of multiple sclerosis (Berger, Liang, & Hudmon, 2005), cardiac rehabilitation intervention (Beckie, 2006), colorectal cancer screening (Zimmerman, Tabbarah, Trauth, Nowalk, & Ricci, 2006), adherence to continuous positive airway pressure treatment in sleep apnea (Stepnowsky, Marler, Palau, & Brooks, 2006), dietary fat modification in breast cancer survivors (Politi, Rabin, & Pinto, 2006), hypercholesterolemia education classes (Kotani, Saiga, Sakane, & Kurozawa, 2005), mammography participation (Hur, Kim, & Park, 2005), a physical activity program for prostate cancer patients (Taylor et al., 2006), smoking cessation (Aveyard et al., 2006; Schumann, John, Rumpf, Hapke, & Meyer,

TABLE 4.4   Examples of Applications of the Transtheoretical Model in Primary Prevention
Acceptance of contraceptives in men
Changing sun protection behaviors
HIV, STD, and pregnancy prevention in adolescents
Increasing fruit and vegetable consumption
Overweight and obesity reduction in primary care
Physical activity promotion
Tobacco cessation counseling by dental hygienists
Training of lay health advisors
Use of food thermometer when cooking meat
Use of hearing protection devices in workers

TABLE 4.5	Examples of Applications of the Transtheoretical Model in Secondary and Tertiary Prevention
Adherence to activity recommendations in chronic low back pain	
Adherence to antiretroviral therapy in AIDS	
Adherence to lipid-lowering drugs	
Adherence to medication for treatment of multiple sclerosis	
Cardiac rehabilitation intervention	
Colorectal cancer screening	
Continuous positive airway pressure (CPAP) treatment adherence in sleep apnea	
Dietary fat modification in breast cancer survivors	
Hypercholesterolemia education classes	
Mammography participation	
Physical activity program for prostate cancer patients	
Smoking cessation	
Web-based physical activity promotion in persons with disabilities	

2006), and Web-based physical activity promotion in persons with disabilities (Kosma, Cardinal, & McCubbin, 2005). Table 4.5 summarizes these applications.

LIMITATIONS OF THE TRANSTHEORETICAL MODEL

Despite the great popularity enjoyed by the transtheoretical model, there have been several criticisms of this model. Some critics have even argued that the model should be completely abandoned (West, 2005). Many critics (Bandura, 1997; Davidson, 1992; Littell & Girvin, 2002; Sutton, 1996; West, 2005) have argued that the stages in the model are arbitrary and that classifying a population into different stages serves little utility. They see change as a continuous process that cannot be categorized. Whitelaw and colleagues (2000) note that classifying people in stages has several problems. First, people can move through the stages of the model in minutes. Second, the validity of self-reported behavior with regard to stage is questionable. Third, a significant number of people cannot be assigned to recognized stages. Herzog (2005, p. 1040) notes "that there has never been a peer-reviewed account of the developmental research that led to the creation of the stages of change algorithm." Littell and Girvin (2002) note that there is little empirical evidence regarding sequential transition between the stages and that no single study has documented movement through the entire spectrum of stages. Etter (2005) notes that classifying people in stages such as precontemplation means lumping different categories together, whereby people who have never thought of changing the behavior are grouped with people who have relapsed after making successful behavior change.

In rejoinder, Prochaska (2006) has clarified that stage of change is a discrete variable that some people mistakenly consider as a theory, which leads to confusion. Migneault, Adams, and Read (2005) also note that most applications of the TTM in the area of substance abuse have focused on the construct of stages of change and very few have focused on other constructs such as processes, decisional balance, and self-efficacy. More constructs of the model need to be used.

Another limitation of the TTM that has been pointed out in the literature is its lack of predictive potential (West, 2005). Migneault, Adams, and Read (2005) note that application of the TTM to substance abuse behaviors has yielded mixed results and that the model is descriptive rather than predictive. There is definitive need to make the model robust in its predictive potential.

Another limitation of the model is that usually theories aim for parsimony, or use of few constructs to predict the phenomenon. The TTM is not parsimonious (West, 2006). There is a need to identify salient constructs that account for the majority of the variance, thereby making TTM parsimonious so that it can be of more practical utility.

Although there are definitive limitations to this model, just like all other models and theories, there is no need to completely abandon its use as some of its critics have suggested. What is needed is better measurement of the constructs of this model, particularly the processes of change; better and more rigorous reification of its constructs; and further refinement of this model.

SKILL-BUILDING ACTIVITY

Let us see how we can apply the transtheoretical model to the issue of smoking cessation. Let us assume that most of the group of smokers are in the precontemplation stage of change. The TTM is an extensive model and is difficult to fully operationalize. Thus, we will choose a few constructs that would be important to move the participants from precontemplation to action: decisional balance, consciousness raising, dramatic relief, self-liberation, and self-efficacy. The scheme is depicted diagrammatically in Figure 4.1.

To modify the construct of decisional balance, the educational process of discussion can be used. In the discussion, the pros of being abstinent from smoking must be

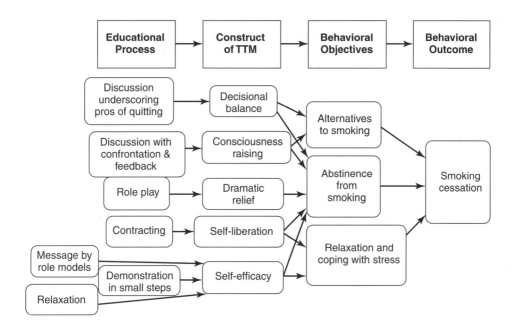

FIGURE 4.1   How the transtheoretical model can be used for smoking cessation

underscored. The pros of alternatives to smoking can also be highlighted. The cons or costs of quitting must be reduced through the discussion. To modify the construct of consciousness raising for quitting smoking and exploring alternatives to smoking, the method of discussion can be used. In the discussion the specific techniques of confrontation about the unhealthy behavior and feedback regarding healthy behaviors need to be used. The construct of dramatic relief can be modified through a role play in which a smoker goes through various kinds of problems because of the habit of smoking. The construct of self-liberation can be modified through use of the method of contracting, in which each participant creates a contract about quitting smoking and agrees to adhere to it. Finally, to modify the construct of self-efficacy, small steps to use for quitting smoking could be outlined and relaxation as an alternative for coping with stress could be demonstrated. Role models can be used to emphasize the message.

Using this approach, you can apply the TTM to a health behavior issue of your choice for any given target population. Table 4.6 provides a set of questions to assist you in choosing an educational method that corresponds to various constructs of the TTM.

TABLE 4.6   Choosing the Educational Method for Planning a Health Education Program Using the Transtheoretical Model

1. What will be the best approach to determine the stage of change?
   - Self-report survey
   - Group discussion
   - Individual interview
   - Other

2. What will be the best educational method to facilitate decisional balance?
   - Lecture
   - Discussion
   - Brainstorming
   - Role play
   - Simulation
   - Other

3. What will be the best educational method to facilitate self-efficacy?
   - Demonstration
   - Role play
   - Video with a credible role model
   - Stress reduction techniques
     - Progressive muscle relaxation
     - Visual imagery
     - Autogenic training
     - Yoga
     - Other
   - Other

4. What will be the best educational method to facilitate overcoming temptations?
   - Demonstration
   - Role play
   - Psychodrama
   - Stress reduction techniques
     - Progressive muscle relaxation
     - Visual imagery
     - Autogenic training
     - Yoga
     - Other
   - Other

TABLE 4.6 *(Continued)*

5. What will be the best educational method to facilitate consciousness raising?
   - Discussion with confrontation
   - Discussion with feedback
   - Discussion with interpretations
   - Lecture
   - Other

6. What will be the best educational method to facilitate dramatic relief?
   - Psychodrama
   - Role play
   - Opportunity to grieve
   - Personal testimonies
   - Other

7. What will be the best educational method to facilitate self-reevaluation?
   - Discussion about values
   - Use of healthy role models
   - Imagery
   - Other

8. What will be the best educational method to facilitate environmental reevaluation?
   - Discussion with empathy
   - Screening of documentaries
   - Lecture
   - Other

9. What will be the best educational method to facilitate self-liberation?
   - Contracting
   - Making resolutions
   - Giving public testimony
   - Brainstorming
   - Other

10. What will be the best educational method to facilitate helping relationships?
    - Alliance with health educator
    - Buddy system
    - Self-help group
    - Other

(Continued)

TABLE 4.6   *(Continued)*

11. What will be the best educational method to facilitate counterconditioning?
    - Stress reduction techniques
        - Progressive muscle relaxation
        - Visual imagery
        - Autogenic training
        - Yoga
        - Other
    - Assertion
    - Positive self-statements
    - Other

12. What will be the best educational method to facilitate reinforcement management?
    - Contracting
    - Discussion
    - Group recognition
    - Other

13. What will be the best health promotion method to facilitate stimulus control?
    - Environmental engineering
    - Avoidance of stimuli
    - Self-help groups
    - Other

14. What will be the best health promotion method to facilitate social liberation?
    - Advocacy
    - Empowerment training
    - Changing policies
    - Other

SUMMARY

The transtheoretical model (TTM) or stages of change (SOC) model, which originated from the field of psychotherapy, is at present the most popular model in research and practice related to health education. The TTM is a model of behavior change that posits that people move through five stages of change, from precontemplation (not thinking about change) to contemplation (thinking about change over the next six months) to preparation (thinking about change in the next month) to action (having made meaningful change but not completed six months) and finally to maintenance (acquisition of the healthy behavior for six or more months).

The TTM identifies ten processes of change and the constructs of decisional balance, self-efficacy, and overcoming temptations, which aid the behavior change. Decisional balance is the construct of TTM that addresses the relative importance placed by an individual on the advantages (pros) of behavior change as opposed to the disadvantages (cons). Self-efficacy is the confidence that a person has in his or her ability to pursue a given behavior. Temptation refers to the urge to engage in unhealthy behavior when confronted with a difficult situation.

The processes of change are categorized as either experiential or behavioral in nature. Experiential processes include consciousness raising, dramatic relief, environmental reevaluation, social liberation, and self-reevaluation. Behavioral processes include stimulus control, counterconditioning, helping relationships, reinforcement management, and self-liberation. The TTM has been widely used in behavioral research, primary prevention, and secondary prevention. Some critics have raised objections to the robustness of TTM, but it continues to be a popular model.

REVIEW QUESTIONS

1. Describe the historical genesis of the transtheoretical model.
2. Discuss the five stages of behavior change in the TTM.
3. List and define the ten key processes of change in the TTM.
4. How can stimulus control be modified?
5. Differentiate between self-liberation and social liberation.
6. Describe the five phases for planning interventions based on the TTM.
7. Discuss the limitations of the TTM.
8. Apply TTM for promoting leisure time physical activity in a group of African American women.

WEBSITE

Go to the Web component of *Theoretical Foundations of Health Education and Health Promotion* at http://health.jbpub.com/foundations for Web exercises, additional resources related to this chapter, and student review tools.

GLOSSARY TERMS

action stage

consciousness raising

contemplation stage

contingency management

counterconditioning

decisional balance

dramatic relief

environmental reevaluation

helping relationships

levels of change

maintenance stage

precontemplation stage

preparation stage

reinforcement management

self-efficacy

self-liberation

self-reevaluation

social liberation

stages of change

stimulus control

temptation

termination

transtheoretical model (TTM)

REFERENCES AND FURTHER READING

Adler, A. (1929). *Problems of neurosis*. London: Kegan Paul.

Arora, N. K., Ayanian, J. Z., & Guadagnoli, E. (2005). Examining the relationship of patients' attitudes and beliefs with their self-reported level of participation in medical decision-making. *Medical Care, 43*(9), 865–872.

Aveyard, P., Lawrence, T., Cheng, K. K., Griffin, C., Croghan, E., & Johnson, C. (2006). A randomized controlled trial of smoking cessation for pregnant women to test the effect of a transtheoretical model-based intervention on movement in stage and interaction with baseline stage. *British Journal of Health Psychology, 11*(Pt. 2), 263–278.

Babcock, J. C., Canady, B. E., Senior, A., & Eckhardt, C. I. (2005). Applying the transtheoretical model to female and male perpetrators of intimate partner violence: Gender differences in stages and processes of change. *Violence and Victims, 20*(2), 235–250.

Bandura, A. (1986). *The social foundations of thought and action: A social cognitive theory*. New Jersey: Prentice Hall.

Bandura, A. (1997). *Self-efficacy: The exercise of control*. New York: W. H. Freeman.

Basler, H. D., Bertalanffy, H., Quint, S., Wilke, A., & Wolf, U. (2007). TTM-based counselling in physiotherapy does not contribute to an increase of adherence to activity recommendations in older adults with chronic low back pain—a randomised controlled trial. *European Journal of Pain, 11*(1), 31–37.

Beckie, T. M. (2006). A behavior change intervention for women in cardiac rehabilitation. *Journal of Cardiovascular Nursing 21*(2), 146–153.

Berger, B. A., Liang, H., & Hudmon, K. S. (2005). Evaluation of software-based telephone counseling to enhance medication persistency among patients with multiple sclerosis. *Journal of the American Pharmacists Association, 45*(4), 466–472.

Berne, E. (1966). *Principles of group treatment*. New York: Oxford University Press.

Binswanger, L. (1958). The existential analysis school of thought. In R. May, E. Angel, & H. Ellenberger (Eds.), *Existence*. New York: Basic Books.

Chacko, M. R., Wiemann, C. M., Kozinetz, C. A., Diclemente, R. J., Smith, P. B., Velasquez, M. M., et al. (2006). New sexual partners and readiness to seek screening for chlamydia and gonorrhoea: Predictors among minority young women. *Sexually Transmitted Infections, 82*(1), 75–79.

Davidson, R. (1992). Prochaska and DiClemente's model of change: A case study? *British Journal of Addiction, 87*, 821–822.

DiClemente, C. C., & Prochaska, J. O. (1998). Toward a comprehensive, transtheoretical model of change. Stages of change and addictive behaviors. In W. R. Miller & N. Heather (Eds.), *Treating addictive behaviors* (2nd ed., pp. 3–24). New York: Plenum Press.

Ellis, A. (1973). *Humanistic psychotherapy: The rational emotive approach*. New York: McGraw Hill.

Etter, J. (2005). Theoretical tools for the industrial era in smoking cessation counseling: A comment on West (2005). *Addiction, 100*, 1041–1042.

Fahrenwald, N. L., & Shangreaux, P. (2006). Physical activity behavior of American Indian mothers. *Orthopaedic Nursing, 25*(1), 22–29.

Freud, S. (1959). The question of lay analysis. In J. Strachey (Ed.), *The standard edition of the complete psychological works of Sigmund Freud*. London: Hogarth Press.

Freud, S. (1960). *The ego and the id*. New York: Norton. (Original work published 1923.)

Freyer, J., Bott, K., Riedel, J., Wedler, B., Meyer, C., Rumpf, H. J., et al. (2006). Psychometric properties of the "Processes of Change" scale for alcohol misuse and its short form (POC-20). *Addictive Behaviors, 31*, 821–832.

Gazabon, S. A., Morokoff, P. J., Harlow, L. L., Ward, R. M., & Quina, K. (2006). Applying the transtheoretical model to ethnically diverse women at risk for HIV. *Health Education and Behavior*, Epub PMID: 16740521.

Ha, B. T., Jayasuriya, R., & Owen, N. (2005). Predictors of men's acceptance of modern contraceptive practice: Study in rural Vietnam. *Health Education and Behavior, 32*(6), 738–750.

Hacker, K., Brown, E., Cabral, H., & Dodds, D. (2005). Applying a transtheoretical behavioral change model to HIV/STD and pregnancy prevention in adolescent clinics. *Journal of Adolescent Health, 37*(3 Suppl.), S80–S93.

Henry, H., Reimer, K., Smith, C., & Reicks, M. (2006). Associations of decisional balance, processes of change, and self-efficacy with stages of change for increased fruit and vegetable intake among low-income, African-American mothers. *Journal of American Dietetic Association, 106*(6), 841–849.

Herzog, T. A. (2005). When popularity outstrips the evidence: Comments on West (2005). *Addiction, 100*, 1040–1041.

Highstein, G. R., Willey, C., & Mundy, L. M. (2006). Development of stage of readiness and decisional balance instruments: Tools to enhance clinical decision-making for adherence to antiretroviral therapy. *AIDS and Behavior, 10*(5), 563–573.

Honda, K., & Gorin, S. S. (2006). A model of stage of change to recommend colonoscopy among urban primary care physicians. *Health Psychology, 25*(1), 65–73.

Hur, H. K., Kim, G. Y., & Park, S. M. (2005). Predictors of mammography participation among rural Korean women age 40 and over. *Taehan Kanho Hakhoe Chi, 35*, 1443–1450.

Janis, I. L., & Mann, L. (1977). *Decision making: A psychological analysis of conflict, choice, and commitment*. New York: Free Press.

Johnson, J. L., Evers, K. E., Paiva, A. L., Van Marter, D. F., Prochaska, J. O., Prochaska, J. M., et al. (2006). Prevention profiles: Understanding youth who do not use substances. *Addictive Behaviors, 31*(9),1593–1606.

Johnson, S. S., Driskell, M. M., Johnson, J. L., Dyment, S. J., Prochaska, J. O., Prochaska, J. M., et al. (2006). Transtheoretical model intervention for adherence to lipid-lowering drugs. *Disease Management, 9*(2), 102–114.

Kobetz, E., Vatalaro, K., Moore, A., & Earp, J. A. (2005). Taking the transtheoretical model into the field: A curriculum for lay health advisors. *Health Promotion Practice, 6*(3), 329–337.

Kosma, M., Cardinal, B. J., & McCubbin, J. A. (2005). A pilot study of a Web-based physical activity motivational program for adults with physical disabilities. *Disability and Rehabilitation, 27*, 1435–1442.

Kotani, K., Saiga, K., Sakane, N., & Kurozawa, Y. (2005). The effects of interval length between sessions in a hypercholesterolemia education class. *Acta Medica Okayama, 59*(6), 271–277.

Kristjansson, S., Ullen, H., & Helgason, A. R. (2004). The importance of assessing the readiness to change sun-protection behaviours: A population-based study. *European Journal of Cancer, 40*, 2773–2780.

Littell, J. H., & Girvin, H. (2002). Stages of change. A critique. *Behavior Modification, 26*, 223–273.

Logue, E., Sutton, K., Jarjoura, D., Smucker, W., Baughman, K., & Capers, C. (2005). Transtheoretical model-chronic disease care for obesity in primary care: A randomized trial. *Obesity Research, 13*, 917–927.

McConnaughy, E. A., DiClemente, C. C., Prochaska, J. O., & Velicer, W. F. (1989). Stages of change in psychotherapy: A follow-up report. *Psychotherapy, 4*, 494–503.

Migneault, J. P., Adams, T. B., & Read, J. P. (2005). Application of the transtheoretical model to substance abuse: Historical development and future directions. *Drug and Alcohol Review, 24*, 437–448.

Migneault, J. P., Velicer, W. F., Prochaska, J. O., & Stevenson, J. F. (1999). Decisional balance for immoderate drinking in college students. *Substance Use and Misuse, 34*, 1325–1346.

Miller, W. R., & Tonigan, J. S. (1996). Assessing drinkers' motivations for change: The Stages of Readiness and Treatment Eagerness Scale (SOCRATES). *Psychology of Addictive Behaviors, 10*, 81–89.

Monson, A. L., & Engeswick, L. M. (2005). Promotion of tobacco cessation through dental hygiene education: A pilot study. *Journal of Dental Education, 69*, 901–911.

Olsen, P. (1976). *Emotional flooding*. New York: Human Sciences Press.

Perls, F. (1969). *Gestalt therapy verbatim*. Lafayette, CA: Real People Press.

Politi, M. C., Rabin, C., & Pinto, B. (2006). Biologically based complementary and alternative medicine use among breast cancer survivors: Relationship to dietary fat consumption and exercise. *Support Care Cancer, 14*(10), 1064–1069.

Popa, M. A. (2005). Stages of change for osteoporosis preventive behaviors: A construct validation study. *Journal of Aging and Health, 17*, 336–350.

Prochaska, J. O. (1979). *Systems of psychotherapy: A transtheoretical analysis*. Homewood, IL: Dorsey Press.

Prochaska, J. O. (1995). An eclectic and integrative approach: Transtheoretical therapy. In A. S. Gurman & S. B. Messer (Eds.), *Essential psychotherapies: Theory and practice* (pp. 403–440). New York: The Guilford Press.

Prochaska, J. O. (1999). How do people change, and how can we change to help many more people? In M. A. Hubble, B. L. Duncan, & S.D. Miller (Eds.), *The heart and soul of change: What works in therapy* (pp. 227–255). Washington, DC: American Psychological Association.

Prochaska, J. O. (2000). Change at differing stages. In C. R. Snyder & R. E. Ingram (Eds.), *Handbook of psychological change: Psychotherapy processes and practices for the 21st century* (pp. 109–127). New York: John Wiley and Sons.

Prochaska, J. O. (2006). Moving beyond the transtheoretical model. *Addiction, 101,* 768–774.

Prochaska, J. O., & DiClemente, C. C. (1983). Stages and processes of self change in smoking: Toward an integrative model of change. *Journal of Consulting and Clinical Psychology, 5,* 390–395.

Prochaska, J. O., DiClemente, C. C., & Norcross, J. C. (1992). In search of how people change: Applications to addictive behaviors. *The American Psychologist, 47,* 1102–1114.

Prochaska, J. O., Redding, C. A., & Evers, K.E. (2002). The transtheoretical model and stages of change. In K. Glanz, B. K. Rimer, & F. M. Lewis (Eds.), *Health behavior and health education:. Theory, research, and practice* (3rd ed., pp. 99–120). San Francisco: Jossey Bass.

Raymond, D. M., 3rd, & Lusk, S. L. (2006). Staging workers' use of hearing protection devices: Application of the transtheoretical model. *AAOHN Journal, 54*(4),165–172.

Rhodes, R. E., & Plotnikoff, R. C. (2006). Understanding action control: Predicting physical activity intention-behavior profiles across 6 months in a Canadian sample. *Health Psychology, 25*(3), 292–299.

Rogers, C. (1951). *Client centered therapy.* Boston: Houghton Mifflin.

Rogers, C. R. (1961). *On becoming a person.* Boston: Houghton Mifflin.

Rollnick, S., Heather N., Gold, R., & Hall, W. (1992). Development of a short readiness to change questionnaire for use in brief opportunistic interventions among excessive drinkers. *British Journal of Addiction, 87,* 743–754.

Schumann, A., John, U., Rumpf, H. J., Hapke, U., & Meyer, C. (2006). Changes in the "stages of change" as outcome measures of a smoking cessation intervention: A randomized controlled trial. *Preventive Medicine, 43*(2), 101–106.

Skinner, B. F. (1953). *Science and human behavior.* New York: The Macmillan Company.

Stepnowsky, C. J., Marler, M. R., Palau, J., & Annette Brooks, J. (2006). Social-cognitive correlates of CPAP adherence in experienced users. *Sleep Medicine, 7*(4), 350–356.

Sutton, S. (1996). Can stages of change provide guidance in the treatment of addictions? A critical examination of Prochaska and DiClemente's model. In G. Edwards & C. Dare (Eds.), *Psychotherapy, psychological treatments and the addictions* (pp. 189–205). Cambridge, UK: Cambridge University Press.

Takeuchi, M. T., Edlefsen, M., McCurdy, S. M., & Hillers, V. N. (2006). Development and validation of stages-of-change questions to assess consumers' readiness to use a food thermometer when cooking small cuts of meat. *Journal of American Dietetic Association, 106*(2), 262–266.

Taylor, C. L., Demoor, C., Smith, M. A., Dunn, A. L., Basen-Engquist, K., Nielsen, I., et al. (2006). Active for life after cancer: A randomized trial examining a lifestyle physical activity program for prostate cancer patients. *Psycho-oncology, 15*(10), 847–862.

Weiss, J., Okun, M., & Quay, N. (2004). Predicting bicycle helmet stage-of-change among middle school, high school, and college cyclists from demographic, cognitive, and motivational variables. *Journal of Pediatrics, 145,* 360–364.

West, R. (2005). Time for a change: Putting the transtheoretical (stages of change) model to rest [Editorial]. *Addiction, 100,* 1036–1039.

West, R. (2006). The transtheoretical model of behavior change and the scientific method. *Addiction, 101,* 774–778.

Whitelaw, S., Baldwin, S., Bunton, R., & Flynn, D. (2000). The status of evidence and outcomes in stages of change research. *Health Education Research, 15,* 707–718.

Wolpe, J. (1973). *The practice of behavior therapy* (2nd ed.). New York: Pergamon Press.

Zhang, A. Y., Harmon, J. A., Werkner, J., & McCormick, R. A. (2006). The long-term relationships between the motivation for change and alcohol use severity among patients with severe and persistent mental illness. *Journal of Addictive Diseases, 25*(1), 121–128.

Zimmerman, R. K., Tabbarah, M., Trauth, J., Nowalk, M. P., & Ricci, E. M. (2006). Predictors of lower endoscopy use among patients at three inner-city neighborhood health centers. *Journal of Urban Health, 83*(2), 221–230.

CHAPTER 5

The Theory of Reasoned Action and Theory of Planned Behavior

KEY CONCEPTS _____

- Attitude toward the behavior
- Behavior
- Behavioral beliefs
- Behavioral intention
- Control beliefs
- Motivation to comply
- Normative beliefs

- Outcome evaluations
- Perceived behavioral control
- Perceived power
- Subjective norm
- Theory of planned behavior
- Theory of reasoned action

AFTER READING THIS CHAPTER YOU SHOULD BE ABLE TO _____

- Describe the historical genesis of the theory of reasoned action (TRA) and the theory of planned behavior (TPB)
- List the constructs of the TRA and TPB
- Summarize the applications of the TRA and TPB in health education and health promotion
- Identify educational methods and match these to modify each construct from the TRA and TPB
- Apply the TRA and TPB in changing a health behavior of your choice

This chapter discusses the **theory of reasoned action (TRA)** and its newer, more evolved version, the **theory of planned behavior (TPB)**. The salient feature of both these theories is that they claim that behavioral intention is the most important determinant of behavior. Both these theories contend that people consider the implications of their actions before deciding to engage or disengage in any given behavior. These theories differ from Freudian theory and other theories that view behavior as being controlled by unconscious motives or desires. Instead, they emphasize the role of thoughts in decision making about engaging in behaviors. The TRA states that a person's intention is determined by two antecedents, one comprising personal factors and the other social influence. However, TRA does not purport that the beliefs and attitudes are necessarily reasonable or correct. That is why it is not called the theory of *reasonable* action. The TPB adds a third predictor, that of control over the behavior. Another important feature of the TRA and TPB is that these two theories provide strong guidance with regard to measurement of their constructs, which is invaluable for both practitioners and researchers.

This chapter begins by describing the historical aspects of the genesis of these theories. Next it describes the various constructs that make up these theories. It then discusses the applications of the TRA and TPB in health education and health promotion. Finally, it discusses the limitations of the TRA and TPB and presents a skill-building application.

> *Theory of Reasoned Action is designed to explain virtually any human behavior, whether we want to understand why a person bought a new car, voted against a school bond issue, was absent from work, or engaged in premarital sexual intercourse.*
>
> —Ajzen & Fishbein
> (1980, p. 4)

HISTORICAL PERSPECTIVES

In the mid- to late-1960s, Martin Fishbein (1965, 1967), a social psychologist at the University of Illinois at Urbana, originated the idea of the relationship between beliefs and attitudes. He defined attitudes as learned predispositions to respond to an object or class of objects in a favorable or unfavorable way. He defined beliefs as hypotheses concerning the nature of objects. He differentiated between beliefs and attitudes and also talked about the distinction between "belief in" an object and "belief about" an object. "Belief in" an object refers to the existence of an object, whereas "belief about" an object deals with the nature of that object. He also differentiated between attitudes toward objects and attitudes toward behaviors. For example, a health educator working with women seeking a Pap test may look at attitudes regarding cervical cancer (object) or at attitudes regarding getting a Pap test (behavior). Emphasis on the latter aspect, attitude toward behavior, served as the origin of the present-day TRA.

In the 1970s Fishbein teamed up with Icek Ajzen of the University of Massachusetts at Amherst to write the book *Belief, Attitude, Intention and Behavior: An Introduction to Theory and Research* (Fishbein & Ajzen, 1975), which formed the basis of the TRA. The theory linked beliefs to attitudes, which in turn were linked to intentions, which led to behaviors. In coming up with this theory, they reviewed several then-existing theories, such as learning theories (Hull, 1943; Spence, 1956), value expectancy theories (Atkinson, 1957; Tolman, 1955; Rotter, 1954), consistency theories such as the balance theory (Heider, 1946), the congruity principle (Osgood & Tannenbaum, 1955), Festinger's theory of cognitive dissonance (1957), and attribution theories (Bem, 1965; Kelley, 1971). Learning theories are those theories that describe when a given response is associated with a given stimulus. Value expectancy theories are those that postulate that a behavior depends upon the value placed by an individual on an outcome (value) and the individual's estimate of the likelihood that a given action will result in that outcome (expectancy). Consistency theories deal with the effects of inconsistencies among beliefs, attitudes, intentions, and behaviors. Attribution theories purport to explain how people make causal explanations and how they answer questions beginning with "why."

In 1980, the team of Icek Ajzen and Martin Fishbein published a second book, *Understanding Attitudes and Predicting Social Behavior*, that simplified the TRA and made it more practical for use in a variety of fields. Throughout the early 1980s, the theory was popular among researchers and practitioners. Sheppard, Hartwick, and Warshaw (1988) performed a meta-analysis on the TRA and found that the theory had strong predictive utility. Still, some researchers, including Professor Ajzen, felt that the theory was deficient in explaining behavior, especially of people who have little power or feel they have little power over their behaviors. As a result, he added a construct to the TRA: perceived behavioral control (Ajzen, 1991). His new thinking was based on Rotter's (1966) locus of control theory, Atkinson's (1964) theory of achievement motivation, and Bandura's (1986) social cognitive theory. The addition of this construct resulted in the theory of planned behavior.

> *The centrality of the attitude concept remains unchallenged and, if anything, its importance has increased.*
>
> —Fishbein and Ajzen (1975, p. v)

In 2004, Francis and colleagues developed a manual for health service researchers to construct questionnaires based on the TPB (Francis et al., 2004). At present both theories seem to be among the popular theories in health education and health promotion. Researchers and practitioners continue to use both theories in several applications.

CONSTRUCTS OF THE THEORY OF REASONED ACTION AND THEORY OF PLANNED BEHAVIOR

Figure 5.1 represents the TRA and TPB diagrammatically. The first construct in the TRA and TPB is **behavior**. Usually this is a single action performed by an individual that is observable. In health education and health promotion we are interested in many such behaviors, such as condom use, eating five servings of vegetables and

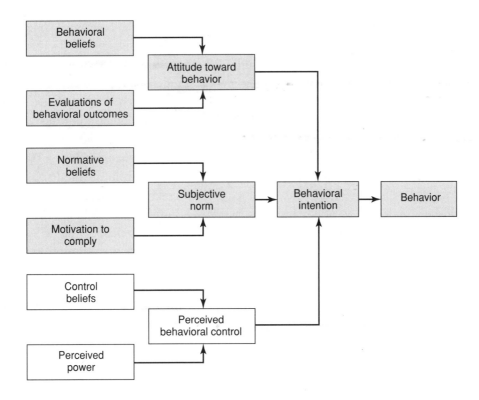

FIGURE 5.1   The theory of reasoned action and theory of planned behavior

Note. The upper shaded section shows the theory of reasoned action; the entire figure shows the theory of planned behavior. From Montano, D. E., & Kasprzyk, D. (2002). The theory of reasoned action and the theory of planned behavior. In K. Glanz, B. Rimer, & F. M. Lewis (Eds.), *Health behavior and health education: Theory, research and practice* (3rd ed., p. 68). San Francisco: Jossey Bass.

fruits, and so on. Ajzen and Fishbein (1980) also talk about behavioral categories that involve sets of actions rather than a single action, which are not easily observable. In health education and health promotion we are interested in many such behaviors, such as being physically active every day, healthy eating, and so on. The behavior should be defined in terms of its target, action, context, and time (TACT). For example, let us consider the behavior of helping sedentary African American women practice 30 minutes of aerobic dancing at a local church. Here the target is the African American women, the action is aerobic dancing, the context is the sedentary nature of the women, and the time is 30 minutes. In TRA and TPB, defining and measuring the behavior accurately is very important. Often the behavior is measured by self-reports.

The second construct in the TRA and TPB is **behavioral intention**. This is the thought to perform the behavior, which is an immediate determinant of the given behavior. This construct is the hallmark of this model, which was the first to posit that intention is a proximal measure of behavior. The intention also has the components of target, action, context, and time (TACT). It is usually measured on a 7-point bipolar scale that includes the categories of extremely probable (+3), quite probable (+2), slightly probable (+1), neither probable nor improbable (0), slightly improbable (−1), quite improbable (−2), and extremely improbable (−3). There should be a high degree of correspondence between intention and behavior. Intentions change over time, so the intention must be measured as close to the occurrence of the behavior as possible. The advantage of measuring behavioral intention is that if actual behavior cannot be easily measured in an intervention, then the behavioral intention serves as a useful indicator.

The third construct in the TRA and TPB is **attitude toward the behavior**, which refers to the overall feeling of like or dislike toward any given behavior. The more favorable a person's attitude is toward a behavior, the more likely it is that he or she will intend to perform the behavior; conversely, the more unfavorable a person's attitude is toward the behavior, the more likely it is that he or she will intend not to perform the behavior. Attitude is usually measured on a 7-point semantic differential scale ranging from favorable to unfavorable or from good to bad. The attitude toward a behavior is shaped by the fourth and fifth constructs of the TRA and TPB, namely, behavioral beliefs and outcome evaluations.

The fourth construct of the TRA and TPB, which is a determinant of attitude toward behavior, is **behavioral beliefs**. Behavioral beliefs are beliefs that performing a given behavior will lead to certain outcomes. The fifth construct of the TRA and TPB is **outcome evaluations**, or the value a person places on each outcome resulting from performance of the behavior. Together the behavioral beliefs and outcome evaluations determine the attitude toward behavior. Behavioral beliefs are usually measured on a 7-point bipolar scale such as extremely likely (+3), quite likely (+2), slightly likely (+1), neither likely nor unlikely (0), slightly unlikely (−1), quite unlikely (−2), and extremely unlikely (−3). Outcome evaluations are usually measured on a 7-point bipolar scale such as extremely good (+3), quite good (+2), slightly good (+1), neither good nor bad (0), slightly bad (−1), quite bad (−2), and extremely bad (−3).

A multiplicative score between the behavioral beliefs and outcome evaluations is derived to assess attitudes toward a behavior. For example, let us look at the behavior of exercising. A person may think of exercising and say that it makes him or her sweaty and thus rates exercise as extremely unlikely (–3) to occur and as quite bad (–2). Such a person would have an attitude score of –5, or a negative attitude toward exercise. Another person might think of exercising and say it gives him or her a feeling of high energy, and thus rate it as quite likely (+2) to occur and as quite good (+2). Such a person would have an attitude score of +4, or a positive attitude toward exercise. To modify behavioral beliefs, a brainstorming of all possible outcomes can be conducted in an educational session. To modify outcome evaluations, a discussion on positive outcomes needs to be undertaken.

The sixth construct in TRA and TPB is **subjective norm**, which refers to one's belief that most of the significant others in one's life think one should or should not perform the behavior. For example, a person might think that if I exercise my spouse would be proud of me. This is the second predictor of behavioral intention. In forming a subjective norm, people consider the normative expectations of others in their environment. It is usually measured on a 7-point bipolar scale with a range of strongly agree (+3), moderately agree (+2), slightly agree (+1), neither agree nor disagree (0), slightly disagree (–1), moderately disagree (–2), and strongly disagree (–3). The subjective norm is shaped by two constructs, namely, normative beliefs and motivation to comply, which form the seventh and eighth constructs of the TRA and TPB.

The seventh construct of the TRA and TPB is **normative beliefs**, which refer to how a person thinks that other people who are significant in his or her life would like him or her to behave. For example, a person might think that his or her spouse, parents, and friends think exercise is good and approve of people who exercise. Normative beliefs are usually measured on a 7-point bipolar scale with a range of strongly agree (+3), moderately agree (+2), slightly agree (+1), neither agree nor disagree (0), slightly disagree (–1), moderately disagree (–2), and strongly disagree (–3). The normative beliefs in educational settings can be influenced by using a role play or psychodrama that makes a person cognizant of how others may think about him or her. They can also be altered by discussion or arranging a panel discussion that makes a person think more critically about the perception of significant others in his or her life.

The eighth construct of TRA and TPB is **motivation to comply**, which refers to the degree to which a person wants to act in accordance with the perceived wishes of those significant in his or her life. For example, a person might think that it matters a lot what his or her spouse, parents, and friends think about that person's plans for exercise. Motivation to comply is usually measured on a 7-point bipolar scale with a range of extremely likely (+3), moderately likely (+2), slightly likely (+1), neither likely nor unlikely (0), slightly unlikely (–1), moderately unlikely (–2), and extremely unlikely (–3). To influence motivation to comply, educational techniques such as role play, psychodrama, or discussion can be used, whereby people may become cognizant of their motivations to comply. With these eight constructs the TRA is complete. Table 5.1 summarizes these constructs and how to modify each one. In subsequent research, Icek Ajzen added constructs to create the TPB.

The ninth, additional, construct in TPB is **perceived behavioral control**, which refers to how much a person feels he or she is in command of enacting the given behavior. It is dependent on the constructs of control belief and perceived power (Montano & Kasprzyk, 2002). Perceived behavioral control is usually measured on a 7-point bipolar scale with a range of strongly agree (+3), moderately agree (+2), slightly agree (+1), neither agree nor disagree (0), slightly disagree (–1), moderately disagree (–2), and strongly disagree (–3).

The tenth construct in TPB is **control beliefs**, which are beliefs about internal and external factors that may inhibit or facilitate the performance of the behavior. For example, a person may believe that he or she can exercise at any time, whereas another person may believe that he or she can exercise only during the times when the gym is open. These are usually measured on 7-point scales with bipolar adjectives ranging from unlikely to likely. To modify control beliefs, one can use discussion about factors that facilitate behavior, provide incentives, and reduce inhibiting factors.

The eleventh, and final, construct in TPB is **perceived power**, which refers to a person's perception about how easy or difficult it is to perform the behavior in each condition identified in that person's control beliefs. For example, a control belief may be that a person is able to exercise only during the times when the gym is open. Perceived power would explore how easy or how difficult it would be for the person to exercise when the gym is open. It is usually measured on a 7-point scale with bipolar adjectives ranging from extremely difficult (–3), moderately difficult (+2), slightly difficult (+1), neither difficult nor easy (0), slightly easy (+1), and moderately easy (+2), to extremely easy (+3). To modify perceived power, educational methods such as having role models model the desired behavior, removing barriers, and breaking down the behavior into small steps could be used. Table 5.2 summarizes the additional constructs of the TPB and how to modify them.

TABLE 5.1 Key Constructs of the Theory of Reasoned Action		
Construct	**Definition**	**How to Modify?**
Behavior	Single, observable action performed by an individual, or a category of actions with a specification of target, action, context, and time (TACT)	By influencing behavioral intention, which is dependent on attitude toward the behavior and subjective norms
Behavioral intention	The thought to perform the behavior, which is an immediate determinant of the given behavior	By influencing attitude toward the behavior and subjective norms
Attitude toward the behavior	Overall feeling of like or dislike toward any given behavior	By influencing behavioral beliefs and outcome evaluations
Behavioral beliefs	Beliefs that performing a given behavior leads to certain outcomes	Brainstorming of all possible outcomes
Outcome evaluations	Value a person places on each outcome resulting from performance of the behavior	Discussion about positive outcomes
Subjective norm	One's belief that most of the significant others in one's life think one should or should not perform the behavior	By influencing normative beliefs and motivation to comply
Normative beliefs	How a person thinks that other people who are significant in his or her life would like him or her to behave	• Role play • Psychodrama • Panel discussion • Discussion
Motivation to comply	Degree to which a person wants to act in accordance with the perceived wishes of those significant in his or her life	• Role play • Psychodrama • Discussion

TABLE 5.2	Additional Constructs of the Theory of Planned Behavior	
Construct	Definition	How to Modify?
Perceived behavioral control	How much a person feels he or she is in command of enacting the given behavior	By influencing control beliefs and perceived power
Control beliefs	Beliefs about internal and external factors that may inhibit or facilitate the performance of the behavior	• Discussion about factors that facilitate behavior • Incentives • Reduction of inhibiting factors
Perceived power	Perception about how easy or difficult it is to perform the behavior in each condition identified in the control beliefs	• Having role models model the behavior • Removing barriers • Breaking down the behavior into small steps

APPLICATIONS OF THE THEORY OF REASONED ACTION AND THE THEORY OF PLANNED BEHAVIOR

It is possible to distinguish between beliefs, attitude, intentions, and behaviors, obtain valid and reliable measures for these, and to show that these are systematically related.

—Fishbein and Ajzen (1975)

Some examples in which the TRA has been used in health education and health promotion are for acceptance of the diagnosis of depression (Van Voorhees et al., 2005), attitudes about genetically modified foods (Silk, Weiner, & Parrott, 2005), colorectal cancer screening (Zimmerman, Tabbarah, Trauth, Nowalk, & Ricci, 2006), condom use behavior (Van-landingham, Suprasert, Grandjean, & Sittitrai, 1995), a developmental care training program for neonatal nurses (Milette, Richard, & Martel, 2005), exercise behavior (Downs, Graham, Yang, Bargainnier, & Vasil, 2006), an HIV prevention program in adolescent mothers (Koniak-Griffin & Stein, 2006), mammography behavior and intention (Ham, 2006), osteoporosis prevention (Tussing & Chapman-Novakofski, 2005), patient compliance during orthodontic treatment (Bos, Hoogstraten, & Prahl-Andersen, 2005), physician intention to prescribe emergency contraception (Sable, Schwartz, Kelly, Lisbon, & Hall, 2006), predicting mothers' infant feeding intentions (Manstead, Proffitt, & Smart, 1983), predicting pneumococcal vaccination (Zimmerman et al., 2005), predicting problem gambling (Moore & Ohtsuka, 1997), promoting milk with 1% or less fat (Booth-Butterfield & Reger, 2004), prostate cancer genetic screening (Doukas, Localio, & Li, 2004), school-based intervention for HIV/AIDS prevention (Kinsler, Sneed, Morisky, & Ang, 2004), substance abuse behavior in pregnant adolescents (Morrison, Spencer, & Gillmore, 1998), sunscreen use behavior (Abroms, Jorgensen, Southwell, Geller, & Emmons, 2003), teaching testicular self-examination by nurse practitioners (Kleier, 2004), and violence prevention (Meyer, Roberto, Boster, & Roberto, 2004). Table 5.3 summarizes these applications.

TABLE 5.3 Examples of Applications of the Theory of Reasoned Action in Health Education and Health Promotion
Acceptance of a diagnosis of depression
Attitudes about genetically modified foods
Colorectal cancer screening
Condom use behavior
Developmental care training program for neonatal nurses
Exercise behavior
HIV prevention program in adolescent mothers
Mammography behavior and intention
Osteoporosis prevention
Patient compliance during orthodontic treatment
Physician intention to prescribe emergency contraception
Predicting mothers' infant feeding intentions
Predicting pneumococcal vaccination
Predicting problem gambling
Promoting milk with 1% or less fat
Prostate cancer genetic screening
School-based intervention for HIV/AIDS prevention
Substance abuse behavior in pregnant adolescents
Sunscreen use behavior
Teaching testicular self-examination by nurse practitioners
Violence prevention

Some examples in which the TPB has been used in health education and health promotion are for condom use (Boer & Mashamba, 2005), controlling preschoolers' sugar snacking (Astrom & Kiwanuka, 2006), exercise behavior (Marsh, Papaioannou, & Theodorakis, 2006), hand washing in health care workers (Whitby, McLaws, & Ross, 2006), healthy eating behaviors (Fila & Smith, 2006), hoist usage for moving a dependent patient among health care workers (Rickett, Orbell, & Sheeran, 2006), hypoglycemic medication among type 2 diabetics (Farmer, Kinmonth, & Sutton, 2006), mammography (Tolma, Reininger, Evans, & Ureda, 2006), mental health problems among prison inmates (Skogstad, Deane, & Spicer, 2006), multivitamin use among women (Pawlak, Connell, Brown, Meyer, & Yadrick, 2005), predicting alcohol use (Quinlan, Jaccard, & Blanton, 2006), predicting binge drinking behavior (Norman & Conner, 2006), predicting fruit consumption (Brug, de Vet, de Nooijer, & Verplanken, 2006), predicting smoking among adolescents (van den Eijnden, Spijkerman, & Engels, 2006), school-based intervention to promote physical activity (Tsorbatzoudis, 2005), self-management of rheumatoid arthritis (Strating, van Schuur, & Suurmeijer, 2006), sexual and reproductive health in early adolescence (Aaro et al., 2006), small business owners' health and safety intentions (Brosseau & Li, 2005), smoking cessation (Bledsoe, 2005), use of assistive devices by home nurses (Roelands, Van Oost, Depoorter, Buysse, & Stevens, 2006), and vaccination against influenza (Gallagher & Povey, 2006). Table 5.4 summarizes these applications.

> *We have long been convinced that it is important to demonstrate the utility of a theory in applied settings as well as in laboratory settings. This has led us to investigate such diverse problems as voting behavior, family planning, consumer behavior, occupational choice, and weight reduction.*
>
> —Ajzen and Fishbein (1980, p. 97)

LIMITATIONS OF THE THEORY OF REASONED ACTION AND THEORY OF PLANNED BEHAVIOR

Both TRA and TPB are theories that predict behavioral intention and behavior but do not necessarily explain behavior change, which is the prime concern in health education and health promotion programs. Hence, they do not provide detailed and specific guidance for behavior modification. Another limitation of the TRA and TPB is that they do not consider personality-related factors, cultural factors, and demographic variables, which also shape behavior. Also, the theory of planned behavior assumes that perceived behavioral control predicts actual behavioral control, which may not always happen. Finally, these theories focus only on rational thoughts and do not account for irrational thoughts or fears, which are also covered by many health educators.

TABLE 5.4   Examples of Applications of the Theory of Planned Behavior in Health Education and Health Promotion

Condom use

Controlling preschoolers' sugar snacking

Exercise behavior

Hand washing in health care workers

Healthy eating behaviors

Hoist usage for moving a dependent patient among health care workers

Hypoglycemic medication among type 2 diabetics

Mammography

Mental health problems among prison inmates

Multivitamin use among women

Predicting alcohol use

Predicting binge drinking behavior

Predicting fruit consumption

Predicting smoking among adolescents

School-based intervention to promote physical activity

Self-management of rheumatoid arthritis

Sexual and reproductive health in early adolescence

Small business owners' health and safety intentions

Smoking cessation

Use of assistive devices by home nurses

Vaccination against influenza

Jane Ogden (2003) noted that the TRA and TPB are pragmatic theories, but criticized their conceptual bases and discussed several limitations of these theories. First, based on literature review, she observed that some studies of TPB reported no role for subjective norms, whereas others showed no predictive role for perceived behavioral control, and some showed no role for attitudes. She contended that these theories may not be predictive or account for low variance, but often investigators rationalize this by arguing that the variables were not adequately operationalized rather than questioning the predictive potential of these theories. Ogden questioned the testability of these theories. Ajzen and Fishbein (2004), in a rejoinder, clarified that the relative importance of attitudes, subjective norms, and perceptions of behavioral control for the prediction of intentions is expected to vary from behavior to behavior and population to population. They argued that of the three theoretical antecedents, sometimes only one or two may be necessary in any given situation.

Ogden (2003) also talked about two types of truth in the philosophy of science, namely, synthetic truth, which can be known through exploration and testing, and analytic truth, which is known by definition. She contended that the TRA and TPB focus on analytic truth, whereby the conclusions are not supported by observation. She also noted that behavior is mostly measured by self-reports rather than objective measures. In their rejoinder, Ajzen and Fishbein (2004) presented evidence from structural equation modeling that supported the path mentioned in the theories. They also defended self-reports by mentioning that it is virtually impossible to obtain objective measurement of some behaviors (such as condom use) and extremely expensive and time consuming for others (such as exercise).

Finally, Ogden (2003) noted that answering questions about an individual's cognition in the operationalization of these theories may change and create an individual's thinking rather than tap into how that person thought to begin with. Ajzen and Fishbein (2004) note that this concern is universal to all behavioral science research.

SKILL-BUILDING ACTIVITY

Let us see how we can apply the TPB to the behavior of condom use. (Application of the TRA would be a subset of the application of the TPB.) This application is depicted in Figure 5.2.

Let us first define the target, which can be college students; the action, which would be condom use; the context, which would be while having sex; and the time, which would be every time an individual had sex. According to the TPB, the behavioral intention would precede the behavior. There would be proximal predictive constructs of intention, which are attitude toward condom use, subjective norm, and perceived be-

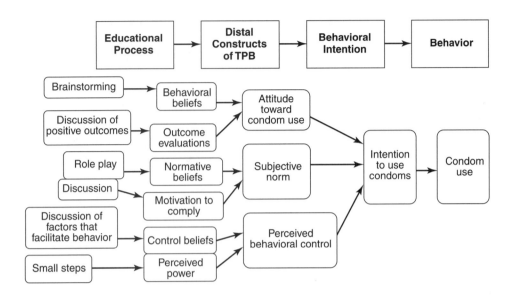

FIGURE 5.2   How the theory of planned behavior can be used for promoting condom use behavior

havioral control. To influence the construct of attitude toward condom use, the constructs of behavioral beliefs and outcome evaluations would need to be modified. To modify behavioral beliefs, a brainstorming session can be organized in which the participants can share their perceived outcomes about condom use. Instead of brainstorming, elicitation interviews with 15 to 20 members of the target audience can also be organized. To modify outcome evaluations, a discussion on the positive outcomes of condom use, such as prevention of diseases and prevention of pregnancy, can be organized that would help all participants develop their outlook about positive effects.

To modify subjective norms, we would need to modify normative beliefs and motivation to comply. Normative beliefs can be modified by use of a role play that depicts the most significant others in a family situation approving of the behavior of condom use. The participants would then perhaps be able to apply that observation to their own lives and make a deduction that significant others in their lives would also approve of the behavior. To modify motivation to comply, a discussion can be organized that would try to sway the participants' belief that parents, friends, teachers, and all other significant others consider using condoms important and that each person must use condoms.

To modify perceived behavioral control, the constructs of control beliefs and perceived power must be modified. To modify control beliefs, we can organize a

TABLE 5.5   Choosing the Educational Method for Health Education Program Planning Using the TRA and TPB

1. How will you define the behavior and behavioral intention?
   - Action: _____
   - Target: _____
   - Context: _____
   - Time: _____

2. What will be the best educational method to facilitate behavioral beliefs?
   - Brainstorming
   - Discussion
   - Elicitation interviews
   - Other

3. What will be the best educational method to facilitate outcome evaluations?
   - Discussion on positive outcomes
   - Lecture
   - Video with a credible role model
   - Other

4. What will be the best educational method to facilitate normative beliefs?
   - Discussion
   - Role play
   - Psychodrama
   - Panel discussion
   - Simulation
   - Other

5. What will be the best educational method to facilitate motivation to comply?
   - Discussion
   - Role play
   - Psychodrama
   - Simulation
   - Other

6. What will be the best educational method to facilitate control beliefs?
   - Discussion about factors that facilitate behavior
   - Incentives
   - Reduction of inhibiting factors
   - Other

7. What will be the best educational method to facilitate perceived power?
   - Demonstration of behavior in small steps
   - Having a role model model the behavior
   - Removing barriers
   - Other

discussion about factors that facilitate condom use behavior, such as keeping condoms readily accessible, having a prior discussion with one's partner, and so on. To modify perceived power, the condom use can be demonstrated in small steps, and role models can demonstrate the behavior of condom use. Using this approach, you can apply the TRA or TPB for any health behavior for a target group of your choice. Table 5.5 provides a set of questions to assist you in choosing an educational method that corresponds to different constructs.

SUMMARY

In the late 1960s and early 1970s, Martin Fishbein and Icek Ajzen propounded the theory of reasoned action (TRA). The theory claims that behavioral intention precedes behavior and is determined by attitude toward the behavior and subjective norm. Attitude toward the behavior is the individual's overall like or dislike of any given behavior and is determined by behavioral beliefs (beliefs that performing a given behavior lead to certain outcomes) and outcome evaluations (the value a person places on each outcome resulting from performance of a given behavior). Subjective norm is one's belief that most of the significant others in one's life think one should or should not perform the behavior and is determined by normative beliefs (a person's beliefs about how other people who are significant in his or her life would like him or her to behave) and motivation to comply (degree to which a person wants to act in accordance with the perceived wishes of those significant in his or her life).

In the late 1980s and early 1990s, Ajzen added the construct of perceived behavioral control (how much a person feels that he or she is in command of enacting the given behavior) and created the theory of planned behavior (TPB). The construct of perceived behavioral control is dependent on control beliefs (beliefs about internal and external factors that may inhibit or facilitate the performance of the behavior) and perceived power (perception about how easy or difficult it is to perform the behavior in each condition identified in the control beliefs).

Both the TRA and TPB have been used widely in health education and health promotion and continue to be applied. Lack of focus on behavior change, not considering all predictors, gap between perceived behavioral control and actual behavioral control, exclusive focus on rational thoughts, variations in predictive constructs, reliance on self-reports, and influences from measuring questionnaires are some identified limitations of the TRA and TPB.

REVIEW QUESTIONS

1. Discuss the historical genesis of the theory of reasoned action (TRA) and the theory of planned behavior (TPB).
2. List and define the constructs of the TRA.
3. List and define the constructs of the TPB.
4. Differentiate between subjective norms and normative beliefs.
5. Discuss the limitations of the TRA and TPB.
6. Apply TPB to the promotion of condom use in college students.

WEBSITE

Go to the Web component of *Theoretical Foundations of Health Education and Health Promotion* at http://health.jbpub.com/foundations for Web exercises, additional resources related to this chapter, and student review tools.

GLOSSARY TERMS

attitude toward the behavior
bchavior
behavioral beliefs
behavioral intention
control beliefs
motivation to comply
normative beliefs

outcome evaluations
perceived behavioral control
perceived power
subjective norm
theory of planned behavior (TPB)
theory of reasoned action (TRA)

REFERENCES AND FURTHER READING

Aaro, L. E., Flisher, A. J., Kaaya, S., Onya, H., Fuglesang, M., Klepp, K. I., et al. (2006). Promoting sexual and reproductive health in early adolescence in South Africa and Tanzania: Development of a theory- and evidence-based intervention programme. *Scandinavian Journal of Public Health*, *34*(2), 150–158.

Abroms, L., Jorgensen, C. M., Southwell, B. G., Geller, A. C., & Emmons, K. M. (2003). Gender differences in young adults' beliefs about sunscreen use. *Health Education and Behavior*, *30*(1), 29–43.

Ajzen, I. (1991). The theory of planned behavior. *Organizational Behavior and Human Decision Process*, *50*, 179–211.

Ajzen, I., & Fishbein, M. (1980). *Understanding attitudes and predicting social behavior*. Englewood Cliffs, NJ: Prentice Hall.

Ajzen, I., & Fishbein, M. (2004). Questions raised by a reasoned action approach: Comment on Ogden (2003). *Health Psychology*, *23*, 431–434.

Astrom, A. N., & Kiwanuka, S. N. (2006). Examining intention to control preschool children's sugar snacking: A study of carers in Uganda. *International Journal of Paediatric Dentistry*, *16*(1), 10–18.

Atkinson, J. W. (1957). Motivational determinants of risk taking behavior. *Psychological Review*, *64*, 359–372.

Atkinson, J. W. (1964). *An introduction to motivation*. Princeton, NJ: Van Nostrand.

Bandura, A. (1986). *Social foundations of thought and action: A social cognitive theory*. Englewood Cliffs, NJ: Prentice Hall.

Bem, D. J. (1965). An experimental analysis of self persuasion. *Journal of Experimental Social Psychology*, *1*, 199–218.

Bledsoe, L. K. (2005). Smoking cessation: An application of theory of planned behavior to understanding progress through stages of change. *Addictive Behaviors*, *31*(7), 1271–1276.

Boer, H., & Mashamba, M. T. (2005). Psychosocial correlates of HIV protection motivation among black adolescents in Venda, South Africa. *AIDS Education and Prevention*, *17*(6), 590–602.

Booth-Butterfield, S., & Reger, B. (2004). The message changes belief and the rest is theory: The "1% or less" milk campaign and reasoned action. *Preventive Medicine*, *39*(3), 581–588.

Bos, A., Hoogstraten, J., & Prahl-Andersen, B. (2005). The theory of reasoned action and patient compliance during orthodontic treatment. *Community Dentistry and Oral Epidemiology*, *33*(6), 419–426.

Brosseau, L. M., & Li, S. Y. (2005). Small business owners' health and safety intentions: A cross-sectional survey. *Environmental Health*, *4*, 23.

Brug, J., de Vet, E., de Nooijer, J., & Verplanken, B. (2006). Predicting fruit consumption: Cognitions, intention, and habits. *Journal of Nutrition Education and Behavior*, *38*(2), 73–81.

Doukas, D. J., Localio, A. R., & Li, Y. (2004). Attitudes and beliefs concerning prostate cancer genetic screening. *Clinical Genetics*, *66*(5), 445–451.

Downs, D. S., Graham, G. M., Yang, S., Bargainnier, S., & Vasil, J. (2006). Youth exercise intention and past exercise behavior: Examining the moderating influences of sex and meeting exercise recommendations. *Research Quarterly for Exercise and Sport*, *77*(1), 91–99.

Farmer, A., Kinmonth, A. L., & Sutton, S. (2006). Measuring beliefs about taking hypoglycaemic medication among people with type 2 diabetes. *Diabetic Medicine*, *23*(3), 265–270.

Festinger, L. (1957). *A theory of cognitive dissonance*. Evanston, IL: Row, Peterson.

Fila, S., & Smith, C. (2006). Applying the theory of planned behavior to healthy eating behaviors in urban Native American youth. *International Journal of Behavioral Nutrition and Physical Activity*, *3*(1), 11.

Fishbein, M. (1965). A consideration of beliefs, attitudes, and their relationship. In I. D. Steiner & M. Fishbein (Eds.), *Current studies in social psychology* (pp. 107–120). New York: Holt Rinehart and Winston.

Fishbein, M. (1967). Attitude and the prediction of behavior. In M. Fishbein (Ed.), *Readings in attitude theory and measurement* (pp. 477–492). New York: John Wiley.

Fishbein, M. (1980). A theory of reasoned action: Some applications and implications. *Nebraska Symposium on Motivation*, *27*, 65–116.

Fishbein, M., & Ajzen, I. (1975). *Belief, attitude, intention and behavior: An introduction to theory and research*. Reading, MA: Addison-Wesley.

Francis, J. J., Eccles, M. P., Johnston, M., Walker, A., Grimshaw, J., Foy, R., et al. (2004). *Constructing questionnaires based on the theory of planned behaviour*. Newcastle upon Tyne, UK: Centre for Health Services Research, University of Newcastle.

Gallagher, S., & Povey, R. (2006). Determinants of older adults' intentions to vaccinate against influenza: A theoretical application. *Journal of Public Health, 28*(2), 139–144.

Ham, O. K. (2006). Factors affecting mammography behavior and intention among Korean women. *Oncology Nursing Forum, 33*(1), 113–119.

Heider, F. (1946). Attitudes and cognitive organization. *Journal of Psychology, 21*, 107–112.

Hull, C. L. (1943). *The principles of behavior*. New York: Appleton-Century-Crofts.

Kelley, H. H. (1971). *Attribution in social interaction*. New York: General Learning Press.

Kinsler, J., Sneed, C. D., Morisky, D. E., & Ang, A. (2004). Evaluation of a school-based intervention for HIV/AIDS prevention among Belizean adolescents. *Health Education Research, 19*(6), 730–738.

Kleier, J. A. (2004). Nurse practitioners' behavior regarding teaching testicular self-examination. *Journal of the American Academy of Nurse Practitioners, 16*(5), 206–208, 210, 212.

Koniak-Griffin, D., & Stein, J. A. (2006). Predictors of sexual risk behaviors among adolescent mothers in a human immunodeficiency virus prevention program. *Journal of Adolescent Health, 38*(3), 297.e1–11.

Manstead, A. S., Proffitt, C., & Smart, J. L. (1983). Predicting and understanding mothers' infant-feeding intentions and behavior: Testing the theory of reasoned action. *Journal of Personality and Social Psychology, 44*(4), 657–671.

Marsh, H. W., Papaioannou, A., & Theodorakis, Y. (2006). Causal ordering of physical self concept and exercise behavior: Reciprocal effects model and the influence of physical education teachers. *Health Psychology, 25*(3), 316–328.

Meyer, G., Roberto, A. J., Boster, F. J., & Roberto, H. L. (2004). Assessing the Get Real About Violence curriculum: Process and outcome evaluation results and implications. *Health Communication, 16*(4), 451–474.

Milette, I. H., Richard, L., & Martel, M. J. (2005). Evaluation of a developmental care training programme for neonatal nurses. *Journal of Child Health Care, 9*(2), 94–109.

Montano, D. E., & Kasprzyk, D. (2002). The theory of reasoned action and the theory of planned behavior. In K. Glanz, B. Rimer, & F. M. Lewis (Eds.), *Health behavior and health education: Theory, research and practice* (3rd ed., pp. 67–98). San Francisco: Jossey Bass.

Moore, S. M., & Ohtsuka, K. (1997). Gambling activities of young Australians: Developing a model of behaviour. *Journal of Gambling Studies, 13*(3), 207–236.

Morrison, D. M., Spencer, M. S., & Gillmore, M. R. (1998). Beliefs about substance use among pregnant and parenting adolescents. *Journal of Research on Adolescence, 8*(1), 69–95.

Norman, P., & Conner, M. (2006). The theory of planned behaviour and binge drinking: Assessing the moderating role of past behaviour within the theory of planned behaviour. *British Journal of Health Psychology, 11*(Pt. 1), 55–70.

Ogden, J. (2003). Some problems with social cognition models: A pragmatic and conceptual analysis. *Health Psychology, 22*, 424–428.

Osgood, C. E., & Tannenbaum, P. H. (1955). The principle of congruity in the prediction of attitude change. *Psychological Review, 62*, 42–55.

Pawlak, R., Connell, C., Brown, D., Meyer, M. K., & Yadrick, K. (2005). Predictors of multivitamin supplement use among African-American female students: A prospective study utilizing the theory of planned behavior. *Ethnicity and Disease, 15*(4), 540–547.

Quinlan, S. L., Jaccard, J., & Blanton, H. (2006). A decision theoretic and prototype conceptualization of possible selves: Implications for the prediction of risk behavior. *Journal of Personality, 74*(2), 599–630.

Rickett, B., Orbell, S., & Sheeran, P. (2006). Social-cognitive determinants of hoist usage among health care workers. *Journal of Occupational Health Psychology, 11*(2), 182–196.

Roelands, M., Van Oost, P., Depoorter, A. M., Buysse, A., & Stevens, V. (2006). Introduction of assistive devices: Home nurses' practices and beliefs. *Journal of Advanced Nursing, 54*(2), 180–188.

Rotter, J. B. (1954). *Social learning and clinical psychology*. New York: Prentice Hall.

Rotter, J. B. (1966). Generalized expectancies for internal versus external control of reinforcement. *Psychological Monographs, 80* (1, No. 609).

Sable, M. R., Schwartz, L. R., Kelly, P. J., Lisbon, E., & Hall, M. A. (2006). Using the theory of reasoned action to explain physician intention to prescribe emergency contraception. *Perspectives on Sexual and Reproductive Health, 38*(1), 20–27.

Sheppard, B. H., Hartwick, J., & Warshaw, P. R. (1988). The theory of reasoned action: A meta-analysis of past research with recommendations for modifications and future research. *Journal of Consumer Research, 15,* 325–343.

Silk, K. J., Weiner, J., & Parrott, R. L. (2005). Gene cuisine or Frankenfood? The theory of reasoned action as an audience segmentation strategy for messages about genetically modified foods. *Journal of Health Communication, 10,* 751–767.

Skogstad, P., Deane, F. P., & Spicer, J. (2006). Social-cognitive determinants of help-seeking for mental health problems among prison inmates. *Criminal Behavior and Mental Health, 16*(1), 43–59.

Spence, K. W. (1956). *Behavior theory and conditioning*. New Haven, CT: Yale University Press.

Strating, M. M., van Schuur, W. H., & Suurmeijer, T. P. (2006). Contribution of partner support in self-management of rheumatoid arthritis patients. An application of the theory of planned behavior. *Journal of Behavioral Medicine, 29*(1), 51–60.

Tolma, E. L., Reininger, B. M., Evans, A., & Ureda, J. (2006). Examining the theory of planned behavior and the construct of self-efficacy to predict mammography intention. *Health Education and Behavior, 33*(2), 233–251.

Tolman, E. C. (1955). Principles of performance. *Psychological Review, 62,* 315–326.

Tsorbatzoudis, H. (2005). Evaluation of a school-based intervention programme to promote physical activity: An application of the theory of planned behavior. *Perceptual and Motor Skills, 101*(3), 787–802.

Tussing, L., & Chapman-Novakofski, K. (2005). Osteoporosis prevention education: Behavior theories and calcium intake. *Journal of American Dietetic Association, 105,* 92–97.

van den Eijnden, R. J., Spijkerman, R., & Engels, R. C. (2006). Relative contribution of smoker prototypes in predicting smoking among adolescents: A comparison with factors from the theory of planned behavior. *European Addiction Research, 12*(3), 113–120.

Vanlandingham, M. J., Suprasert, S., Grandjean, N., & Sittitrai, W. (1995). Two views of risky sexual practices among northern Thai males: The health belief model and the theory of reasoned action. *Journal of Health and Social Behavior, 36,* 195–212.

Van Voorhees, B. W., Fogel, J., Houston, T. K., Cooper, L. A., Wang, N. Y., & Ford, D. E. (2005). Beliefs and attitudes associated with the intention to not accept the diagnosis of depression among young adults. *Annals of Family Medicine, 3*(1), 38–46.

Whitby, M., McLaws, M. L., & Ross, M. W. (2006). Why healthcare workers don't wash their hands: A behavioral explanation. *Infection Control and Hospital Epidemiology, 27*(5), 484–492.

Zimmerman, R. K., Tabbarah, M., Nowalk, M. P., Raymund, M., Jewell, I. K., Block, B., et al. (2005). Predictors of pneumococcal polysaccharide vaccination among patients at three inner-city neighborhood health centers. *American Journal of Geriatric Pharmacotherapy, 3*(3), 149–159.

Zimmerman, R. K., Tabbarah, M., Trauth, J., Nowalk, M. P., & Ricci, E. M. (2006). Predictors of lower endoscopy use among patients at three inner-city neighborhood health centers. *Journal of Urban Health, 83*(2), 221–230.

CHAPTER 6

Theories of Stress and Coping

KEY CONCEPTS

- Challenge
- Chronic strains
- Chronic stressors
- Commitment
- Community-wide strains
- Comprehensibility
- Control
- Coping
- Daily hassles
- Emotion-focused coping
- Event-based model
- General adaptation syndrome
- Hardiness
- Life events or life change events
- Manageability
- Meaningfulness

- Nonevents
- Optimism
- Persistent life difficulties
- Problem-focused coping
- Recent life events
- Remote life events
- Response-based model
- Role strains
- Sense of coherence
- Social support
- Stress
- Stressors
- Transactional model
- Type A personality
- Type B personality

AFTER READING THIS CHAPTER YOU SHOULD BE ABLE TO

- Describe the historical genesis of theories of stress and coping
- List the constructs of the expanded transactional model, the theory of hardiness, and the theory of sense of coherence
- Summarize the applications of theories of stress and coping in health education and health promotion
- Identify educational methods and match these to modify each construct from theories of stress and coping
- Apply the theories of stress and coping in reducing stress

This chapter discusses theories of stress and coping. Stress is an integral part of any behavior change. One experiences some amount of stress with changing any given behavior. If this stress is very high, then new behavior cannot be acquired. Stress can be produced by a variety of external and internal events other than acquiring a new behavior. Often this stress is harmful and causes negative sequelae. Various theories, models, and constructs have been developed that explain the stress process. Some of these theories and models focus on the effects of stress, some on the causes of stress, others on personality characteristics, and some on coping responses. This chapter integrates the understanding of stress across these various models and theories. In health education and health promotion, we are interested in understanding the stress process as well as in finding ways to reduce negative stress, so the emphasis is on the modifiability of constructs that can be altered.

The chapter begins by describing the historical aspects of the genesis of these theories. Next it describes the various constructs that make up these theories and discusses the applications of theories of stress and coping in health education and health promotion. The chapter then discusses the limitations of the theories of stress and coping and presents a skill-building application.

> *It is not the stressor but your perception of the stress that is important.*
>
> —Romas and Sharma (2007, p. 1)

HISTORICAL PERSPECTIVES

The concept of **stress** in physiology and psychology was not known prior to 1932. Prior to that time this term was used mainly in physical sciences to denote cracks in the structure of buildings caused by pressure. Walter Cannon (1932), a physiologist, first defined stress as a "fight or flight" syndrome. He stated that when an organism is presented with a stressful stimulus, it responds by either fighting with it or running away from it. This was the origin of **response-based models** of stress.

The response-based concept was further elaborated by the work of Swedish physiologist Hans Selye (1936, 1974a, 1974b, 1982), who described the **general adaptation syndrome**. While trying to isolate a new sex hormone in rats, Selye observed that exposing rats to events such as cold, heat, injury, infection, loss of blood, pain, and other noxious stimuli resulted in their adrenal glands secreting corticoid hormones (a steroid) and their bodies going through three stages that he called the general adaptation syndrome (Figure 6.1). He labeled the first stage the *alarm reaction*, in which a living organism's homeostasis, or balance, is disrupted by the noxious stimuli.

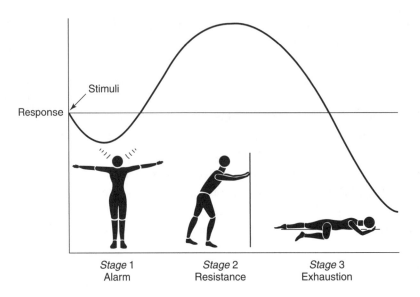

FIGURE 6.1   Stages of Selye's General Adaptation Syndrome

Note: From Romas, J. A., & Sharma, M. (2007). *Practical stress management. A comprehensive work-book for managing change and promoting health* (4th ed., p. 10). San Francisco: Benjamin Cummings. Reproduced with permission.

In this phase the endocrine glands (ductless glands that pour their secretions directly into the blood), especially the adrenal glands, start secreting their hormones (corticosteroids), which help in supplying more energy to the body. This is accompanied by a shrinkage of lymphatic structures, decrease in blood volume, and development of ulcers in the stomach. The second stage is the *stage of resistance*, in which the body tries to resist the noxious stimuli. In this stage the adaptation energy continues to get depleted. The third and final stage of the general adaptation syndrome is *exhaustion*. Exhaustion causes permanent damage to the system; if the noxious agent is not removed, the organism's energy becomes depleted, and death may ensue.

The response-based modeling of stress that originated from the work of physiologists and discussed hormonal and physiological responses remained the major model of stress until the 1960s, when **event-based models** and the concept of **coping** became understood in psychology. Thomas Holmes and Richard Rahe (1967) developed the Social Readjustment Rating Scale, which listed 43 life events, each with a predetermined weight, and asked a person to identify events he or she had experienced in the past year. They empirically found that the higher a person's score was on the scale, the greater were the chances of that individual developing sickness in the subsequent year. The event-based models changed the paradigm from the effect (response) to the cause (stressor).

Alongside the event-based models, the concept of coping also developed, which led to the establishment of the transactional model of coping. The term *coping* can be traced back to the concept of **defense mechanisms** described in the psychoanalytical model by the famous Austrian neurologist Sigmund Freud (1923). In the 1920s, Freud described the mechanisms of defense that a person's mind uses to protect itself. These include methods such as introjection, isolation, projection reversal, reaction formation, regression, repression, sublimation, turning against the self, and undoing. According to Freud, defense mechanisms were the devices that the mind used to alter the individual's perception of situations that disturbed the internal milieu or mental balance. He applied the concept in identifying sources of anxiety through the free association technique on patients.

In the 1930s one of Freud's associates, Austrian-born physician Alfred Adler, differed from Freud and argued that defense mechanisms were protective against external threats or challenges (Sharma, 2003). Sigmund Freud's daughter and renowned psychologist, Anna Freud (1937), included both these viewpoints and underscored the role of defense mechanisms as being protective against both internal and external threats. She also extended the repertoire of defense mechanisms to include denial, intellectualization, ego restriction, and identifying with the aggressor. Therefore, it appears that the concept of defense mechanisms is very similar to that of coping, which it preceded. However, in the 1970s, psychologist Norma Haan (1977) distinguished defense mechanisms from coping. She explained that coping is purposive and involves choices, whereas defense mechanisms are rigid and set. Coping, according to Haan, is focused on the present, whereas defense mechanisms are premised on the past and distort the present.

Using the concept of coping, Richard Lazarus (1966, 1984), a professor of psychology at the University of California–Berkley, came up with the **transactional model**. According to this model, all stressful experiences, including chronic illnesses, are perceived as person-environment transactions. In these transactions, the person undertakes a four-stage assessment known as *appraisal* (Lazarus & Folkman, 1984). When confronted with any stressor, the first stage is the *primary appraisal* of the event. In this stage, the person internally determines the severity of the stressor and whether he or she is in trouble. If the stressor is perceived to be severe or threatening, has caused harm or loss in the past, or has affected someone known to the person, then the stage of secondary appraisal occurs. If, on the other hand, the stressor is judged to be irrelevant or poses minimal threat, then stress does not develop any further, and no further coping occurs. The *secondary appraisal* determines how much control the person has over the stressor. Based on this understanding, the individual ascertains what means of control are available to him or her. This is the stage known as *coping*. According to the transactional model, there are two broad categories of coping: problem-focused coping and emotion-focused coping. Finally, the fourth stage is *reappraisal*, during which the person determines whether the effects of the stressor have been effectively negated.

In the 1970s Suzanne Kobasa (1979a, 1979b) conducted an eight-year study of executives undergoing the major stress of losing their jobs or being reassigned and found that individuals who displayed a certain set of personality characteristics remained healthier and happier during the crisis. She labeled such personality traits **hardiness**. Friedman and Rosenman (1974) classified people into type A and type B personalities. The **type A personality** was characterized by hurrying, exercising control over people and things, a sense of urgency, and a challenging nature. The **type B personality** was more laid back and had a more relaxed disposition. It was found that type B personalities had less stress and type A had more stress. In the late 1970s and 1980s, a medical sociologist, Aaron Antonovsky (1979, 1987), proposed the theory of **sense of coherence**, which postulated that people who possess a higher sense of coherence tend to cope with life better. In the 1980s another construct that moderates the influence of stressors was discovered, namely, social support. Scheier and Carver (1985) also suggested the construct of optimism as having a beneficial effect on coping.

> *The nature and severity of the stress disorder could depend on at least three factors: (1) the formal characteristics of the environmental demands, (2) the quality of the emotional response generated by the demands, or in particular individuals facing these demands, and (3) the process of coping mobilized by the stressful commerce.*
>
> —Lazarus (1974, p. 327)

CONSTRUCTS OF THEORIES OF STRESS AND COPING

The primary construct of theories of stress and coping is that of **stressors**, which are demands from the internal or external environment that an individual perceives as being harmful or threatening (Lazarus & Folkman, 1984). These are generally divided into three general classes: discrete, major life events; ongoing, everyday chronic stressors; and the absence of major happenings, or nonevents (Romas & Sharma, 2007).

Life events, or **life change events**, are discrete, observable, and objectively reportable events that require some social or psychological adjustment, or both, on the part of the individual (Wheaton, 1994). Examples of such events are the death of a family member, starting a new job, and buying a new home. If these happened in the recent past (within the last year), they are called **recent life events**; if they occurred further in the past (such as childhood events) and are bothersome as memories, they are called **remote life events**.

McLean and Link (1994) classified **chronic stressors** into five types:

1. **Persistent life difficulties:** Life events lasting longer than 6 months, such as long-term disability
2. **Role strains:** Strain from either performing a specific role (such as parenting, working, or being in a relationship) or performing a multiplicity of roles at the same time
3. **Chronic strains:** Responses of one social group to another, such as overt or covert, intentional or unintentional discriminatory behavior due to race, ethnicity, and so on
4. **Daily hassles:** Everyday problems, such as getting stuck in traffic
5. **Community-wide strains:** Stressors that operate at an ecological level, such as residing in a high-crime neighborhood

Nonevents are of three kinds: (1) when desired or anticipated events do not occur (e.g., wanting to graduate but not having enough credits), (2) when desired events do not occur even though their occurrence is normative for people of a certain group (e.g., a person does not get married when most people of his or her age are married), and (3) not having anything to do (e.g., being bored).

Most of the time stressors cannot be modified and have to be endured. However, what can be changed in these cases is a person's perception of the stressors. Some stressors can be changed by modification of the environment. For example, if one is stressed about taking a class from a certain instructor and that class is being offered by another instructor, then making a change to the second instructor can alleviate the stress.

The second construct of the theories of stress and coping is that of **primary appraisal**, in which the person determines the severity of the stressor and makes an assessment regarding whether he or she is in trouble. To modify this construct in an educational program, participants could be asked to keep a stress diary, or they could participate in a brainstorming session to identify the stressors that are affecting them at any given time, or they could discuss the stressors and their severity.

In **secondary appraisal**, the person determines how much control he or she has over the stressor. If control is high, then no stress develops; if control is low, then stress develops. To modify secondary appraisal in an educational program, stress diaries, brainstorming, or discussion can be helpful.

The construct of **problem-focused coping** is based on a person's capability to think and to alter the environmental event or situation. Examples of this strategy at the thought process level include utilization of problem-solving skills, interpersonal conflict resolution, advice seeking, time management, goal setting, and gathering more information about what is causing the stress. Problem solving requires thinking through various alternatives, evaluating the pros and cons of different solutions, and then implementing a solution that seems most advantageous to reduce the stress. Examples of this strategy at the behavioral or action level include activities such as joining a smoking cessation program, compliance with a prescribed medical treatment, adherence to a diabetic diet plan, and scheduling and prioritizing tasks for managing time.

In the construct of **emotion-focused coping**, the focus is on altering the way one thinks or feels about a situation or an event. Examples of this strategy at the thought process level include denying the existence of the stressful situation, freely expressing emotions, avoiding the stressful situation, making social comparisons, and looking at the bright side of things. Examples of this strategy at the behavioral or action level include seeking social support to negate the influence of the stressful situation; use of exercise, relaxation, or meditation; joining support groups; and practicing religious rituals. Negative examples include escaping through the use of alcohol and drugs.

The final construct of theories of stress and coping is **reappraisal**, which is the feedback loop by which the person determines whether the effects of the stressor have been effectively negated. To modify this construct, techniques such as stress diaries, brainstorming, or discussion can again be helpful. Table 6.1 summarizes the constructs.

As we have seen, the theory of hardiness also originated in the 1970s. Hardiness has three constructs (Taylor & Aspinwall, 1996): control, commitment, and challenge (Table 6.2). **Control** refers to a person's belief that he or she causes the events of his or her life and can influence the environment. The greater a person's belief in his or her control, the better that person is able to endure the adverse effects of stress. Control can be modified in an educational program by conducting a discussion on this topic or by having participants role play situations in which they experience control and relate it to their lives.

TABLE 6.1 Key Constructs of Theories of Stress and Coping		
Construct	**Definition**	**How to Modify?**
Stressors	Demands from the internal or external environment that one perceives as being harmful or threatening. These are of three kinds: life events, chronic stressors, and nonevents.	Most stressors cannot be modified and must be endured. What can be modified is the person's perception of the stressors. Some stressors can be modified by environmental engineering.
Primary appraisal	Person determines the severity of the stressor and makes an assessment regarding whether he or she is in trouble.	• Stress diary • Brainstorming • Discussion
Secondary appraisal	Person determines how much control he or she has over the stressor.	• Stress diary • Brainstorming • Discussion
Problem-focused coping	Method of dealing with a given stressor by one's ability to think and to alter the environmental event or situation.	• Problem-solving skills • Interpersonal conflict resolution • Advice seeking • Time management • Goal setting • Discussion to gather more information about what is causing the stress
Emotion-focused coping	Method of dealing with a stressor in which the focus is on altering the way one thinks or feels about a situation or an event.	• Exercise • Relaxation • Meditation • Joining support groups
Reappraisal	Feedback loop in which the person determines whether the effects of the stressor have been effectively negated.	• Stress diary • Brainstorming • Discussion

TABLE 6.2	Key Constructs of the Theory of Hardiness	
Construct	**Definition**	**How to Modify?**
Control	Belief that one causes the events of one's life and can influence the environment	• Discussion • Role play
Commitment	Tendency to involve oneself in whatever one encounters, or a feeling of deep involvement in the activities of life	• Discussion • Role play
Challenge	Willingness to undertake change, confront new activities, and obtain opportunities for growth	• Goal setting

Commitment refers to a person's tendency to become involved in whatever he or she encounters or to a feeling of deep involvement in the activities of life. The higher a person's commitment, the higher that person's ability to cope with stress. To modify commitment in an educational program, the educator can facilitate a discussion on the topic, or the effects of commitment can be portrayed in a role play.

The mechanism whereby stressful life events produce illness is presumably physiological. Whatever this physiological response is, the personality characteristics of hardiness may cut into it, decreasing the likelihood of breakdown into illness.

—Kobasa (1985, p. 187)

Challenge refers to a person's willingness to undertake change, confront new activities, and obtain opportunities for growth. The greater a sense of challenge a person has, the easier he or she is able to cope with stress. To modify the construct of challenge, one can use goal setting, whereby participants set incrementally challenging goals for themselves.

Another theory that originated in the 1970s was that of the sense of coherence (Antonovsky, 1979, 1987). The three constructs of the sense of coherence are comprehensibility, manageability, and meaningfulness (Table 6.3). **Comprehensibility** refers to the extent to which one perceives that the stressors that confront one make cognitive sense, implying that there is some set structure, consistency, order, clarity, and predictability. To modify comprehensibility in an educational program, there should be a discussion session that clarifies the stressors and interprets them so as to give them clarity and predictability.

TABLE 6.3 Key Constructs of the Theory of Sense of Coherence		
Construct	**Definition**	**How to Modify?**
Comprehensibility	The extent to which one perceives that the stressors that confront one make cognitive sense, implying that there is some set structure, consistency, order, clarity, and predictability	By clarifying the stressors and interpreting them such that they have clarity and predictability
Manageability	The extent to which one feels that the resources under one's control are adequate to meet the demands posed by the stressors	• Brainstorming of all resources • Support group to increase resources
Meaningfulness	The extent to which one feels that life makes sense emotionally and that at least some of the stressors in life are worth investing energy in and are worthy of commitment and engagement	Discussion about perspective toward stressors

Manageability refers to the extent to which one feels that the resources under one's control are adequate to meet the demands posed by the stressors. To modify this construct in educational sessions, the educator can facilitate a brainstorming session in which all the potential resources can be enlisted. A support group that is able to provide additional resources can also be built into the educational program.

Meaningfulness refers to the extent to which one feels that life makes sense emotionally and that at least some of the stressors in life are worth investing energy in and are worthy of commitment and engagement. It entails looking at challenges in life as something welcome rather than burdensome. It can be modified in an educational session by organizing a discussion about changing one's perspective regarding stressors.

Another construct that has been found to moderate the negative effects of stressors is **social support**, which is the help obtained through social relationships and interpersonal exchanges (Heaney & Israel, 2002). House (1981) classified social support into four types: (1) emotional support, which entails providing understanding, love, caring, and reliance; (2) informational support, which entails providing information, guidance, and counsel; (3) instrumental support, which entails providing concrete assistance and support; and (4) appraisal support, which entails providing evaluative assistance. Social support can be naturally occurring, in the form of parents, spouse, other family members, and friends, or it can be created artificially by the health educator. Social support buffers the effect of stressors and shields a person from negative consequences.

A final construct that has been linked to resistance to stress is **optimism** (Scheier & Carver, 1985), which is the tendency to expect the best possible outcome or to think about the most hopeful aspects of any situation. Several studies have linked optimism to better coping and health. Optimism acts by several pathways to ensure better health. First, optimism affects a person's efforts to avoid illness by increasing attention to information about potential health threats. Second, optimism directly improves coping. Third, optimism acts through its influence on the maintenance of positive mood. Martin Seligman has talked about the modifiability of this construct in his books *Learned Optimism* (1990) and *What You Can Change and What You Can't* (1994). To modify the construct of optimism in an educational program, the educator can facilitate a lecture or discussion on its value.

APPLICATIONS OF THE THEORIES OF STRESS AND COPING

Theories of stress and coping have been used in a variety of health education and promotion applications, such as for cardiac rehabilitation following myocardial infarction (Macinnes, 2005), coping following traumatic brain injury (Anson & Ponsford, 2006), coping in breast cancer survivors (Wonghongkul, Dechaprom, Phumivichuvate, & Losawatkul, 2006), coping in the elderly (Poderico, Ruggiero, Iachini, & Iavarone, 2006), coping in the elderly with arthritis (Tak, 2006), coping in head and neck cancer patients (Vidhubala, Latha, Ravikannan, Mani, & Karthikesh, 2006), coping in newly incarcerated adolescents (Brown & Ireland, 2006), coping in old-age psychosis (Berry, Barrowclough, Byrne, & Purandare, 2006), coping in survivors of domestic violence (Lewis et al., 2006; Watlington & Murphy, 2006), coping with exacerbation of psoriasis and eczema (Wahl, Mork, Hanestad, & Helland, 2006), prevention of atherosclerosis (Jedryka-Goral et al., 2006), prevention of recurrent depression (Bockting et al., 2006), quality of life assessment for stroke caregivers (Van Puymbroeck & Rittman, 2005), smoking cessation (Friis, Forouzesh, Chhim, Monga, & Sze, 2006), and a worksite stress management program (Shimazu, Umanodan, & Schaufeli, 2006). Table 6.4 summarizes these applications.

The theory of hardiness has been used in a variety of health education and promotion applications, such as for adaptation in families of young children with chronic

TABLE 6.4   Examples of Applications of Theories of Stress and Coping in Health Education and Health Promotion
Cardiac rehabilitation following myocardial infarction
Coping following traumatic brain injury
Coping in breast cancer survivors
Coping in the elderly
Coping in the elderly with arthritis
Coping in head and neck cancer patients
Coping in newly incarcerated adolescents
Coping in old-age psychosis
Coping in survivors of domestic violence
Coping with exacerbation of psoriasis and eczema
Prevention of atherosclerosis
Prevention of recurrent depression
Quality of life assessment for stroke caregivers
Smoking cessation
Worksite stress management program

asthma (Svavarsdottir, Rayens, & McCubbin, 2005), family-level intervention for parents of children with cancer (Svavarsdottir & Sigurdardottir, 2005), military cadets participating in survival training (Eid & Morgan, 2006), modeling coping in spousal caregivers of persons with dementia (DiBartolo & Soeken, 2003), modeling for mental health among mothers of adult children with intellectual disability (Ben-Zur, Duvdevany, & Lury, 2005), modeling health in women with physical and sexual abuse (Heckman & Clay, 2005), modeling psychological status and physical function in osteoarthritis patients (Kee, 2003), modeling well-being in older women (Smith, Young, & Lee, 2004), modeling work stress and job satisfaction (McCalister, Dolbier, Webster, Mallon, & Steinhardt, 2006), organizational and psychological adjustment in managers (Ghorbani & Watson, 2005), qualitative study of adults aging with HIV

(Vance & Woodley, 2005), qualitative study of hardiness in intensive care unit nurses (Hurst & Koplin-Baucum, 2005), qualitative study of women with paraplegia (Kinder, 2005), and workplace stress reduction (Lambert, Lambert, & Yamase, 2003). Table 6.5 summarizes these applications.

The theory of sense of coherence has been used in a variety of health education and promotion applications, such as for an addiction recovery program (Chen, 2006), associations with quality of life among women with systemic lupus erythematosus (Abu-Shakra et al., 2006), coping in the next of kin of cancer patients who are in palliative home care (Milberg & Strang, 2003), coping with serious accidental injury (Hepp, Moergeli, Buchi, Wittmann, & Schnyder, 2005), couple therapy aimed at reducing marital distress and psychiatric symptoms (Lundblad & Hansson, 2005), an educational program after breast cancer surgery (Koinberg, Langius-Eklof, Holm-

---

TABLE 6.5   Examples of Applications of the Theory of Hardiness in Health Education and Health Promotion

Adaptation in families of young children with chronic asthma

Family-level intervention for parents of children with cancer

Military cadets participating in survival training

Modeling coping in spousal caregivers of persons with dementia

Modeling for mental health among mothers of adult children with intellectual disability

Modeling health in women with physical and sexual abuse

Modeling psychological status and physical function in osteoarthritis patients

Modeling well-being in older women

Modeling work stress and job satisfaction

Organizational and psychological adjustment in managers

Qualitative study of adults aging with HIV

Qualitative study of hardiness in intensive care unit nurses

Qualitative study of women with paraplegia

Workplace stress reduction

berg, & Fridlund, 2006), modeling sick leave absence in parents of children with Down syndrome (Hedov, Wikblad, & Anneren, 2006), pain management in spinal cord injury patients (Norrbrink Budh, Kowalski, & Lundeberg, 2006), predicting depression in mass-evacuated adults from Kosovo (Roth & Ekblad, 2006), predicting quality of life among spouses of stroke patients (Larson et al., 2005), quality of life in older people (Borglin, Jakobsson, Edberg, & Hallberg, 2006), relationship with stress in parents of children with developmental disabilities (Oelofsen & Richardson, 2006), and relationship with tobacco use (Glanz, Maskarinec, & Carlin, 2005). Table 6.6 summarizes these applications.

> *Each person must find a way to relieve his pent-up energy without creating conflicts with his fellow men. Such an approach not only insures peace of mind but also earns the goodwill, respect, and even love of our neighbors, the highest degree of security and the noblest status symbol to which the human being can aspire.*
>
> —Selye (1985, p. 28)

TABLE 6.6 Examples of Applications of the Theory of Sense of Coherence in Health Education and Health Promotion
Addiction recovery program
Associations with quality of life among women with systemic lupus erythematosus
Coping in the next of kin of cancer patients who are in palliative home care
Coping with serious accidental injury
Couple therapy aimed at reducing marital distress and psychiatric symptoms
Educational program after breast cancer surgery
Modeling sick leave absence in parents of children with Down syndrome
Pain management in spinal cord injury patients
Predicting depression in mass-evacuated adults from Kosovo
Predicting quality of life among spouses of stroke patients
Quality of life in older people
Relationship with stress in parents of children with developmental disabilities
Relationship with tobacco use

LIMITATIONS OF THE THEORIES OF STRESS AND COPING

We have seen that there are three major kinds of theories of stress and coping. The strength of response-based models is that they explicate the physiological relationships involved in stress, but some of the limitations of this model are the nonspecificity of stimuli, the lack of accounting for individual variations, the lack of accounting for differences in stressors, and lack of attention to cognitive processing of stressors. Event-based models are strong in terms of clarifying stressors, introducing the notion of coping, and explaining the differences in stressors, but have the limitations of not covering physiological mechanisms and not distinguishing between cause and effect (e.g., disease is an event that produces stress as well as an outcome of stress).

The strengths of the transactional model of stress are that it explains coping in steps; underscores the importance of thinking, perception, and determination of controllability; emphasizes the role of chronic stressors or daily hassles as being more important than once-in-a-while life events; takes into account the interaction between individual and environment; and has a feedback mechanism or "closed loop" system in the form of reappraisal. The chief limitations of this model are that coping is not measured objectively, that it does not cover personality characteristics, and that it does not cover physiological mechanisms. Table 6.7 summarizes the strengths and weaknesses of the three major kinds of models of stress and coping.

SKILL-BUILDING ACTIVITY

Let us see how we can apply the transactional model of stress and coping for developing healthy coping behavior in a group of college students. Figure 6.2 depicts each of the constructs of the transactional model of coping and links these with the educational processes and behavioral objectives in this example.

The health education intervention would start with the construct of primary appraisal, or stressor identification. This can be done by keeping a stress diary. Secondary appraisal can be modified through a brainstorming session. Problem-focused coping can be used to build problem-solving skills in the students. A demonstration of how to apply the steps of problem solving to help participants think through many solutions and identify the pros and cons of each solution before

TABLE 6.7 Comparison of Response-Based, Event-Based, and Transactional Models of Stress and Coping		
Model	**Strengths**	**Weaknesses**
Response-based models	• Explicates the physiological mechanisms	• Nonspecificity of stimuli/stressors • Does not account for individual variations • Multiplicity of stressors not addressed • No attention to the cognitive processing of the stressor(s)
Event-based models	• Clarifies stressors • Introduces the notion of coping (or dealing with environmental events) • Explains multiplicity of stressors	• Does not cover physiological mechanisms • Does not distinguish between cause and effect (e.g., disease is an event that produces stress as well as being considered an outcome of stress)
Transactional model	• Explains coping in steps • Underscores the importance of thinking, perception, and determination of controllability • Emphasizes the role of chronic stressors or daily hassles as being more important than once-in-a-while life events • Takes into account the communication process or interaction between individual and environment, including other people • Existence of a feedback mechanism, or "closed loop" system, in this model (reappraisal)	• Lack of objective measurement of coping • Does not consider personality characteristics • Does not cover physiological mechanisms

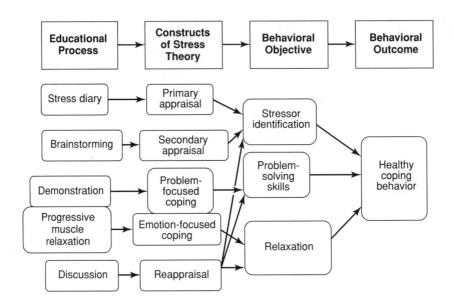

FIGURE 6.2   How the transactional model can be used to develop healthy coping

choosing one solution will be used as an educational method. Emotion-focused coping would involve teaching the behavioral skill of relaxation to the students. The technique of progressive muscle relaxation can be taught in this regard. The final construct, reappraisal, can be facilitated through a discussion in which the participants think about how successful they have been with identifying stressors, using problem-solving skills, and learning relaxation. Using this approach, you can plan a coping intervention either as a standalone as shown in this example or as an adjuvant to another behavior change program. Table 6.8 provides a set of questions.

TABLE 6.8   Choosing the Educational Methods for Health Education Program Planning Using Theories of Stress and Coping

1. What will be the best method to facilitate primary appraisal?
   - Stress diary
   - Brainstorming
   - Discussion
   - Other

2. What will be the best educational method to facilitate secondary appraisal?
   - Stress diary
   - Brainstorming
   - Discussion
   - Other

3. What will be the best educational method to facilitate problem-focused coping?
   - Demonstration of problem-solving skills
   - Interpersonal conflict resolution
   - Advice seeking
   - Time management
   - Goal setting
   - Discussion
   - Other

4. What will be the best educational method to facilitate emotion-focused coping?
   - Exercise
   - Relaxation
   - Meditation
   - Support groups
   - Other

5. What will be the best educational method to facilitate reappraisal?
   - Stress diary
   - Brainstorming
   - Discussion
   - Other

6. What will be the best educational method to facilitate control (theory of hardiness)?
   - Discussion
   - Role play
   - Simulation
   - Other

(Continued)

TABLE 6.8   *(Continued)*

7. What will be the best educational method to facilitate commitment (theory of hardiness)?
   - Discussion
   - Role play
   - Simulation
   - Other

8. What will be the best educational method to facilitate challenge (theory of hardiness)?
   - Discussion
   - Goal setting
   - Other

9. What will be the best educational method to facilitate comprehensibility (sense of coherence)?
   - Discussion clarifying the stressors
   - Lecture
   - Other

10. What will be the best educational method to facilitate manageability (sense of coherence)?
    - Brainstorming
    - Support groups
    - Other

11. What will be the best educational method to facilitate meaningfulness (sense of coherence)?
    - Lecture
    - Discussion
    - Other

12. What will be the best educational method to facilitate optimism?
    - Lecture
    - Discussion
    - Other

SUMMARY

In physiology and psychology, the concept of stress originated in the 1930s with the response-based models based on the work of Walter Cannon and Hans Selye. These models looked at a myriad of physiological effects of stress on the body. This conceptualization was followed by the event-based models, which looked at the role of life events or discrete stressors in the causation of stress. Between the 1960s and 1980s,

Richard Lazarus proposed the transactional model of stress, in which a person interacts with the environment while going through four stages: primary appraisal, secondary appraisal, coping, and reappraisal.

Besides these models, several sets of personality characteristics were also identified as predictors of healthier coping. One such personality trait, identified by Suzanne Kobasa, is hardiness, which comprises three factors: commitment, control, and challenge. Similarly, Friedman and Rosenman classified personality into types A and B and found that type B personalities had less stress compared with type A. Aaron Antonovsky proposed a theory of the sense of coherence, which suggested that people who possess a higher sense of coherence tend to cope better in life. A sense of coherence comprises comprehensibility, manageability, and meaningfulness. Another construct is social support, which entails the help obtained through social relationships and interpersonal exchanges and is protective against negative effects arising from stressors. Finally, the construct of optimism (a personality disposition that refers to the tendency to expect the best possible outcome) has been found to have a beneficial effect on coping.

REVIEW QUESTIONS

1. Differentiate between response-based and event-based models.
2. Describe the transactional model.
3. Discuss the general adaptation syndrome.
4. Define stressors. Provide a classification of stressors.
5. Describe the constructs of hardiness.
6. Describe the constructs of the sense of coherence.
7. Differentiate between problem-focused and emotion-focused coping.
8. Apply the transactional model of stress and coping for developing healthy coping behavior in a group of college students.

WEBSITE

Go to the Web component of *Theoretical Foundations of Health Education and Health Promotion* at http://health.jbpub.com/foundations for Web exercises, additional resources related to this chapter, and student review tools.

GLOSSARY TERMS

challenge
chronic strains
chronic stressors
commitment
community-wide strains
comprehensibility
control
coping
daily hassles
defense mechanisms
emotion-focused coping
event-based models
general adaptation syndrome
hardiness
life events (life change events)
manageability
meaningfulness
nonevents

optimism
persistent life difficulties
primary appraisal
problem-focused coping
reappraisal
recent life events
remote life events
response-based model
role strains
secondary appraisal
sense of coherence
social support
stress
stressors
transactional model
type A personality
type B personality

REFERENCES AND FURTHER READING

Abu-Shakra, M., Keren, A., Livshitz, I., Delbar, V., Bolotin, A., Sukenik, S., et al. (2006). Sense of coherence and its impact on quality of life of patients with systemic lupus erythematosus. *Lupus*, *15*(1), 32–37.

Anson, K., & Ponsford, J. (2006). Coping and emotional adjustment following traumatic brain injury. *Journal of Head Trauma Rehabilitation*, *21*(3), 248–259.

Antonovsky, A. (1979). *Health, stress, and coping*. San Francisco: Jossey-Bass.

Antonovsky, A. (1987). *Unraveling the mystery of health: How people manage stress and stay well*. San Francisco: Jossey-Bass.

Ben-Zur, H., Duvdevany, I., & Lury, L. (2005). Associations of social support and hardiness with mental health among mothers of adult children with intellectual disability. *Journal of Intellectual Disability Research*, *49*(Pt. 1), 54–62.

Berry, K., Barrowclough, C., Byrne, J., & Purandare, N. (2006). Coping strategies and social support in old age psychosis. *Social Psychiatry and Psychiatric Epidemiology*, *41*(4), 280–284.

Bockting, C. L., Spinhoven, P., Koeter, M. W., Wouters, L. F., Visser, I., & Schene, A. H. (2006). Differential predictors of response to preventive cognitive therapy in recurrent depression: A 2-year prospective study. *Psychotherapy and Psychosomatics*, *75*(4), 229–236.

Borglin, G., Jakobsson, U., Edberg, A. K., & Hallberg, I. R. (2006). Older people in Sweden with various degrees of present quality of life: Their health, social support, everyday activities and sense of coherence. *Health and Social Care in the Community*, *14*(2), 136–146.

Brown, S. L., & Ireland, C. A. (2006). Coping style and distress in newly incarcerated male adolescents. *Journal of Adolescent Health, 38*(6), 656–661.

Cannon, W. B. (1932). *The wisdom of the body.* New York: Norton.

Chen, G. (2006). Social support, spiritual program, and addiction recovery. *International Journal of Offender Therapy and Comparative Criminology, 50*(3), 306–323.

DiBartolo, M. C., & Soeken, K. L. (2003). Appraisal, coping, hardiness, and self-perceived health in community-dwelling spouse caregivers of persons with dementia. *Research in Nursing and Health, 26*(6), 445–458.

Eid, J., & Morgan, C. A., 3rd. (2006). Dissociation, hardiness, and performance in military cadets participating in survival training. *Military Medicine, 171*(5), 436–442.

Freud, A. (1937). *The ego and mechanism of defense.* London: Hogarth Press.

Freud, S. (1923). *The ego and the id.* New York: Norton.

Friedman, M., & Rosenman, R. H. (1974). *Type A behavior and your heart.* New York: Fawcett Crest.

Friis, R. H., Forouzesh, M., Chhim, H. S., Monga, S., & Sze, D. (2006). Sociocultural determinants of tobacco use among Cambodian Americans. *Health Education Research, 21*(3), 355–365.

Ghorbani, N., & Watson, P. J. (2005). Hardiness scales in Iranian managers: Evidence of incremental validity in relationships with the five factor model and with organizational and psychological adjustment. *Psychological Reports, 96*(3 Pt. 1), 775–781.

Glanz, K., Maskarinec, G., & Carlin, L. (2005). Ethnicity, sense of coherence, and tobacco use among adolescents. *Annals of Behavioral Medicine, 29*(3), 192–199.

Haan, N. (1977). *Coping and defending: Processes of self-environment organization.* New York: Academic Press.

Heaney, C. A., & Israel, B. A. (2002). Social networks and social support. In K. Glanz, B. K. Rimer, & F. M. Lewis (Eds.), *Health behavior and health education: Theory, research and practice* (pp. 185–209). San Francisco: Jossey-Bass.

Heckman, C. J., & Clay, D. L. (2005). Hardiness, history of abuse and women's health. *Journal of Health Psychology, 10*(6), 767–777.

Hedov, G., Wikblad, K., & Anneren, G. (2006). Sickness absence in Swedish parents of children with Down's syndrome: Relation to self-perceived health, stress and sense of coherence. *Journal of Intellectual Disability Research, 50*(7), 546–552.

Hepp, U., Moergeli, H., Buchi, S., Wittmann, L., & Schnyder, U. (2005). Coping with serious accidental injury: A one-year follow-up study. *Psychotherapy and Psychosomatics, 74*(6), 379–386.

Holmes, T. H., & Rahe, R. H. (1967). The social readjustment rating scale. *Journal of Psychosomatic Research, 11*, 213–218.

House, J. S. (1981). *Work stress and social support.* Reading, MA: Addison-Wesley.

Hurst, S., & Koplin-Baucum, S. (2005). A pilot qualitative study relating to hardiness in ICU nurses: Hardiness in ICU nurses. *Dimensions of Critical Care Nursing, 24*(2), 97–100.

Jedryka-Goral, A., Pasierski, T., Zabek, J., Widerszal-Bazyl, M., Radkiewicz, P., Szulczyk, G. A., et al. (2006). Risk factors for atherosclerosis in healthy employees—a multidisciplinary approach. *European Journal of Internal Medicine, 17*(4), 247–253.

Kee, C. C. (2003). Older adults with osteoarthritis. Psychological status and physical function. *Journal of Gerontological Nursing, 29*(12), 26–34.

Kinder, R. A. (2005). Psychological hardiness in women with paraplegia. *Rehabilitation Nursing, 30*(2), 68–72.

Kobasa, S. C. (1979a). Personality and resistance to illness. *American Journal of Community Psychology*, 7, 413–423.

Kobasa, S. C. (1979b). Stressful life events, personality, and health: An inquiry into hardiness. *Journal of Personality and Social Psychology*, 37, 1–11.

Kobasa, S. C. (1985). Stressful life events, personality, and health: An inquiry into hardiness. In A. Monat & R. S. Lazarus (Eds.), *Stress and coping: An anthology* (pp. 174–188). New York: Columbia University Press.

Koinberg, I., Langius-Eklof, A., Holmberg, L., & Fridlund, B. (2006). The usefulness of a multidisciplinary educational program after breast cancer surgery: A prospective and comparative study. *European Journal of Oncology Nursing*, 10(4), 273–282.

Lambert, V. A., Lambert, C. E., & Yamase, H. (2003). Psychological hardiness, workplace stress and related stress reduction strategies. *Nursing and Health Sciences*, 5(2), 181–184.

Larson, J., Franzen-Dahlin, A., Billing, E., Arbin, M., Murray, V., & Wredling, R. (2005). Predictors of quality of life among spouses of stroke patients during the first year after the stroke event. *Scandinavian Journal of Caring Science*, 19(4), 439–445.

Lazarus, R. S. (1966). *Psychological stress and the coping process*. New York: McGraw Hill.

Lazarus, R. S. (1974). Psychological stress and the coping in adaptation and illness. *International Journal of Psychiatry in Medicine*, 5, 321–333.

Lazarus, R. S. (1984). Puzzles in the study of daily hassles. *Journal of Behavioral Medicine*, 7, 375–389.

Lazarus, R. S., & Folkman, S. (1984). *Stress, appraisal, and coping*. New York: Springer.

Lewis, C. S., Griffing, S., Chu, M., Jospitre, T., Sage, R. E., Madry, L., et al. (2006). Coping and violence exposure as predictors of psychological functioning in domestic violence survivors. *Violence Against Women*, 12(4), 340–354.

Lundblad, A. M., & Hansson, K. (2005). Outcomes in couple therapy: Reduced psychiatric symptoms and improved sense of coherence. *Nordic Journal of Psychiatry*, 59(5), 374–380.

Macinnes, J. D. (2005). The illness perceptions of women following acute myocardial infarction: Implications for behaviour change and attendance at cardiac rehabilitation. *Women and Health*, 42(4), 105–121.

McCalister, K. T., Dolbier, C. L., Webster, J. A., Mallon, M. W., & Steinhardt, M. A. (2006). Hardiness and support at work as predictors of work stress and job satisfaction. *American Journal of Health Promotion*, 20(3), 183–191.

McLean, D. E., & Link, B. G. (1994). Unraveling complexity: Strategies to refine concepts, measures, and research designs in the study of life events and mental health. In W. R. Avison & I. H. Gotlib (Eds.), *Stress and mental health: Contemporary issues and prospects for the future* (pp. 15–42). New York: Plenum Press.

Milberg, A., & Strang, P. (2003). Meaningfulness in palliative home care: An interview study of dying cancer patients' next of kin. *Palliative and Supportive Care*, 1(2), 171–180.

Norrbrink Budh, C., Kowalski, J., & Lundeberg, T. (2006). A comprehensive pain management programme comprising educational, cognitive and behavioural interventions for neuropathic pain following spinal cord injury. *Journal of Rehabilitation Medicine*, 38(3), 172–180.

Oelofsen, N., & Richardson, P. (2006). Sense of coherence and parenting stress in mothers and fathers of preschool children with developmental disability. *Journal of Intellectual and Developmental Disability*, 31(1), 1–12.

Poderico, C., Ruggiero, G., Iachini, T., & Iavarone, A. (2006). Coping strategies and cognitive functioning in elderly people from a rural community in Italy. *Psychological Reports, 98*(1), 159–168.

Romas, J. A., & Sharma, M. (2007). *Practical stress management. A comprehensive workbook for managing change and promoting health* (4th ed.). San Francisco: Benjamin Cummings.

Roth, G., & Ekblad, S. (2006). A longitudinal perspective on depression and sense of coherence in a sample of mass-evacuated adults from Kosovo. *Journal of Nervous and Mental Disease, 194*(5), 378–381.

Scheier, M. F., & Carver, C. S. (1985). Optimism, coping, and health: Assessment and implications of generalized outcome expectancies. *Health Psychology, 4,* 219–247.

Seligman, M. E. P. (1990). *Learned optimism.* New York: Pocket Books.

Seligman, M. E. P. (1994). *What you can change and what you can't: The complete guide to self improvement.* New York: Alfred A. Knopf.

Selye, H. (1936). A syndrome produced by diverse nocuous agents. *Nature, 138,* 32.

Selye, H. (1974a). *Stress without distress.* Philadelphia: Lippincott.

Selye, H. (1974b). *The stress of life.* New York: McGraw Hill.

Selye, H. (1982). History and present status of stress concept. In L. Goldberger & S. Breznitz (Eds.), *Handbook of stress: Theoretical and clinical aspects* (pp. 7–17). New York: Free Press.

Selye, H. (1985). History and present status of the stress concept. In A. Monat & R. S. Lazarus (Eds.), *Stress and coping: An anthology* (pp. 17–29). New York: Columbia University Press.

Sharma, M. (2003). Coping: Strategies. In N. A. Pitrowski (Ed.), *Magill's encyclopedia of social science: Psychology* (pp. 442–446). Pasadena, CA: Salem Press.

Shimazu, A., Umanodan, R., & Schaufeli, W. B. (2006). Effects of a brief worksite stress management program on coping skills, psychological distress and physical complaints: A controlled trial. *International Archives of Occupational and Environmental Health, 80*(1), 60–69.

Smith, N., Young, A., & Lee, C. (2004). Optimism, health-related hardiness and well-being among older Australian women. *Journal of Health Psychology, 9*(6), 741–752.

Svavarsdottir, E. K., Rayens, M. K., & McCubbin, M. (2005). Predictors of adaptation in Icelandic and American families of young children with chronic asthma. *Family and Community Health, 28*(4), 338–350.

Svavarsdottir, E. K., & Sigurdardottir, A. (2005). The feasibility of offering a family level intervention to parents of children with cancer. *Scandinavian Journal of Caring Sciences, 19*(4), 368–372.

Tak, S. H. (2006). An insider perspective of daily stress and coping in elders with arthritis. *Orthopaedic Nursing, 25*(2), 127–132.

Taylor, S. E., & Aspinwall, L. G. (1996). Mediating and moderating processes in psychosocial stress. Appraisal, coping, resistance, and vulnerability. In H. B Kaplan (Ed.), *Psychosocial stress: Perspectives on structure, theory, life course and methods* (pp. 71–110). San Diego: Academic Press.

Vance, D. E., & Woodley, R. A. (2005). Strengths and distress in adults who are aging with HIV: A pilot study. *Psychological Reports, 96*(2), 383–386.

Van Puymbroeck, M., & Rittman, M. R. (2005). Quality-of-life predictors for caregivers at 1 and 6 months poststroke: Results of path analyses. *Journal of Rehabilitation Research and Development, 42*(6), 747–760.

Vidhubala, E., Latha, Ravikannan, R., Mani, C. S., & Karthikesh, M. (2006). Coping preferences of head and neck cancer patients—Indian context. *Indian Journal of Cancer, 43*(1), 6–11.

Wahl, A. K., Mork, C., Hanestad, B. R., & Helland, S. (2006). Coping with exacerbation in psoriasis and eczema prior to admission in a dermatological ward. *European Journal of Dermatology, 16*(3), 271–275.

Watlington, C. G., & Murphy, C. M. (2006). The roles of religion and spirituality among African American survivors of domestic violence. *Journal of Clinical Psychology, 62*(7), 837–857.

Wheaton, B. (1994). Sampling the stress universe. In W. R. Avison & I. H. Gotlib (Eds.), *Stress and mental health: Contemporary issues and prospects for the future* (pp. 15–42). New York: Plenum Press.

Wonghongkul, T., Dechaprom, N., Phumivichuvate, L., & Losawatkul, S. (2006). Uncertainty appraisal coping and quality of life in breast cancer survivors. *Cancer Nursing, 29*(3), 250–257.

CHAPTER 7

Social Cognitive Theory

KEY CONCEPTS

- Emotional coping
- Environment
- Forethought capability
- Goal setting or self-control
- Knowledge
- Outcome expectations
- Outcome expectancies
- Reciprocal determinism
- Self-efficacy

- Self-efficacy in overcoming impediments
- Self-reflective capability
- Self-regulatory capability
- Situational perception
- Social cognitive theory
- Social learning theory
- Symbolizing capability
- Vicarious capability

AFTER READING THIS CHAPTER YOU SHOULD BE ABLE TO

- Identify the five basic human capabilities according to social cognitive theory
- List the constructs of social cognitive theory
- Summarize the applications of social cognitive theory in health education and health promotion
- Identify educational methods and match these to modify each construct from social cognitive theory
- Apply social cognitive theory for changing a health behavior of your choice

This chapter discusses **social cognitive theory (SCT)**, which was earlier known as the social learning theory (SLT). The word *social* refers to the social origins of thought and action. *Cognitive* refers to the influential causal contributions of thought processes to human motivation, affect, and action. The word *theory* alludes to the fact that this model has been empirically tested and that the set of constructs in this model can explain, describe, predict, or control behavior.

Social cognitive theory posits that human behavior can be explained as a triadic reciprocal causation. One angle of the tripod consists of the behavior. The second angle consists of environmental factors, and the third angle consists of personal factors such as cognitions, affect, and biological events. The unique interaction among these three dimensions results in behavior change. Hence, all three dimensions—personal factors, behavioral factors, and environmental factors—must be targeted in designing health education and health promotion interventions. This is known as **reciprocal determinism**. Over the past three decades many research studies, articles, and books by Albert Bandura and other research workers have sub-stantiated the application of this theory in predicting, ex-plaining, and changing behavior in a variety of settings. Some examples are clinical psychology for the treatment of phobias, counseling for parenting, career development, educational programs, and health education and health promotion.

> *A theory that denies that thoughts can regulate actions does not lend itself readily to the explanation of complex human behavior.*
>
> —Bandura (1986)

This chapter begins by describing the historical aspects of the genesis of SCT. Next it describes the underpinnings of SCT and the various constructs that make up this theory and discusses the applications of SCT in health education and health promotion. Finally, it discusses the limitations of SCT and provides a skill-building application.

HISTORICAL PERSPECTIVES

Historically, social cognitive theory superseded several earlier theories developed to explain behavior. The first such theory, proposed in the early part of the twentieth century, was the psychodynamic theory of Sigmund Freud (1923/1960), which proposed that behavior was shaped by a dynamic interplay of subconscious and unconscious needs, drives, impulses, and instincts. However, this theory lacked predictive value, was difficult to test, and entailed no social dimension, thereby offering limited utility. Another theory was Gordon Allport's (1937) trait theory, which emphasized determination of behavior through broad, enduring dispositions. Weak empirical support and inconsistency of behavior across situations and over time did not provide much credence to this line of thought.

Learning theories were also popular in psychology, such as those by Dollard and Miller (1950), Rotter (1954), and Skinner (1953). A major limitation of these theories was that they were tested either on animal models or on human subjects in one-person situations and therefore did not consider the social aspects of learning.

In 1963 Albert Bandura at Stanford University, in collaboration with Richard Walters of the University of Waterloo, Ontario, proposed the **social learning theory**

(Bandura & Walters, 1963), which described the existence of three important influences on learning. The first is the role of imitation. Imitation provides three possible effects that contribute to learning: (1) a modeling effect, whereby the person directly copies the behavior; (2) an inhibitory or disinhibitory effect, whereby there is an increase or decrease in the behavior as a result of the observation; and (3) an eliciting effect, whereby imitation serves as a cue for releasing similar responses in the observer.

The second important influence in learning, according to Bandura and Walters (1963), is that of reinforcement patterns. Positive reinforcement, in the form of verbal approval or material rewards, tends to reinforce the occurrence of the behavior. Negative reinforcement, in the form of verbal or physical punishment by an authority figure, inhibits aggression as long as the punitive agent is present; however, children who receive a great deal of negative reinforcement display aggression toward objects other than the punitive agent.

The third important influence in learning is that of self-control. There are three forms of self-controlling behavior: (1) resistance to deviation, (2) regulation of self-administered rewarding resources, and (3) postponement of immediate reinforcements in lieu of some more valued reward in the future. Self-control is acquired and maintained by direct reinforcement that takes the form of disciplinary interventions, both negative and positive.

In 1969 Bandura wrote a book, *Principles of Behavior Modification*, that made the social learning theory more applicable to a variety of behaviors. The approach delineated in this book was used in designing the Stanford three-community study, which began in 1972 in three northern California communities (Farquhar et al., 1977; Farquhar, 1978). The intervention targeted three risk factors: smoking, high serum cholesterol, and high blood pressure. The primary objectives of the intervention were to make comparisons among a mass media campaign alone in one community; a mass media campaign with high-risk screening and face-to-face instruction for high-risk individuals in the second community; and no health education with regard to knowledge and behavior related to cardiovascular disease, and measurement of various physiological indicators in the third community (Farquhar et al., 1977; Farquhar, 1978). The health education approach of this project had three distinct features: (1) mass media materials focused on teaching specific behavioral skills and affecting attitudes and motivation, (2) traditional behavior and self-control training, and (3) assessment of the knowledge deficits and media consumption patterns of intended audiences before the intervention. The study was able to demonstrate that mass media campaigns can increase knowledge and change habits, and that the approach is cost effective.

In 1977, Bandura refined his approach and published the book entitled *Social Learning Theory*. This refined approach formed the basis of the Stanford five-city project, which began in 1978 (Farquhar et al., 1985; Young, Haskell, Jatulis, & Fortmann, 1993). This intervention was implemented in northern California for six years in two treatment cities and two control cities, and in one city for surveillance only. The use of social learning theory in these two trials popularized this theory in health education and health promotion. In the 1980s, it was used in the Minnesota Heart Health Program (Luepker et al., 1994) and the Pawtucket Heart Health Program (Carleton, Lasater, Assaf, Feldman, & McKinlay, 1995), among other applications.

In 1986, Bandura renamed the theory *social cognitive theory* in his book *Social Foundations of Thought and Action*. Social cognitive theory continues to be popular today. In 1995, Bandura published the book *Self-Efficacy in Changing Societies*, which underscored the role of the construct that usually accounts for the largest proportion of variance in work with this theory. In his recent works (1997, 2001a, 2001b, 2002, 2004, 2005), Bandura has emphasized an agentic perspective, that is, the role of a person as an agent shaping and controlling his or her own life. In 2002 he was awarded the Healthtrac Award. He delivered a lecture at the convention of the Society for Public Health Education that focused mainly on the theory's applications in health education and promotion (Bandura, 2004).

> *Self-efficacy is the belief in one's capabilities to organize and execute the sources of action required to manage prospective situations.*
>
> —Bandura (1986)

UNDERPINNINGS OF SOCIAL COGNITIVE THEORY

One of the distinctive features of SCT is the importance it places on the potential of human beings. According to this theory, five basic human capabilities describe human beings. The first such capability is the **symbolizing capability**, which refers to the use of symbols in attributing meaning to experiences. It is an important tool for understanding, creating, and managing one's environment. Most environmental events act through cognitive interpretation rather than directly. By using symbols, people give structure, meaning, and continuity to their experiences. The symbolizing capability also helps in communicating with others at any distance in time and space.

The **vicarious capability** refers to the ability to learn from observing other people's behavior and the consequences they face. This ability is important because it enables people to generate and regulate behavior without tedious trial and error. Some complex skills can be mastered only through modeling. Modeling is not simply a process of response mimicry but entails creativity and innovativeness as well.

Forethought capability refers to the fact that most behavior is purposive and regulated by prior thoughts. Human beings motivate themselves and plan their actions using their forethought capability. Although future events do not have actual existence, they can be imagined and can serve as motivators in the present. Usually the course of action that is likely to bring positive rewards is easily adopted, whereas the course that is likely to produce negative outcomes is not adopted.

Self-regulatory capability refers to setting internal standards and self-evaluative reactions for one's behavior. Self-satisfaction is gained from meeting desirable standards, and dissatisfaction results from below-standard performance. Human beings are proactive and constantly form challenging goals for themselves, which also plays an important role in self-regulation.

The final capability is **self-reflective capability**, which is the analysis of experiences and examination of one's own thought processes. Human beings are not just agents of action but also self-examine and critique their own actions. They generate ideas, act upon them based on an anticipated outcome, and then in retrospect judge the accuracy and value of the outcomes, finally modifying their thinking as needed. According to Bandura (2001a), verification of one's thought processes happens in four ways: (1) enactive verification, in which one looks at the closeness between one's thoughts and the results of one's action; (2) vicarious verification, in which one looks at other people's actions and compares that with one's thinking; (3) persuasive verification, in which one evaluates one's beliefs against what others believe; and (4) logical verification, in which one compares one's thinking against knowledge that is known.

> *People are not only agents of action but self examiners of their own functioning.*
>
> —Bandura (2001a, p. 10)

CONSTRUCTS OF SOCIAL COGNITIVE THEORY

The constructs of Bandura's theory have been delineated in the literature in several ways. This chapter uses the depiction elaborated by Bandura in his presentation regarding the application of SCT in health promotion (Bandura, 2004). The constructs, their definitions, and ways to modify each construct are summarized in Table 7.1.

The first construct of SCT is *knowledge*, which is learning facts and gaining insights related to an action, idea, object, person, or situation. Knowledge is the essential component for any behavior change. It is a necessary precondition for change, but is often not

TABLE 7.1   Key Constructs of Social Cognitive Theory

Construct	Definition	How to Modify?
Knowledge	Learning facts and gaining insights related to an action, idea, object, person, or situation	• Lecture • Informational talk • Providing fact sheets
Outcome expectations	Anticipation of the probable outcomes that would ensue as a result of engaging in the behavior under discussion	• Discussion of benefits • Brainstorming • Role play
Outcome expectancies	Value a person places on the probable outcomes that result from performing a behavior	• Discussion of values • Brainstorming • Role play
Situational perception	How one perceives and interprets the environment around oneself	• Rectifying misperceptions
Environment	Physical or social circumstances or conditions that surround a person	• Providing opportunities to overcome personal and situational impediments • Providing access to the health system • Building social support around the person
Self-efficacy	Confidence in one's ability to pursue a behavior	• Practicing in small steps (e.g., breaking down the complex behavior of physical activity into doable small steps) • Having a role model demonstrate (e.g., having a video of a well-known movie star with whom the target audience can associate performing the same behaviors) • Using persuasion and reinforcement (e.g., telling the participants that they have what it takes to perform the behavior, and attributing past failures to external reasons)

(Continued)

TABLE 7.1   *(Continued)*

Construct	Definition	How to Modify?
		• Reducing stress associated with implementing a new behavior (e.g., having women take a relaxing shower before doing a breast self-examination)
Self-efficacy in overcoming impediments	Confidence that a person has in overcoming barriers while performing a given behavior	• Practicing overcoming barriers in small steps • Having a role model demonstrate overcoming barriers • Using persuasion and reinforcement in overcoming barriers • Reducing stress while overcoming barriers
Goal setting or self-control	Setting goals and developing plans to accomplish chosen behaviors	• Providing opportunities for setting goals • Self-monitoring • Providing personal rewards to reinforce accomplishment of goals
Emotional coping	Techniques employed by the person to control the emotional and physiological states associated with acquisition of a new behavior	• Progressive muscle relaxation • Yoga/meditation • Autogenic training • Visual imagery • Other stress management techniques

sufficient for making the behavior change. In the context of health education and health promotion, knowledge of the risks and benefits of different health practices is required for behavior change interventions. To modify knowledge, the health educator can provide information in the form of a lecture, a demonstration, or fact sheets on the topic.

The second construct of SCT is **outcome expectations**, which is the anticipation of the probable outcomes that would ensue as a result of engaging in the behavior under discussion. Bandura (2004) identifies three types of outcomes: (1) physical outcomes, which include positive and negative consequences of the behavior, (2) the outcome of social approval or disapproval of engaging or disengaging in the behavior, and (3) positive and negative self-evaluations. For example, a person who is being motivated to be physically active may think of losing weight, looking attractive, being able to make more friends, having less chances of acquiring heart disease, and improving self-image as some possible outcome expectations. The higher the expectations, the greater the likelihood of acquiring the behavior. To modify outcome expectations, the health educator can facilitate a discussion on possible outcomes that may ensue from engaging in the desired behavior. Other methods could be brainstorming or a role play that depicts the effects of the behavior on a person.

The construct of SCT that goes hand-in-hand with outcome expectations is **outcome expectancies**, which refers to the value a person places on the probable outcomes that result from performing a behavior. The higher the expectancies, the higher the chances of indulging in the behavior. For example, in motivating students, possible outcomes of getting an A grade could be to graduate early, to have more friends, to learn more about the subject, and so on. If students value these outcomes and getting an A in the course, they are likely to work harder. On the contrary, some students may not value getting an A and its associated outcomes and would be likely to put in less effort. Measurement of outcome expectations and outcome expectancies is usually reified using Likert scales. The expectations are multiplied with corresponding expectancies and then summed to arrive at a score of expectations (outcome expectations plus outcome expectancies). To modify expectancies, a discussion or brainstorming on values associated with outcomes can be organized. Expectancies can also be influenced by a psychodrama or role play.

The fourth construct of SCT is **situational perception**, which refers to how one perceives and interprets the environment around oneself (Baranowski, Perry, & Parcel, 2002). Any misperceptions hinder the behavior change. Thus, efforts must be made to remove misperceptions and to promote social norms that are healthy. For example, in a teen pregnancy program, a large number of teens may think that it is normative for most teens to be sexually active, whereas the statistical evidence points to the contrary. Providing correct information and explaining it would rectify the situational perception. To modify situational perception, misperceptions can be modified in either a discussion or a lecture.

The fifth construct of SCT, **environment**, refers to the physical or social circumstances or conditions that surround a person. Whereas situational perception involves a person's interpretation of his or her surroundings, environment consists of the actual conditions. Some effective means of modifying this construct are creating opportunities to overcome personal and situational impediments, providing access to the health system, and building social support around the person. Example applications of this construct are creating facilities for physical activity in the community (physical environment) and creating learning experiences for eliciting and maintaining social support from friends to maintain exercise behavior (social environment).

The sixth construct of SCT is *self-efficacy*, which is the confidence a person has in his or her ability to pursue a behavior. Self-efficacy is behavior specific and is in the present. It is not about the past or future. Self-efficacy plays a central role in behavior change. Bandura (2004) notes that unless people believe that they can produce the desired changes by their own efforts, there will be very little incentive to put in that effort. Four strategies can be used in building self-efficacy:

1. *Break down the complex behavior into practical and doable small steps.* For example, instead of telling people to be physically active, the educator may teach participants an aerobic sequence in small steps.

2. *Use a demonstration from credible role models.* For example, in facilitating an educational program about quitting alcohol, having a movie star who has himself or herself successfully gone through the process share his or her story would help in enhancing the self-efficacy of the participants.

3. *Use persuasion and reassurance.* If a person has failed in the past to make a behavior change, those failures can be attributed to external reasons. If the person has succeeded in related fields, those successes can be compared with the behavior the person is trying to change. For example, in a smoking cessation program, the health educator could ask participants to identify one instance where they have been successful in changing a negative behavior or in acquiring a positive behavior and then could state that they can do the same thing with the smoking behavior.

4. *Reduce stress.* Any behavior change is associated with some amount of stress, which hinders the change process. Reducing stress is thus an effective means of building self-efficacy. For example, if women find breast self-examination to be stressful, they should be instructed to relax either by taking a shower, listening to music, or practicing progressive muscle relaxation before performing the behavior.

The seventh construct is **self-efficacy in overcoming impediments**, which refers to the confidence that a person has in overcoming barriers while performing a given behavior. This construct is related to self-efficacy in terms of being situation specific, pertaining to the present, and being a confidence level. Sometimes it is considered as a subset of self-efficacy, but it is better to consider it as a separate construct. For example, to become more physically active, one must overcome several barriers, such as being tired, feeling depressed, feeling anxious, encountering bad weather, and having other interesting things to do rather than exercising. To modify the construct of self-efficacy in overcoming barriers, helpful techniques include practicing to overcome each barrier in small steps, having role models demonstrate success, using persuasion, and reducing stress.

The eighth construct is **goal setting** or **self-control**, which refers to setting goals and developing plans to accomplish chosen behaviors. When one sets goals and develops concrete plans, accomplishment of the behavior becomes easier. Goals are proximal and distal. Proximal goals are immediate accomplishments, whereas distal goals set the course of making change. To modify the construct of goal setting or self-control, educators need to provide opportunities for setting goals, show individuals how to monitor their progress, and provide personal rewards to reinforce the attainment of goals.

The final construct in SCT is **emotional coping**, which refers to the techniques employed by the person to control the emotional and physiological states associated with acquisition of a new behavior. This construct is often reified in association with self-efficacy. To modify emotional coping, stress management techniques such as progressive muscle relaxation, yoga, autogenic training, and visual imagery are useful. For example, a program that teaches aerobics to a group of sedentary employees at a worksite may also need to utilize stress management techniques that reduce the anxiety associated with learning a new skill.

> *Social cognitive theory acknowledges the influential role of evolved factors in human adaptation and change, but it rejects one-sided evolutionism in which evolved biology shapes behavior but the selection pressures of social and technological innovations on biological evolution get ignored.*
>
> —Bandura (2001a, p. 20)

APPLICATIONS OF SOCIAL COGNITIVE THEORY

Some examples of behavior research in which SCT has been used are as follows: assessing medication adherence among low-literacy patients (Kalichman et al., 2005), defining correlates of physical activity in fibromyalgia patients (Oliver & Cronan, 2005), defining predictors of exercise participation (Kaewthummanukul, Brown, Weaver, & Thomas, 2006), identifying perceptions of whole-grain foods and the factors influencing their intake by children (Burgess-Champoux, Marquart, Vickers, & Reicks, 2006), modeling adolescents' sexual behavior on exposure to sexual content on television (Martino, Collins, Kanouse, Elliott, & Berry, 2005), modeling father-son communication about sex (Diiorio, McCarty, & Denzmore, 2006), predicting bullying and victimization (Mouttapa, Valente, Gallaher, Rohrbach, & Unger, 2004), predicting condom use among university students (Mashegoane, Moalusi, Peltzer, &

Ngoepe, 2004), predicting fruit and vegetable intake in children (Bere & Klepp, 2005), predicting heavy drinking in college students (Gilles, Turk, & Fresco, 2006), predicting physical activity behavior (Rhodes & Plotnikoff, 2005), predicting physician behavior to recommend colonoscopy (Honda & Gorin, 2006), predicting reproductive health behavioral intention in adolescent women with diabetes (Wang, Charron-Prochownik, Sereika, Siminerio, & Kim, 2006), predicting sexually risky behaviors among adolescent mothers (Koniak-Griffin & Stein, 2006), and profiling community-based rehabilitation volunteers (Sharma & Deepak, 2003). Table 7.2 summarizes these applications.

Some examples in which SCT has been used for primary prevention are for an active ergonomics training program in computer users (Greene, DeJoy, & Olejnik, 2005), family planning decision making (Ha, Jayasuriya, & Owen, 2005), an HIV prevention program in adolescents (Diiorio et al., 2006), a nutrition education program

TABLE 7.2   Examples of Applications of Social Cognitive Theory in Behavioral Research
Assessing medication adherence among low-literacy patients
Defining correlates of physical activity in fibromyalgia patients
Defining predictors of exercise participation
Identifying perceptions of whole-grain foods and the factors influencing their intake by children
Modeling adolescents' sexual behavior on exposure to sexual content on television
Modeling father-son communication about sex
Predicting bullying and victimization
Predicting condom use among university students
Predicting fruit and vegetable intake in children
Predicting heavy drinking in college students
Predicting physical activity behavior
Predicting physician behavior to recommend colonoscopy
Predicting reproductive health behavioral intention in adolescent women with diabetes
Predicting sexually risky behaviors among adolescent mothers
Profiling community-based rehabilitation volunteers

(Powers, Struempler, Guarino, & Parmer, 2005), a poison prevention education program (Schwartz, Howland, Mercurio-Zappala, & Hoffman, 2003), prevention and reduction of aggressive behavior (Orpinas & Horne, 2004), problem-solving skills (Sharma, Petosa, & Heaney, 1999; Shimazu, Kawakami, Irimajiri, Sakamoto, & Amano, 2005), a self-help physical activity intervention at the workplace (Griffin-Blake & DeJoy, 2006), a self-help weight management intervention (Tufano & Karras, 2005), self-regulation of driving among high-risk older drivers (Stalvey & Owsley, 2003), a sun protection intervention in preschoolers (Gritz et al., 2006), a smoking cessation program (Ramelson, Friedman, & Ockene, 1999), smoking prevention programs (Langlois, Petosa, & Hallam, 1999), a walking program (Rovniak, Hovell, Wojcik, Winett, & Martinez-Donate, 2005), and Web-assisted instruction for physical activity (Suminski & Petosa, 2006). Table 7.3 summarizes these applications.

TABLE 7.3   Examples of Applications of Social Cognitive Theory in Primary Prevention
Active ergonomics training program in computer users
Family planning decision making
HIV prevention program in adolescents
Nutrition education program
Poison prevention education program
Prevention and reduction of aggressive behavior
Problem-solving skills
Self-help physical activity intervention at the workplace
Self-help weight management intervention
Self-regulation of driving among high-risk older drivers
Smoking cessation program
Smoking prevention programs
Sun protection intervention in preschoolers
Walking program
Web-assisted instruction for physical activity

> *The field of health is changing from a disease model to a health model. It is just as meaningful to speak of levels of vitality and healthfulness as of degrees of impairment and debility. Health promotion should begin with goals not means. If health is the goal, biomedical interventions are not the only means to it.*
>
> —Bandura (2004, p.143)

Some examples in which SCT has been used for secondary and tertiary prevention are for adherence to continuous positive airway pressure (CPAP) treatment for sleep apnea (Stepnowsky, Marler, Palau, & Annette Brooks, 2006), behavior change intervention after knee replacement (Harnirattisai & Johnson, 2005), a childhood asthma management program (McGhan, Wells, & Befus, 1998), a diabetes education program (Chapman-Novakofski & Karduck, 2005), dietary approaches to reducing hypertension (Rankins, Sampson, Brown, & Jenkins-Salley, 2005), intervention to improve the quality of life for women with breast cancer (Graves, Carter, Anderson, & Winett, 2003), a lifestyle program for leg ulcer patients (Heinen, Bartholomew, Wensing, Kerkhof, & Achterberg,

TABLE 7.4   Examples of Applications of Social Cognitive Theory in Secondary and Tertiary Prevention
Adherence to continuous positive airway pressure (CPAP) treatment for sleep apnea
Behavior change intervention after knee replacement
Childhood asthma management program
Diabetes education program
Dietary approaches to reducing hypertension
Intervention to improve the quality of life for women with breast cancer
Lifestyle program for leg ulcer patients
Mammography screening among American Indian women
Medication self-management among people with epilepsy
Physical activity program for prostate cancer patients
Promotion of female condom use in a sexually transmitted disease clinic
Rehabilitation following myocardial infarction and coronary artery bypass grafting
Skin self-examination by patients at high risk for melanoma
Weight loss in overweight and obese low-income mothers

2006), mammography screening among American Indian women (Dignan et al., 2005), medication self-management among people with epilepsy (Diiorio et al., 2005), a physical activity program for prostate cancer patients (Taylor et al., 2006), promotion of female condom use in a sexually transmitted disease clinic (Artz et al., 2005), rehabilitation following myocardial infarction and coronary artery bypass grafting (Hiltunen et al., 2005), skin self-examination by patients at high risk for melanoma (Hay et al., 2006), and weight loss in overweight and obese low-income mothers (Klohe-Lehman et al., 2006). Table 7.4 summarizes these applications.

LIMITATIONS OF SOCIAL COGNITIVE THEORY

Social cognitive theory is a robust behavioral theory, and its biggest advantage is that it can be applied easily. The other important dimension of this theory is that social structural factors are integrated with personal determinants, which is often not the case with other theories of behavior. However, like all theories, this theory also has some limitations. Some critics have noted that the theory is about learning and is therefore more applicable for children. The theory is not specifically designed for changing behavior. For example, the stages of change theory is specific about changing behaviors and provides indications of the different stages through which a person moves. SCT provides no such guidance.

The theory has many constructs, and often it is not possible to reify all these constructs, which tends to limit the theory's usage. Ideally, a theory should be parsimonious. Also, the single most important predictor of the theory is identified as self-efficacy. Often the items that measure self-efficacy are very similar to the items that measure the behavior, thus adding to measurement bias. Further, questions meant to measure an individual's cognition in SCT often change and create the responder's thinking rather than tapping into how exactly that individual thinks to begin with. Prochaska (2006) has criticized SCT as lacking arrangement of constructs in mathematical relationships. As a result, different practitioners use different sets of constructs in different combinations. Finally, Prochaska (2006) notes that SCT-based interventions mainly target those who are prepared to change the behavior; in the process, such interventions miss a large majority of the population. A theory should provide guidance for change for people with varying levels of readiness.

SKILL-BUILDING ACTIVITY

Let us see how we can apply SCT to the issue of developing problem-solving skills in upper elementary school children. Figure 7.1 depicts each of the constructs from

SCT and links these with educational processes and behavioral objectives to develop problem-solving skills.

We need to be parsimonious in our selection of constructs from the theory, so let's choose six constructs. The health education intervention would start by modifying the construct of situational perception by brainstorming about potential stressors that would require problem solving by the children. A lecture to build knowledge about stressors and the steps of problem solving can be given. To modify outcome expectations, a discussion on the benefits of problem-solving skills can be organized. Some examples of these benefits could include increased popularity with friends, faster learning, better grades, more fun with family, and more fun at school. To modify outcome expectancies, the relevance of the anticipated outcomes to the students' personal lives can be discussed.

To modify self-efficacy, the steps of problem solving can be broken down into small steps. These steps could be as follows: (1) identify the stressor, (2) think of many ways to deal with each stressor, (3) think of all the good points about each way, (4)

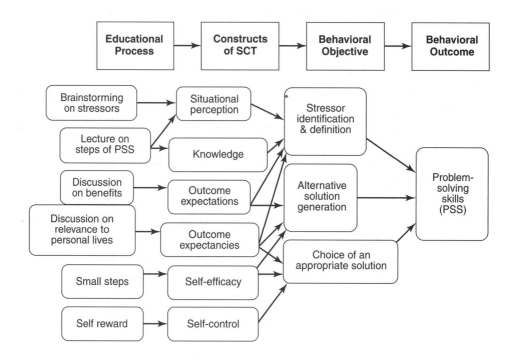

FIGURE 7.1   How Social Cognitive Theory (SCT) Has Been Used to Modify Problem-Solving Skills

think of all the bad points about each way, and (5) choose one solution after looking at the good and bad points for several possible solutions. Messages that role models use these steps of problem solving can be used to reinforce self-efficacy. Stress management techniques can be practiced while applying the steps of problem solving, which also reinforces self-efficacy. Finally, to modify self-control, the children can be instructed to write goals for applying problem-solving skills and then reward themselves upon accomplishing those goals.

Using this approach, you can plan a health education program for a behavior issue of your choice. Table 7.5 provides a set of questions to assist you in choosing educational methods that correspond to different constructs of social cognitive theory.

TABLE 7.5   Choosing the Educational Methods for Health Education Program Planning Using Social Cognitive Theory

1. What will be the best educational method to facilitate knowledge?
   - Lecture
   - Informational talk
   - Fact sheets
   - Other

2. What will be the best educational method to facilitate outcome expectations?
   - Discussion
   - Brainstorming
   - Role play
   - Simulation
   - Other

3. What will be the best educational method to facilitate outcome expectancies?
   - Discussion
   - Brainstorming
   - Role play
   - Simulation
   - Other

4. What will be the best educational method to facilitate situational perception?
   - Discussion
   - Brainstorming
   - Role play
   - Simulation
   - Other

(Continued)

TABLE 7.5   (Continued)

5. What will be the best educational method to facilitate changes in environment?
   - Making physical changes in the environment
   - Building social support
   - Providing access to health care
   - Other

6. What will be the best educational method to facilitate self-efficacy?
   - Demonstration
   - Role play
   - Video with a credible role model
   - Stress reduction techniques
       - Progressive muscle relaxation
       - Visual imagery
       - Autogenic training
       - Yoga/meditation
       - Other
   - Other

7. What will be the best educational method to facilitate self-efficacy in overcoming impediments?
   - Demonstration
   - Role play
   - Video with a credible role model
   - Stress reduction techniques
       - Progressive muscle relaxation
       - Visual imagery
       - Autogenic training
       - Yoga/meditation
       - Other
   - Other

8. What will be the best educational method to facilitate self-control?
   - Group formation
   - Coalition building
   - Registration of not-for-profit organization
   - Other

9. What will be the best educational method to facilitate emotional coping?
   - Progressive muscle relaxation
   - Autogenic training
   - Yoga/meditation
   - Visual imagery
   - Other

SUMMARY

Albert Bandura, a professor of psychology at Stanford University, is the originator of social cognitive theory (previously called social learning theory). This theory explains human behavior as a triadic reciprocal causation among behavior, environment, and personal factors (such as cognitions, affect, and biological events). Five basic human capabilities describe human beings according to this theory: symbolizing capability (use of symbols in attributing meaning to experiences), vicarious capability (learning from observing other people's behavior and the consequences they face), forethought capability (most behavior is purposive and regulated by prior thoughts), self-regulatory capability (setting of internal standards and self-evaluative reactions for one's behavior), and self-reflective capability (analysis of experiences and thinking about one's own thought processes).

The constructs of the theory include knowledge (learning of facts and gaining insights related to an action, idea, object, person, or situation), outcome expectations (the anticipation of the probable outcomes that would ensue as a result of engaging in the behavior), outcome expectancies (the value a person places on the probable outcomes that result from performing a behavior), situational perception (how a person perceives and interprets the environment around himself or herself), environment (physical or social circumstances or conditions that surround a person), self-efficacy (the confidence that a person has in his or her ability to pursue a behavior), self-efficacy in overcoming impediments (the confidence that a person has in overcoming barriers while performing a given behavior), goal setting or self-control (setting goals and developing plans to accomplish chosen behaviors), and emotional coping (techniques employed by the person to control the emotional and physiological states associated with acquisition of a new behavior). The constructs are amenable to modification by different educational methods. Social cognitive theory has been applied over the past 30 years in a variety of applications within health promotion and education.

REVIEW QUESTIONS

1. Describe the historical genesis of social cognitive theory.
2. Discuss reciprocal determinism.
3. Discuss the underpinnings of social cognitive theory.
4. What is self-efficacy and how can it be built?
5. Describe the constructs of social cognitive theory.

6. Discuss the limitations of social cognitive theory.
7. Apply social cognitive theory in changing a behavior of your choice for a target population of your choice.

WEBSITE

Go to the Web component of *Theoretical Foundations of Health Education and Health Promotion* at http://health.jbpub.com/foundations for Web exercises, additional resources related to this chapter, and student review tools.

GLOSSARY TERMS

emotional coping

environment

forethought capability

goal setting

outcome expectancies

outcome expectations

reciprocal determinism

self-control

self-efficacy in overcoming impediments

self-reflective capability

self-regulatory capability

situational perception

social cognitive theory (SCT)

social learning theory

symbolizing capability

vicarious capability

REFERENCES AND FURTHER READING

Allport, G. W. (1937). *Personality: A psychological interpretation*. New York: Holt and Company.

Artz, L., Macaluso, M., Kelaghan, J., Austin, H., Fleenor, M., Robey, L., et al. (2005). An intervention to promote the female condom to sexually transmitted disease clinic patients. *Behavior Modification, 29*(2), 318–369.

Bandura, A. (1969). *Principles of behavior modification*. New York: Prentice Hall.

Bandura, A. (1977). *Social learning theory*. Englewood Cliffs, NJ: Prentice Hall.

Bandura, A. (1986). *Social foundations of thought and action*. Englewood Cliffs, NJ: Prentice Hall.

Bandura, A. (Ed.) (1995). *Self-efficacy in changing societies*. New York: Cambridge University Press.

Bandura, A. (1997). *Self-efficacy: The exercise of control*. New York: W. H. Freeman.

Bandura, A. (2001a). Social cognitive theory: An agentic perspective. *Annual Review of Psychology, 52,* 1–26.

Bandura, A. (2001b). Social cognitive theory of mass communication. *Mediapsychology, 3,* 265–299.

Bandura, A. (2002). Social cognitive theory in cultural context. *Applied Psychology: An International Review, 51*(2), 269–290.

Bandura, A. (2004). Health promotion by social cognitive means. *Health Education and Behavior, 31,* 143–164.

Bandura, A. (2005). The primacy of self regulation in health promotion. *Applied Psychology: An International Review*, *54*(2), 245–254.

Bandura, A., & Walters, R. H. (1963). *Social learning and personality development*. New York: Holt, Rinehart and Winston.

Baranowski, T., Perry, C. L., & Parcel, G. S. (2002). How individuals, environments, and health behavior interact. Social cognitive theory. In K. Glanz, B. K. Rimer, & F. M. Lewis (Eds.), *Health behavior and health education: Theory, research, and practice* (3rd ed., pp. 165–184). San Francisco: Jossey-Bass.

Bere, E., & Klepp, K. I. (2005). Changes in accessibility and preferences predict children's future fruit and vegetable intake. *International Journal of Behavioral Nutrition and Physical Activity*, *2*, 15.

Burgess-Champoux, T., Marquart, L., Vickers, Z., & Reicks, M. (2006). Perceptions of children, parents, and teachers regarding whole-grain foods, and implications for a school-based intervention. *Journal of Nutrition Education and Behavior*, *38*(4), 230–237.

Carleton, R. A., Lasater, T. M., Assaf, A. R., Feldman, H. A., & McKinlay, S. (1995). The Pawtucket Heart Health Program: Community changes in cardiovascular risk factors and projected disease risk. *American Journal of Public Health*, *85*, 777–785.

Chapman-Novakofski, K., & Karduck, J. (2005). Improvement in knowledge, social cognitive theory variables, and movement through stages of change after a community-based diabetes education program. *Journal of the American Dietetic Association*, *105*(10), 1613–1616.

Dignan, M. B., Burhansstipanov, L., Hariton, J., Harjo, L., Rattler, T., Lee, R., et al. (2005). A comparison of two Native American Navigator formats: Face-to-face and telephone. *Cancer Control*, *12*(Suppl. 2), 28–33.

Diiorio, C., McCarty, F., & Denzmore, P. (2006). An exploration of social cognitive theory mediators of father-son communication about sex. *Journal of Pediatric Psychology*, *31*(9), 917–927.

Diiorio, C., Resnicow, K., McCarty, F., De, A. K., Dudley, W. N., Wang, D. T., et al. (2006). Keepin' it R.E.A.L.! Results of a mother-adolescent HIV prevention program. *Nursing Research*, *55*(1), 43–51.

Diiorio, C., Shafer, P. O., Letz, R., Henry, T. R., Schomer, D. L., Yeager, K., et al. (2005). Project EASE: A study to test a psychosocial model of epilepsy medication management. *Epilepsy and Behavior*, *5*(6), 926–936.

Dollard, J., & Miller, N. E. (1950). *Personality and psychotherapy*. New York: McGraw Hill.

Farquhar, J. W. (1978). The community-based model of life-style intervention trials. *American Journal of Epidemiology*, *108*, 103–111.

Farquhar, J. W., Fortmann, S. P., Maccoby, N., Haskell, W. I., Williams, P., Flora, J., et al. (1985). The Stanford five-city project: Design and methods. *American Journal of Epidemiology*, *108*, 103–111.

Farquhar, J. W., Maccoby, N., Wood, P. D., Alexander, J. K., Breitrose, H., Brown, Jr., et al. (1977). Community education for cardiovascular health. *Lancet*, *1*, 1192–1195.

Freud, S. (1960). *The ego and the id*. New York: Norton. (Original work published 1923.)

Gilles, D. M., Turk, C. L., & Fresco, D. M. (2006). Social anxiety, alcohol expectancies, and self-efficacy as predictors of heavy drinking in college students. *Addictive Behaviors*, *31*(3), 388–398.

Graves, K. D., Carter, C. L., Anderson, E. S., & Winett, R. A. (2003). Quality of life pilot intervention for breast cancer patients: Use of social cognitive theory. *Palliative and Support Care, 1*(2), 121–134.

Greene, B. L., DeJoy, D. M., & Olejnik, S. (2005). Effects of an active ergonomics training program on risk exposure, worker beliefs, and symptoms in computer users. *Work, 24*(1), 41–52.

Griffin-Blake, C. S., & DeJoy, D. M. (2006). Evaluation of social-cognitive versus stage-matched, self-help physical activity interventions at the workplace. *American Journal of Health Promotion, 20*(3), 200–209.

Gritz, E. R., Tripp, M. K., James, A. S., Harris, R. B., Mueller, N. H., Chamberlain, R. M., et al. (2006). Effects of a preschool staff intervention on children's sun protection: Outcomes of Sun Protection Is Fun! *Health Education and Behavior*, Epub PMID: 16740505.

Ha, B. T., Jayasuriya, R., & Owen, N. (2005). Increasing male involvement in family planning decision making: Trial of a social-cognitive intervention in rural Vietnam. *Health Education Research, 20*(5), 548–556.

Harnirattisai, T., & Johnson, R. A. (2005). Effectiveness of a behavioral change intervention in Thai elders after knee replacement. *Nursing Research, 54*(2), 97–107.

Hay, J. L., Oliveria, S. A., Dusza, S. W., Phelan, D. L., Ostroff, J. S., & Halpern, A. C. (2006). Psychosocial mediators of a nurse intervention to increase skin self-examination in patients at high risk for melanoma. *Cancer Epidemiology Biomarkers and Prevention, 15*(6), 1212–1216.

Heinen, M. M., Bartholomew, L. K., Wensing, M., Kerkhof, P., & Achterberg, T. (2006). Supporting adherence and healthy lifestyles in leg ulcer patients: Systematic development of the Lively Legs program for dermatology outpatient clinics. *Patient Education and Counseling, 61*(2), 279–291.

Hiltunen, E. F., Winder, P. A., Rait, M. A., Buselli, E. F., Carroll, D. L., & Rankin, S. H. (2005). Implementation of efficacy enhancement nursing interventions with cardiac elders. *Rehabilitation Nursing, 30*(6), 221–229.

Honda, K., & Gorin, S. S. (2006). A model of stage of change to recommend colonoscopy among urban primary care physicians. *Health Psychology, 25*(1), 65–73.

Kaewthummanukul, T., Brown, K. C., Weaver, M. T., & Thomas, R. R. (2006). Predictors of exercise participation in female hospital nurses. *Journal of Advanced Nursing, 54*(6), 663–675.

Kalichman, S. C., Cain, D., Fuhrel, A., Eaton, L., Di Fonzo, K., & Ertl, T. (2005). Assessing medication adherence self-efficacy among low-literacy patients: Development of a pictographic visual analogue scale. *Health Education Research, 20*(1), 24–35.

Klohe-Lehman, D. M., Freeland-Graves, J., Anderson, E. R., McDowell, T., Clarke, K. K., Hanss-Nuss, H., et al. (2006). Nutrition knowledge is associated with greater weight loss in obese and overweight low-income mothers. *Journal of American Dietetic Association, 106*(1), 65–75.

Koniak-Griffin, D., & Stein, J. A. (2006). Predictors of sexual risk behaviors among adolescent mothers in a human immunodeficiency virus prevention program. *Journal of Adolescent Health, 38*(3), 297.e1-11.

Langlois, M. A., Petosa, R., & Hallam, J. S. (1999). Why do effective smoking prevention programs work? Student changes in social cognitive theory constructs. *Journal of School Health, 69*(8), 326–331.

Luepker, R. V., Murray, D. M., Jacobs, D. R., Mittelmark, M. B., Bracht, N., Carlaw, R., et al. (1994). Community education for cardiovascular disease prevention: Risk factor changes in the Minnesota Heart Health Program. *American Journal of Public Health, 84*, 1383–1393.

Martino, S. C., Collins, R. L., Kanouse, D. E., Elliott, M., & Berry, S. H. (2005). Social cognitive processes mediating the relationship between exposure to television's sexual content and adolescents' sexual behavior. *Journal of Personality and Social Psychology, 89*(6), 914–924.

Mashegoane, S., Moalusi, K. P., Peltzer, K., & Ngoepe, M. A. (2004). The prediction of condom use intention among South African university students. *Psychological Reports, 95*(2), 407–417.

McGhan, S. L., Wells, H. M., & Befus, A. D. (1998). The "Roaring Adventures of Puff": A childhood asthma education program. *Journal of Pediatric Health Care, 12*(4), 191–195.

Mouttapa, M., Valente, T., Gallaher, P., Rohrbach, L. A., & Unger, J. B. (2004). Social network predictors of bullying and victimization. *Adolescence, 39*(154), 315–335.

Oliver, K., & Cronan, T. A. (2005). Correlates of physical activity among women with fibromyalgia syndrome. *Annals of Behavioral Medicine, 29*(1), 44–53.

Orpinas, P., & Horne, A. M. (2004). A teacher-focused approach to prevent and reduce students' aggressive behavior: The GREAT Teacher Program. *American Journal of Preventive Medicine, 26* (Suppl. 1), 29–38.

Powers, A. R., Struempler, B. J., Guarino, A., & Parmer, S. M. (2005). Effects of a nutrition education program on the dietary behavior and nutrition knowledge of second-grade and third-grade students. *Journal of School Health, 75*(4), 129–133.

Prochaska, J. O. (2006). Is social cognitive theory becoming a transtheoretical model? A comment on Dijkstra et al. (2006). *Addiction, 101*, 916–917.

Ramelson, H. Z., Friedman, R. H., & Ockene, J. K. (1999). An automated telephone-based smoking cessation education and counseling system. *Patient Education and Counseling, 36*(2), 131–144.

Rankins, J., Sampson, W., Brown, B., & Jenkins-Salley, T. (2005). Dietary Approaches to Stop Hypertension (DASH) intervention reduces blood pressure among hypertensive African American patients in a neighborhood health care center. *Journal of Nutrition Education and Behavior, 37*(5), 259–264.

Rhodes, R. E., & Plotnikoff, R. C. (2005). Can current physical activity act as a reasonable proxy measure of future physical activity? Evaluating cross-sectional and passive prospective designs with the use of social cognition models. *Preventive Medicine, 40*(5), 547–555.

Rotter, J. B. (1954). *Social learning and clinical psychology.* Englewood Cliffs, NJ: Prentice Hall.

Rovniak, L. S., Hovell, M. F., Wojcik, J. R., Winett, R. A., & Martinez-Donate, A. P. (2005). Enhancing theoretical fidelity: An e-mail-based walking program demonstration. *American Journal of Health Promotion, 20*(2), 85–95.

Schwartz, L., Howland, M. A., Mercurio-Zappala, M., & Hoffman, R. S. (2003). The use of focus groups to plan poison prevention education programs for low-income populations. *Health Promotion Practice, 4*(3), 340–346.

Sharma, M., & Deepak, S. (2003). An intercountry study of expectations, roles, attitudes and behaviors of community-based rehabilitation volunteers. *Asia Pacific Disability Rehabilitation Journal, 14*, 179–190.

Sharma, M., Petosa, R., & Heaney, C. A. (1999). Evaluation of a brief intervention based on social cognitive theory to develop problem solving skills among sixth grade children. *Health Education and Behavior, 26,* 465–477.

Shimazu, A., Kawakami, N., Irimajiri, H., Sakamoto, M., & Amano, S. (2005). Effects of Web-based psychoeducation on self-efficacy, problem solving behavior, stress responses and job satisfaction among workers: A controlled clinical trial. *Journal of Occupational Health, 47*(5), 405–413.

Skinner, B. F. (1953). *Science and human behavior.* New York: Macmillan.

Stalvey, B. T., & Owsley, C. (2003). The development and efficacy of a theory-based educational curriculum to promote self-regulation among high-risk older drivers. *Health Promotion Practice, 4*(2), 109–119.

Stepnowsky, C. J., Marler, M. R., Palau, J., & Annette Brooks, J. (2006). Social-cognitive correlates of CPAP adherence in experienced users. *Sleep Medicine, 7*(4), 350–356.

Suminski, R. R., & Petosa, R. (2006). Web-assisted instruction for changing social cognitive variables related to physical activity. *Journal of American College Health, 54*(4), 219–225.

Taylor, C. L., Demoor, C., Smith, M. A., Dunn, A. L., Basen-Engquist, K., Nielsen, I., et al. (2006). Active for Life After Cancer: A randomized trial examining a lifestyle physical activity program for prostate cancer patients. *Psychooncology, 15*(10), 847–862.

Tufano, J. T., & Karras, B. T. (2005). Mobile eHealth interventions for obesity: A timely opportunity to leverage convergence trends. *Journal of Medical Internet Research, 7*(5), e58.

Wang, S. L., Charron-Prochownik, D., Sereika, S. M., Siminerio, L., & Kim, Y. (2006). Comparing three theories in predicting reproductive health behavioral intention in adolescent women with diabetes. *Pediatric Diabetes, 7*(2), 108–115.

Young, D. R., Haskell, W. L., Jatulis, D. E., & Fortmann, S. P. (1993). Associations between changes in physical activity and risk factors for coronary heart disease in a community-based sample of men and women: The Stanford Five-City Project. *American Journal of Epidemiology, 138,* 205–216.

CHAPTER 8

Social Marketing

KEY CONCEPTS _____

- Audience segmentation
- Exchange theory
- Marketing mix
- Partnership
- Place
- Policy

- Price
- Product
- Promotion
- Publics
- Purse strings
- Social marketing

AFTER READING THIS CHAPTER YOU SHOULD BE ABLE TO _____

- Describe the historical genesis of social marketing
- List the constructs of social marketing
- Differentiate between commercial marketing and social marketing
- Summarize the applications of social marketing in health education and health promotion
- Identify key constructs from the social marketing model
- Apply the social marketing model for influencing a health behavior of your choice

This chapter discusses the social marketing model. **Social marketing** is the use of commercial marketing techniques to help a target population acquire a beneficial health behavior (Weinreich, 1999). Social marketing is becoming popular in the governmental sector as well as the not-for-profit sector in the United States and many other countries around the world for influencing behaviors. In the field of health, some important applications of social marketing include family planning, recruiting blood donors, reducing infant mortality through oral rehydration, and preventing smoking in adolescents (Andreasen & Kotler, 2003). The primary difference between social marketing and commercial marketing is in their objectives. In social marketing, the primary purpose is to benefit the target audience and change behaviors that have social implications.

This chapter begins by describing the historical aspects of the genesis of social marketing. Next it delineates the differences between commercial marketing and social marketing and describes the social marketing approach and the various constructs that make up this model. It then discusses the applications of social marketing in health education and health promotion. Finally, it discusses the limitations of social marketing and presents a skill-building application.

HISTORICAL PERSPECTIVES

Social marketing had its origins in India, where it was used in the 1960s to promote the family planning program, particularly the use of condoms (Harvey, 1999). The process entailed subsidizing condoms and supplying them through existing commercial distribution networks, using the mass media and other retail marketing techniques (Thapa, Prasad, Rao, Severy, & Rao, 1994). Partnerships were formed with corporations such as Unilever and Brooke Bond Tea Company to market the Nirodh brand of condoms. Under the program the sales of condoms reached over one billion in the mid-1990s, a multifold jump from the

> *Social marketing is the application of commercial marketing techniques to the analysis, planning, execution, and evaluation of programs designed to influence the voluntary behavior of target audiences in order to improve their personal welfare and that of their society.*
>
> —Andreasen (1995, p. 7)

initial years of the program. The program continues to be one of the largest applications of social marketing in the world and has been expanded to include other products such as oral contraceptives, oral rehydration solution, iron folate, and female condoms.

In the United States, a sociologist, G. D. Wiebe, first suggested in the 1950s that marketing might be applied to things such as "selling brotherhood" and other social applications (Wiebe, 1951–1952). This suggestion was incorporated into the work of Philip Kotler in the late 1960s. Kotler and Levy (1969) suggested that marketing was a pervasive societal activity that included all transactions. Kotler and Zaltman (1971, p. 5) first defined social marketing as "the design, implementation, and control of programs calculated to influence the acceptability of social ideas and involving considerations of product planning, pricing, communication, distribution, and marketing research." However, interest in social marketing was lukewarm throughout the 1970s and most of the 1980s (Andreasen, 2003). The main type of social marketing that occurred was marketing of contraceptives, in which the product was just like a product in commercial marketing and a nominal price was involved. Not much marketing of ideas was done.

Social marketing made major advancements in the late 1980s and throughout the 1990s. In 1989 the first textbook on social marketing was published by Kotler and

Roberto. They defined social marketing as a "social change technology involving the design, implementation, and control of programs aimed at increasing the acceptability of a social idea or practice in one or more groups of target adopters" (Kotler & Roberto, 1989, p. 24), thus placing social marketing in synchrony with health education and health promotion. In 1995, Andreasen defined social marketing as "the application of commercial marketing techniques to the analysis, planning, execution, and evaluation of programs designed to influence the voluntary behavior of target audiences in order to improve their personal welfare and that of their society" (p. 7). This definition brought the idea closer to health education and health promotion, where the purpose is also behavior change.

In 1994 the journal *Social Marketing Quarterly* was founded. In 1999, the Social Marketing Institute was founded in Washington, DC, with a mission to advance the science and art of social marketing. Some of the major social marketing initiatives in the 1990s were the U.S. Department of Agriculture's 5-a-Day campaign; the Centers for Disease Control and Prevention's campaign to inform health care professionals and the public that stomach ulcers were caused by the bacterium *Helicobacter pylori* and could be cured with antibiotics; North Carolina's statewide seat belt enforcement campaign, the "Click It or Ticket" program, which is still in use in other states; and a national breast-feeding promotional campaign through the Women, Infants and Children (WIC) program (Social Marketing Institute, 2006).

> *Social marketing consists of voluntary exchange between two or more parties, in which each is trying to further its own perceived self-interest while recognizing the need to accommodate the perceived self-interest of the other to achieve its own ends.*
>
> —Rothschild (1999)

Alan Andreasen (2006) laments in his book *Social Marketing in the 21st Century* that at present social marketing is in danger of being "pigeonholed as a downstream approach." He believes that most social marketing applications are geared toward rectifying bad behaviors, such as smoking, neglecting prenatal care, and so on. As a result, opportunities for using social marketing to foster positive behaviors are being lost. In any case, the social marketing approach is quite strong, as evidenced by the growing number of publications and diverse applications using this model.

DIFFERENCES BETWEEN COMMERCIAL MARKETING AND SOCIAL MARKETING

The primary difference between social marketing and commercial marketing is their objectives. In social marketing, the primary purpose is to benefit the target audience and change behaviors that have social implications. Andreasen and Kotler (2003) have identified additional differences between commercial marketing and social marketing (Table 8.1). The expectations in social marketing are more demanding, the scrutiny is done from a variety of sources, the idea that is sold is often totally new, and the educational level of the target audience is usually low. Social marketing often has to address what people do not want to change, has a high level of involvement between the marketer and

TABLE 8.1	**Differences Between Commercial Marketing and Social Marketing**	
Attribute	**Commercial Marketing**	**Social Marketing**
Purpose	Making profits	Making behavior change for social causes
Expectations	Modest	Demanding, such as complete eradication of a problem or universal adoption of a behavior
Scrutiny	Usually done in the private sector	Done from a variety of sources: government, public, and funders
Novelty	Usually selling a known product	Sometimes selling an idea that is totally new (e.g., bacteria cause ulcers)
Educational level of audiences	Variable and includes different sections	Usually vulnerable sections with low literacy
Distasteful behaviors	Usually caters to what public likes	Often has to address what people do not want to change (e.g., wearing a seat belt)
Involvement between marketer and public	Less	Often very high
Benefits	Clear in profits	Often invisible
Third parties	Direct benefits to people using the product	Often the benefits are to third parties, such as poor people
Self-rewards	Usually the rewards are external (e.g., discount, better product)	Usually the rewards offered are internal or self-rewards (e.g., weight loss)
Budgets	Generous	Limited
Funding	Usually private	Usually government or not-for-profit foundations
Choices of products	Numerous	Limited

the public, and often has invisible benefits or benefits that go to third parties. The rewards offered for making the recommended change are usually self-rewards, and budgets and the choice of products are limited.

APPROACH AND CONSTRUCTS OF SOCIAL MARKETING

A core concept in marketing is that of **exchange theory** (Thackeray & Brown, 2005). Exchange theory implies the transfer or transaction of something valuable between two individuals or groups (Flora, Schooler, & Pierseon, 1997). In social marketing, this transaction is voluntary and must be of benefit to the consumer (Lefebvre & Flora, 1988). Benefits as viewed by the target audience must outweigh the costs for making the behavior change. For example, in a health promotion program that encourages participants to engage in physical activity, the costs to individuals would be loss of free time, loss of time to watch television, and so on. The benefits the social marketer offers must be more appealing than these losses, such as more energy to do things, the ability to lose weight, and so on.

Different authors have described different steps in social marketing. There is no universal consensus regarding a social marketing model among social marketing professionals. Andreasen (1995) has defined six stages:

1. *Listening stage.* Background analysis and listening to the target audience are done.
2. *Planning stage.* The marketing mission, objectives, goals, and strategy are defined.
3. *Structuring stage.* A marketing organization, procedures, benchmarks, and feedback mechanisms are established.
4. *Pretesting stage.* Key program elements are tested.
5. *Implementing stage.* The strategy is put into effect.
6. *Monitoring stage.* Program progress is tracked.

Andreasen (1995) notes that the movement across these six stages is not linear but is an upward spiral process. The target audience is central in this planning process.

The National Cancer Institute (2005) has suggested four steps in a wheel of planning for social marketing: (1) planning and strategy development; (2) developing and pretesting concepts, messages, and materials; (3) implementing the program; and (4) assessing effectiveness and making refinements.

Weinreich (1999) has described a somewhat similar sequence of five steps: (1) planning, (2) message and material development, (3) pretesting, (4) implementation, and (5) evaluation. The first step, planning, entails four components: formative research, analysis, segmenting the target audience, and strategy development. **Formative research** involves collecting quantitative and qualitative data about the problem, its context, the attitudes and behaviors of the target audience, ways to reach the target audience, and existing messages and materials. In the analysis component, the problem, environment, and resources available for the program are analyzed. In **audience segmentation**, distinct groups of people who are similar to each other in particular characteristics and are thus likely to respond to messages in a similar way are identified. Segments may be based on such factors as geography, demography, medical history, personality characteristics, attitudes, behaviors, and so on. After identifying the segments, data about the target audience's knowledge, attitudes, and behavior is collected. Qualitative methods such as focus groups, in-depth interviews, or case studies or quantitative methods such as surveys are used in this component. The fourth component in the first step is *strategy development*, in which the goals and objectives are set and the social marketing mix is chosen. In marketing, the four Ps that define the **marketing mix** are product, price, place, and promotion. Weireich (1999) has defined four additional Ps for social marketing: publics, partnership, policy, and purse strings.

The first P is **product**. In social marketing, the product is the behavior or offering that is intended to be adopted by the target audience. The product can be a physical product, such as condoms; a service, such as mammography; a practice, such as eating five or more servings of fruits and vegetables a day; or an intangible idea, such as environmental protection. The product must be able to fill a need felt by people and must be appealing and attractive. It is important to link potential benefits and subsequent benefits to the product, thereby making it attractive to the target audience. It is also important to find out about competing ideas (products) and why the target audience would prefer the product being socially marketed. For example, if one were marketing physical activity, the competition would be from sedentary activities such as watching television or surfing the Internet. Knowing the competition allows one to plan counterarguments.

Price refers to the tangible and intangible things that the target audience has to give up in order to adopt the new idea (product). The price could be money, which is tangible, but often it is an intangible cost such as time, effort, or giving up an old way of life. Formative research should find out what the target audience considers to be the price for adopting the new behavior. This research should include an assessment of all barriers that confront the target population. Ways to minimize the costs and remove barriers must be considered in designing the strategy.

In commercial marketing, **place** refers to the distribution channels, or where and how the customers will get the product. In social marketing, it refers to where the target audience will be exposed to messages about the behavior. For example, if we were advocating physical activity, we would need to determine whether the message would be delivered at the home of the person by a television spot, a newspaper article, or through the Internet. The message could also be given at the workplace, either on a bulletin board or by e-mail. The message could be given in community forums, such as the grocery store, local church, community center, or doctor's office. After deciding the place, the messages need to be targeted to that particular place to be effective. Along with the messages, the product (idea or behavior) should also be made available at that particular place. For example, if physical activity is to be done at home, then a stationary bike or treadmill should be available so that the person can exercise while watching television. Distribution channels, or who will deliver the message, need to be decided. For example, if we want to promote physical activity, we could use a peer-to-peer network or we could use counseling sessions through phone calls from the doctor's office.

Promotion is the mechanism by which one gets the message across to the target audience. Various techniques are used. Examples are advertisements, such as public service announcements (PSAs); public relations, such as writing letters to the editor or creating press releases; promotions, such as having a contest; media advocacy, such as holding a press event for policy change; personal selling, such as by having a counseling session; special events, such as organizing a health fair; and entertainment, such as organizing a psychodrama.

The fifth P, **publics**, refers to both the primary and secondary audiences involved in the program. The primary audience is the target audience to whom the behavior change is targeted. In making their decisions, the members of the primary target audience may depend on other people. For example, in a smoking prevention program for adolescents, their parents, peers, and teachers would all be secondary audiences who need to provide the same messages. Policy makers are another secondary group that influence any decision and need to be involved.

Partnership refers to collaborating with multiple individuals or organizations who work on the same issue. No single organization has sufficient resources to significantly influence the huge outcome usually expected in social marketing. As a result, it makes sense for different organizations to form a coalition around the issue and then target it from different angles. Such collaborations can occur if two organizations either share the same goal or share the same target population.

Policy refers to creating the environmental supports needed to sustain the behavior change. For example, for promoting five or more servings of fruits and vegetables, there must be policies in place that allow for vending machines to dispense such items and that make fruits and vegetables available at affordable rates. Some effective approaches for modifying policies are techniques such as advocacy, media advocacy, lobbying, and working with policy makers or legislators.

The final P is the **purse strings**, which refers to the amount of money available for the campaign. In social marketing, there is no profit to sustain the efforts. All efforts in social marketing depend on resources in the form of donations or grants; therefore, grant writing is an important aspect of running a social marketing campaign. Other sources of funding, including selling a tangible product, must also be considered. Table 8.2 summarizes the eight Ps of social marketing.

The second step in social marketing is message and materials development. This step has three components: identifying appropriate channels, developing effective messages, and developing creative strategy. Identifying appropriate channels entails identifying where the target population will be performing the behavior (place) and then matching the channels. For example, if physical activity is to be performed at community centers, then the channels of health fairs at the community center, community center newsletter announcements, billboard announcements, and so on, would need to be organized. The step of developing effective messages needs to use some of the behavioral theories elaborated in this book, such as the health belief model, transtheoretical model, theory of reasoned action, theory of planned behavior, social cognitive theory, and the diffusion of innovations model. Developing creative strategy entails being creative in packaging the set of messages and materials.

The third step in social marketing is pretesting. Some of the aspects that need to be checked while pretesting the materials are their acceptability by the target audience, attractiveness to the target population, comprehension by the target population, completeness, and appropriateness for the target population. Techniques such as focus groups, nominal groups, central location interviews, questionnaires, and expert review can be used.

The fourth step in social marketing is implementation, in which the strategy is put into action. The final stage is evaluation. A variety of designs and methods can be used in the evaluation step, such as a post-test only design, a single group pretest/post-test design, or an experimental design with a control group. In terms of methods, one can use self-reports as well as observational methods.

> *Social marketing is a larger idea than social promotion and advertising. We need to highlight the importance of the other three Ps, product, price, and place, in determining whether a social marketing campaign will be successful. We must add the idea that client behavior analysis, segmentation, and positioning are critical concepts in developing our social marketing approach.*
>
> —Kotler (2005, p. 147)

TABLE 8.2   Key Constructs of Social Marketing

Construct	Definition	How to Modify?
Product	Behavior or offering that is intended for the target audience to adopt	• Matching with a need felt by the target audience • Making it appealing and attractive • Linking potential benefits and subsequent benefits to the product • Finding out about the competing ideas (products) and why the target audience would prefer the product being socially marketed
Price	Tangible and intangible things that the target audience has to give up in order to adopt the new idea (product)	• Finding ways to minimize the costs • Finding ways to eliminate barriers
Place	Where the target audience will perform the behavior	• Targeting messages at the particular place where the behavior will be performed • Making the product (idea or behavior) available at that particular place • Choosing appropriate distribution channels, or who will deliver the message
Promotion	Mechanism by which one gets the message across to the target audience	• Advertising • Public relations • Promotions • Media advocacy • Personal selling • Special events • Entertainment
Publics	Primary and secondary audiences involved in the program	• Involving primary audiences • Involving secondary audiences

TABLE 8.2 *(Continued)*		
Partnership	Establishing collaboration with multiple individuals or organizations who work on the same issue	• Building coalitions
Policy	Creating the environmental supports needed to sustain the behavior change	• Advocating, lobbying, and creating policies regarding the issue
Purse strings	Amount of money available for the campaign	• Writing grants • Selling a tangible product

APPLICATIONS OF SOCIAL MARKETING

Social marketing has been used in a variety of applications in health education and health promotion. Some examples of these applications are an antitobacco campaign (Lin & Hullman, 2005), a campaign to improve antibiotic use (Goossens et al., 2006), a campaign to reduce the stigma of mental illness (Corrigan & Gelb, 2006), a community-wide physical activity campaign (Reger-Nash et al., 2006), designing a cancer prevention program (Miner, White, Lubenow, & Palmer, 2005), a diabetes prevention program (Bachar et al., 2006), an educational program aimed at improving prescribing for hypertension (Horn et al., 2006), family health advocacy for pregnant and parenting women (Baffour, Jones, & Contreras, 2006), increasing cervical cancer screening (Millett, Zelenyanszki, Furlong, & Binysh, 2005), increasing condom use (Meekers, Agha, & Klein, 2005), increasing female condom use (Meekers & Richter, 2005), increasing syphilis awareness (Vega & Roland, 2005), increasing use of bicycle helmets (Ludwig, Buchholz, & Clarke, 2005), iron-folic acid supplementation in Cambodian women (Crape et al., 2005), leprosy elimination in Sri Lanka (Williams, Dewapura, Gunawardene, & Settinayake, 1998), nutrition education in preschoolers (Young, Anderson, Beckstrom, Bellows, & Johnson, 2004), physical activity promotion in adolescent girls (Staten, Birnbaum, Jobe, & Elder, 2006), promoting insecticide-treated nets in Tanzania (Maxwell, Rwegoshora, Magesa, & Curtis, 2006), promoting iron nutrition for at-risk infants (Verrall, Napash,

> *For decades the health sector has watched as big companies have used marketing to wreak havoc on public health. Social marketing enables us to fight fire with fire.*
>
> —Hastings and McDermott (2006, p. 1212)

Leclerc, Mercure, & Gray-Donald, 2006), promoting preconceptional use of folic acid (Quinn, Hauser, Bell-Ellison, Rodriguez, & Frias, 2006), recruiting men who have sex with men for HIV research (Silvestre et al., 2006), reducing marijuana and alcohol use among adolescents (Slater et al., 2006), and a self-help weight management intervention (Tufano & Karras, 2005). Table 8.3 summarizes these applications.

TABLE 8.3   Examples of Applications of Social Marketing in Health Education and Health Promotion

Antitobacco campaign

Campaign to improve antibiotic use

Campaign to reduce the stigma of mental illness

Community-wide physical activity campaign

Designing cancer prevention programs

Diabetes prevention program

Educational program aimed at improving prescribing for hypertension

Family health advocacy for pregnant and parenting women

Increasing cervical cancer screening

Increasing condom use

Increasing female condom use

Increasing syphilis awareness

Increasing use of bicycle helmets

Iron-folic acid supplementation in Cambodian women

Leprosy elimination in Sri Lanka

Nutrition education in preschoolers

Physical activity promotion in adolescent girls

Promoting insecticide-treated nets in Tanzania

Promoting iron nutrition for at-risk infants

Promoting preconceptional use of folic acid

Recruiting men who have sex with men for HIV research

Reducing marijuana and alcohol use among adolescents

Self-help weight management intervention

LIMITATIONS OF SOCIAL MARKETING

Social marketing is a useful model that is still being refined. There are definitive advantages to this approach, such as extensive formative research, pretesting of the components before implementation, and the use of the marketing mix. However, like all other models and theories, social marketing has some limitations. First, in public health, the goal is to reach as many people as possible; however, in social marketing, audience segmentation and the use of tailored messages filter out many people who may be in need of the services or behavior change. Second, social marketing requires a lot of lead time for extensive formative research and pretesting (Marshall, Bryant, Keller, & Fridinger, 2006). Often the program planners do not have that much time and need to implement the intervention faster; they also often do not have the resources to expend on preplanning.

Social marketing has been labeled "motivational manipulation," especially by thinkers from third world countries (Banerji, 1986). Delivery of health education programs as social marketing campaigns that rely on technomanagerial approaches often drains resources that could be used to build the basic infrastructure in developing country contexts. Sometimes the solutions advocated by social marketing in these situations are Band-Aid solutions that do not address the root causes and do not involve community participation. Almost always, the social marketer decides what behaviors will constitute improvement; community members do not have much say. This unequal playing field between marketers and public poses ethical dilemmas as well (Grier & Bryant, 2005).

Andreasen (2006) notes that social marketing as an approach to social change lacks clarity. There are multiple definitions, the field is not well differentiated and lacks academic stature, and there is a lack of appreciation of social marketing at top levels. These observations are based on empirical research from over 300 personal interviews, 100 field questionnaires, and two focus groups conducted by Social Marketing Institute researchers.

Social marketing is usually effective for behaviors that need to be changed once or only a few times, but is not effective for behaviors that must be repeated and maintained over a period of time (Evans, 2006). Finally, Peattie and Peattie (2003) note that social marketing depends too much on commercial marketing for its theoretical underpinnings and must formulate its own

> *Social marketing needs to be marketed to major social action groups, both governmental and nongovernmental, so that these groups will seek more social marketing consultants and offer more funding for social marketing campaigns. This will convince marketing students and marketing professionals that they can find a challenging and remunerative career in social marketing.*
>
> —Kotler (2005, p. 147)

theoretical basis. They suggest that the four Ps should be renamed as follows: social proposition (product), costs (price), accessibility (place), and communication (promotion).

SKILL-BUILDING ACTIVITY

Let us see how we can apply the social marketing model to the issue of promoting physical activity among middle-aged women. Let us assume that formative research and audience segmentation have identified the target audience as African American women. Figure 8.1 provides a diagrammatic depiction of the application of social marketing to this example.

The first construct that needs to be determined is product. We need to articulate a specific behavior, which could be defined as 30 minutes of moderate-intensity physical activity on at least five days of a week (preferably all days). Some activities that might appeal to this audience are brisk walking, doing yard work, swimming, riding a bicycle, and dancing. A brief message that could appeal is "Work out for 30 minutes-a-day." The message would need to be pretested and refined with the members of the target audience

The second construct that needs to be reified is price. Modification of costs and barriers needs to be done. Some potential costs are time, child care, health club dues, discomfort, and missing a favorite TV show. These could be countered by emphasizing that the activity takes only 30 minutes, initially reimbursing child care costs, offering a subsidized fee for health clubs or finding activities that can be done at home, clarifying that discomfort disappears with regular activity, and designing activities around the TV. Some potential barriers include lack of motivation, lack of skills, having no one to exercise with, and unsafe neighborhoods. These could be countered by having self-rewards, providing free lessons, having participants exercise in pairs or with a peer or a spouse, and stressing that participants should exercise at times and places when it is safe.

The place for giving out the message could be at home through television, newspaper, or the Internet. Or it could be at the workplace through a bulletin board, e-mail, or a supervisor's memo. It could also be community outlets such as a grocery store, shopping mall, church, community center, or doctor's office. Community outlets, especially churches or community centers, would generally be good for this target audience.

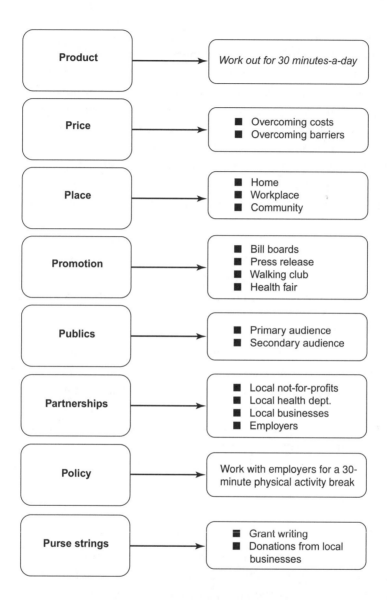

FIGURE 8.1   How the Social Marketing Mix Can Be Used to Promote Physical Activity

Promotion can be done through a billboard campaign in the community that shows the message "Work out for 30 minutes-a-day" and the image of an African American woman engaged in physical activity. Additional promotion can be done through a press release for all community outlets, such as newspapers, television channels, and radio shows. In addition, a walking club can be formed and promoted in the community. A community-based event such as a health fair can be used to launch the walking club.

The fifth construct is publics. The primary audience for this campaign would be African American women, who would be targeted with the message. The secondary audience would be peers and spouses, who would need to be mobilized to help participants adhere to the physical activity routine.

To modify the construct of partnership, the organization initiating this program would need to work with local nonprofit agencies, such as the American Heart Association, American Cancer Society, local health department, local businesses, employers, and local gyms. Ideally, it would be nice to form a coalition to which everyone can contribute systematically.

To modify policy, if feasible, the organization can work with employers to allow time for being physically active while at work. For example, a break of 30 minutes can be given to women for walking while they are at the office. The final construct is purse strings, which would involve the organization writing a grant to obtain funding. In-kind donations from local businesses can also be obtained.

Using this approach, you can plan to work on designing a social marketing–based campaign for a health behavior issue in a target audience of your choice. Table 8.4 provides a set of questions to assist you in shaping the constructs of the social marketing mix.

SUMMARY

Social marketing is the use of commercial marketing techniques to help a target population acquire a beneficial health behavior. Social marketing had its origins in India in the 1960s for promoting the family planning program by marketing condoms. In the United States the approach began to be used in the 1970s; it is at present a useful technique for behavior change.

Social marketing differs from commercial marketing in that social marketing is more demanding, the scrutiny is done from a variety of sources, the idea that is sold is often totally new, and the educational level of the target audience is usually low. Also, social marketing often has to address what people do not want to change, has

TABLE 8.4 Shaping the Constructs of the Social Marketing Mix for Health Education Program Planning

1. What should be considered while developing the product?
   - One-time behavior or continuing behavior
   - Low-involvement behavior or high-involvement behavior
   - Individual decision involved in behavior or group decision involved in behavior
   - Creativity of the message
   - Appeal of the message
   - Attractiveness of the message

2. What should be considered while developing the price?
   - Costs
   - Ways to counteract costs
   - Barriers
   - Ways to counteract barriers

3. What should be considered while developing the place?
   - Home avenues
     - Television
     - Newspaper
     - Mail
     - Internet
   - Community avenues
     - Supermarkets
     - Shopping malls
     - Community centers
     - Churches
   - Workplace avenues
     - Bulletin boards
     - E-mail
     - Memos
   - Other avenues

4. What should be considered while developing the promotion?
   - Advertising options
   - Public relations opportunities
   - Promotional avenues
   - Media advocacy opportunities
   - Personal selling options
   - Special events
   - Entertainment events

(Continued)

TABLE 8.4 *(Continued)*

5. What should be considered while developing the publics?
   - Primary audience delineation
   - Secondary audience delineation

6. What should be considered while developing the partnerships?
   - Local health department
   - Local not-for-profit organizations working on same or similar topics
   - Local not-for-profit organizations working with same target audience
   - Local businesses
   - Other

7. What should be considered while developing the policy?
   - Agenda framing
   - Identifying policy makers
   - Opportunities to meet policy makers and legislators
   - Other

8. What should be considered while developing the purse strings?
   - Grant writing
   - Donations from local businesses
   - Selling tangible products
   - Other

high involvement between the marketer and the public, and often has invisible benefits or benefits that go to third parties. The rewards offered for making the recommended change are self-rewards, and budgets and the choice of products are limited. A salient concept in social marketing is that of exchange theory, which implies the voluntary transfer or transaction of something valuable between two parties. The benefits to the consumer must be underscored.

Social marketing goes through five steps: (1) planning, (2) message and material development, (3) pretesting, (4) implementation, and (5) evaluation. In planning, audience segmentation and marketing mix are important. In audience segmentation, distinct groups of people who are similar to each other in particular characteristics and are thus likely to respond to messages in a similar way are identified. In marketing mix, the product (behavior), price (costs and barriers), place, and promotion are considered. Social marketing adds a further four Ps: publics, partnership, policy, and purse strings. The social marketing model has been widely applied in health education and health promotion programs.

REVIEW QUESTIONS

1. Describe the historical genesis of social marketing.
2. Differentiate between social marketing and commercial marketing.
3. Define audience segmentation.
4. Describe the constructs of the social marketing model.
5. Apply the social marketing model for influencing a health behavior of your choice.
6. Discuss the limitations of the social marketing model.

WEBSITE

Go to the Web component of *Theoretical Foundations of Health Education and Health Promotion* at http://health.jbpub.com/foundations for Web exercises, additional resources related to this chapter, and student review tools.

GLOSSARY TERMS

audience segmentation	price
exchange theory	product
formative research	promotion
marketing mix	publics
partnership	purse strings
place	social marketing
policy	

REFERENCES AND FURTHER READING

Andreasen, A. A. (1995). *Marketing social change: Changing behavior to promote health, social development, and the environment.* San Francisco: Jossey-Bass.

Andreasen, A. A. (2003). The life trajectory of social marketing. Some implications. *Marketing Theory, 3*(3), 293–303.

Andreasen, A. A. (2006). *Social marketing in the 21st century.* Thousand Oaks, CA: Sage Publications.

Andreasen, A. R., & Kotler, P. (2003). *Strategic marketing for non profit organizations* (6th ed.). Upper Saddle River, NJ: Prentice Hall.

Bachar, J. J., Lefler, L. J., Reed, L., McCoy, T., Bailey, R., & Bell, R. (2006). Cherokee Choices: A diabetes prevention program for American Indians. *Preventing Chronic Disease, 3*(3), A103.

Baffour, T. D., Jones, M. A., & Contreras, L. K. (2006). Family health advocacy: An empowerment model for pregnant and parenting African American women in rural communities. *Family and Community Health, 29*(3), 221–228.

Banerji, D. (1986). *Social sciences and health service development in India: Sociology of formation of an alternative paradigm.* New Delhi, India: Lok Paksh.

Corrigan, P., & Gelb, B. (2006). Three programs that use mass approaches to challenge the stigma of mental illness. *Psychiatric Services, 57*(3), 393–398.

Crape, B. L., Kenefick, E., Cavalli-Sforza, T., Busch-Hallen, J., Milani, S., & Kanal, K. (2005). Positive impact of a weekly iron-folic acid supplement delivered with social marketing to Cambodian women: Compliance, participation, and hemoglobin levels increase with higher socioeconomic status. *Nutrition Reviews, 63*(12 Pt. 2), S134–S138.

Evans, W. D. (2006). How social marketing works in health care. *British Medical Journal, 332,* 1207–1210.

Flora, J. A., Schooler, C., & Pierseon, R. M. (1997). Effective health promotion among communities of color: The potential of social marketing. In M. E. Goldberg, M. Fishbein, & S. E. Middlestadt (Eds.), *Social marketing: Theoretical and practical perspectives* (pp. 353–373). Mahwah, NJ: Lawrence Erlbaum.

Goossens, H., Guillemot, D., Ferech, M., Schlemmer, B., Costers, M., van Breda, M., et al. (2006). National campaigns to improve antibiotic use. *European Journal of Clinical Pharmacology, 62*(5), 373–379.

Grier, S., & Bryant, C. A. (2005). Social marketing in public health. *Annual Review of Public Health, 26,* 319–339.

Harvey, P. D. (1999). *Let every child be wanted: How social marketing is revolutionizing contraceptive use around the world.* Westport, CT: Auburn House.

Hastings, G., & McDermott, L. M. (2006). Putting social marketing into practice. *British Medical Journal, 332,* 1210–1212.

Horn, F. E., Mandryk, J. A., Mackson, J. M., Wutzke, S. E., Weekes, L. M., & Hyndman, R. J. (2006). Measurement of changes in antihypertensive drug utilization following primary care educational interventions. *Pharmacoepidemiology and Drug Safety,* Epub PMID: 16634120.

Kotler, P. (2005). *According to Kotler: The world's foremost authority on marketing answers your questions.* New York: American Management Association.

Kotler, P., & Levy, S. J. (1969). Broadening the concept of marketing. *Journal of Marketing, 33,* 10–15.

Kotler, P., & Roberto, E. (1989). *Social marketing: Strategies for changing public behavior.* New York: The Free Press.

Kotler, P., & Zaltman, G. (1971). Social marketing: An approach to planned social change. *Journal of Marketing, 35,* 3–12.

Lefebvre, R. C., & Flora, J. A. (1988). Social marketing and public health intervention. *Health Education Quarterly, 15,* 299–315.

Lin, C. A., & Hullman, G. A. (2005). Tobacco-prevention messages online: Social marketing via the Web. *Health Communication, 18*(2), 177–193.

Ludwig, T. D., Buchholz, C., & Clarke, S. W. (2005). Using social marketing to increase the use of helmets among bicyclists. *Journal of American College Health, 54*(1), 51–58.

Marshall, R. J., Bryant, C., Keller, H., & Fridinger, F. (2006). Marketing social marketing: Getting inside those "big dogs' heads" and other challenges. *Health Promotion Practice, 7,* 206–212.

Maxwell, C., Rwegoshora, R., Magesa, S., & Curtis, C. (2006). Comparison of coverage with insecticide-treated nets in a Tanzanian town and villages where nets and insecticide are either marketed or provided free of charge. *Malaria Journal, 5*(1), 44.

Meekers, D., Agha, S., & Klein, M. (2005). The impact on condom use of the "100% Jeune" social marketing program in Cameroon. *Journal of Adolescent Health, 36*(6), 530.

Meekers, D., & Richter, K. (2005). Factors associated with use of the female condom in Zimbabwe. *International Family Planning Perspectives, 31*(1), 30–37.

Millett, C., Zelenyanszki, C., Furlong, C., & Binysh, K. (2005). An evaluation of a social marketing campaign to reduce the number of London women who have never been screened for cervical cancer. *Journal of Medical Screening, 12*(4), 204–205.

Miner, J. W., White, A., Lubenow, A. E., & Palmer, S. (2005). Geocoding and social marketing in Alabama's cancer prevention programs. *Preventing Chronic Disease, 2*, A17.

National Cancer Institute. (2005). *Theory at a glance: A guide for health promotion practice* (2nd ed.). Washington, DC: U.S. Department of Health and Human Services. Retrieved May 20, 2006, from http://www.nci.nih.gov/theory/pdf.

Peattie, S., & Peattie, K. (2003). Ready to fly solo? Reducing social marketing's dependency on commercial marketing theory. *Marketing Theory, 3*, 365–385.

Quinn, G. P., Hauser, K., Bell-Ellison, B. A., Rodriguez, N. Y., & Frias, J. L. (2006). Promoting pre-conceptional use of folic acid to Hispanic women: A social marketing approach. *Maternal and Child Health Journal, 10*(5), 403–412.

Reger-Nash, B., Fell, P., Spicer, D., Fisher, B. D., Cooper, L., Chey, T., et al. (2006). BC Walks: Replication of a communitywide physical activity campaign. *Preventing Chronic Disease, 3*(3), A90.

Rothschild, M. L. (1999). Carrots, sticks, and promises: A conceptual framework for the management of public health and social issue behaviors. *Journal of Marketing, 63*, 24–37.

Silvestre, A. J., Hylton, J. B., Johnson, L. M., Houston, C., Witt, M., Jacobson, L., et al. (2006). Recruiting minority men who have sex with men for HIV research: Results from a 4-city campaign. *American Journal of Public Health, 96*(6), 1020–1027.

Slater, M. D., Kelly, K. J., Edwards, R. W., Thurman, P. J., Plested, B. A., Keefe, T. J., et al. (2006). Combining in-school and community-based media efforts: Reducing marijuana and alcohol uptake among younger adolescents. *Health Education Research, 21*(1), 157–167.

Social Marketing Institute. (2006). Success stories. Retrieved July 10, 2006, from http://www.social-marketing.org/success.html.

Staten, L. K., Birnbaum, A. S., Jobe, J. B., & Elder, J. P. (2006). A typology of middle school girls: Audience segmentation related to physical activity. *Health Education and Behavior, 33*(1), 66–80.

Thackeray, R., & Brown, K. M. (2005). Social marketing's unique contributions to health promotion practice. *Health Promotion Practice, 6*, 365–368.

Thapa, S., Prasad, C. V., Rao, P. H., Severy, L. J., & Rao, S. R. (1994). Social marketing of condoms in India. *Advances in Population: Psychosocial Perspective, 2*, 171–204.

Tufano, J. T., & Karras, B. T. (2005). Mobile eHealth interventions for obesity: A timely opportunity to leverage convergence trends. *Journal of Medical Internet Research, 7*(5), e58.

Vega, M. Y., & Roland, E. L. (2005). Social marketing techniques for public health communication: A review of syphilis awareness campaigns in 8 US cities. *Sexually Transmitted Diseases, 32* (Suppl. 10), S30–S36.

Verrall, T., Napash, L., Leclerc, L., Mercure, S., & Gray-Donald, K. (2006). Community-based communication strategies to promote infant iron nutrition in northern Canada. *International Journal of Circumpolar Health*, *65*(1), 65–78.

Weinreich, N. K. (1999). *Hands on social marketing: A step-by-step guide.* Thousand Oaks, CA: Sage Publishers.

Wiebe, G. D. (1951–1952). Merchandising commodities and citizenship on television. *Public Opinion Quarterly*, *15*, 679–691.

Williams, P. G., Dewapura, D., Gunawardene, P., & Settinayake, S. (1998). Social marketing to eliminate leprosy in Sri Lanka. *Social Marketing Quarterly*, *4*(4), 27–31.

Young, L., Anderson, J., Beckstrom, L., Bellows, L., & Johnson, S. L. (2004). Using social marketing principles to guide the development of a nutrition education initiative for preschool-aged children. *Journal of Nutrition Education and Behavior*, *36*(5), 250–257.

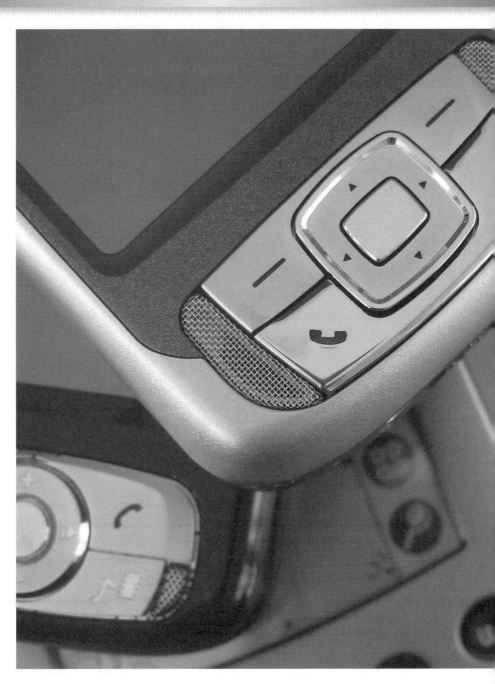

CHAPTER 9

Diffusion of Innovations

KEY CONCEPTS

- Change agent
- Clarity of results
- Communication channels
- Compatibility
- Complexity
- Costs
- Demonstrability
- Diffusion
- Homophily

- Innovation
- Opinion leaders
- Perceived relative advantage
- Pervasiveness
- Reinvention
- Reversibility
- Time
- Social networks
- Social system

AFTER READING THIS CHAPTER YOU SHOULD BE ABLE TO

- Describe the historical genesis of the diffusion of innovations theory
- List the constructs of the diffusion of innovations theory
- Summarize the applications of the diffusion of innovations theory in public health
- Identify methods to modify constructs from the diffusion of innovations theory
- Apply the diffusion of innovations theory for changing a health behavior of your choice

This chapter discusses the diffusion of innovations theory. The term **diffusion** refers to the process by which a new idea, object, or practice filters through various channels in a community over time (Rogers, 2003). It is a special form of communication in which the idea that is being conveyed is new. The term **innovations** refers to the new ideas, objects, or practices that are to be adopted. The term *theory* indicates that this model has been tested thoroughly. The hallmark of the diffusion of innovations theory is that it deals with the dissemination of new ideas and their adoption by people in a systematic manner. In addition, diffusion of innovations theory is a tool for social change. Once a new idea is infused into a community, the latter does not remain the same; therefore, change becomes inevitable.

This chapter begins by describing the historical aspects of the genesis of the diffusion of innovations theory. It then describes the approach taken by the diffusion of innovations theory and the various constructs that make up this theory. The applications of the diffusion of innovations theory in public health and the limitations of the theory are discussed next, and a skill-building application is presented.

> *Communication is essential for social change.... Social change is the process by which alteration occurs in the structure and function of a social system. National revolution, invention of a new manufacturing technique, founding of a village improvement council, adoption of birth control methods by a family—all are examples of social change.*
>
> —Rogers and Shoemaker (1971, p. 7)

HISTORICAL PERSPECTIVES

The diffusion of innovations theory can be traced back to the early 1900s, when Gabriel Tarde, a French sociologist and legal scholar, wrote *The Laws of Imitation* (Tarde, 1903/1969), which looked at factors that made innovations spread. He used the term *imitation*, which is similar to the present-day term *adoption* (Rogers, 2003), to describe how innovations were accepted. Georg Simmel, a German philosopher and sociologist who was a contemporary of Tarde, introduced the notion of a *stranger*, who is a member of a system but not strongly attached to it. This concept was used later on in diffusion of innovations theory. Tarde and Simmel's propositions were followed by the work of anthropologist Clark Wissler (1923), who studied the diffusion of horses from Spanish explorers to American Indian tribes in the plains. Wissler's work found that the introduction of horses caused the peaceful Indian tribes to go to war with neighboring tribes.

Empirical work with the diffusion of innovations theory began with a hybrid seed corn study conducted by rural sociologists Bryce Ryan and Neal Gross at Iowa State University (Ryan & Gross, 1943; Valente & Rogers, 1995). Hybrid seeds were developed in 1928. Their use increases a harvest by over 20%, yet only a small number of farmers had initially adopted the hybrid corn. Full diffusion of this innovation took almost 12 years, with the average farmer taking 7 years to progress from initial awareness to full-scale adoption of planting the whole field with hybrid seed. The main dependent variable was innovativeness (the degree to which an individual adopts early as compared with others). The cumulative number of farmers adopting the hybrid corn plotted against time formed an S-shaped curve; when plotted on a frequency basis, it formed a normal bell-shaped curve. Mass media were found to be important in the awareness stage, whereas interpersonal communication was more important at the persuasion stage (Rogers & Singhal, 1996).

Throughout the 1940s and 1950s, the diffusion of innovations theory was popular in rural sociology. In the 1950s, Everett Rogers, while pursuing his doctoral studies in rural sociology at Iowa State, became interested in the diffusion theory and worked on his dissertation in that area. In 1962, he wrote the book *Diffusion of Innovations*; at that time there were 405 publications on this theory (Rogers, 2004). In 2003, when the fifth edition of this book was published, over 5,200 applications of this theory in various fields had been published (Rogers, 2003). Interested readers may consult this book for detailed information on this theory. Everett Rogers is the foremost authority on this theory and teaches at the University of New Mexico.

The applications of the diffusion of innovations theory in public health, health promotion, and health education began with immunization campaigns and family planning programs. From the 1960s onward, the diffusion of innovations theory was used to speed up the adoption of family planning methods in Latin America, Africa, and Asia. Recent impetus for applying the diffusion of innovations theory in public health has come from the HIV/AIDS epidemic. In the mid-1980s, the STOP AIDS intervention based on the diffusion of innovations theory was implemented and tested in San Francisco (Rogers & Shefner-Rogers, 1999). One of the components of this intervention was identification of opinion leaders by bartenders at gay bars who were trained in prevention of HIV among gay men. This approach is now being evaluated in developing countries. In 2000, Malcolm Gladwell wrote *The Tipping Point: How Little Things Can Make a Big Difference*, in which he defined *tipping point* as the moment when something unique becomes common. This is the purpose of diffusion of innovations.

> *The diffusion model has now been around for a long time, almost 60 years. Is diffusion dead or dying? It is not declining. The number of diffusion publications completed per year continues to hold steady. Unlike most models of human behavior that begin to fade after some years of use, the diffusion model continues to attract strong interest from scholars.*
>
> —Rogers (2004, p. 19)

CONSTRUCTS OF THE DIFFUSION OF INNOVATIONS THEORY

An *innovation* refers to an idea, practice, or product (including services) that is perceived as new by an individual or other unit of adoption (Rogers, 2003). It does not matter how long this idea, practice, or product has been around. What matters is that the person who is adopting it *perceives* it as new. The newness of an innovation can be with regard to knowledge, persuasion, or decision to adopt. Newness regarding knowledge refers to the situation in which the potential adopter was not previously aware of the product, practice, or idea. Newness regarding persuasion refers to the situation in which the potential adopter has not been previously contacted by anyone about the product, practice, or idea. Finally, newness regarding decision to adopt pertains to the situation in which the potential adopter has not formed a positive or negative attitude about using the product, practice, or idea. Innovations are of three types: (1) *incremental innovations*, which reflect a relatively small improvement over previous products; (2) *distinctive innovations*, which represent significant improvement but do not entail any new technology or approach; and (3) *breakthrough innovations*, which are based on a new technology or approach (Schumann, Prestwood, Tong, & Vanston, 1994).

Innovations have several attributes (Frerichs, 1994; Greenhalgh, Robert, Bate, Macfarlane, & Kyriakidou, 2005; Rogers, 2003; Tornatzky & Klein, 1982). Some important attributes are as follows (Table 9.1):

- **Perceived relative advantage:** Perception regarding how much better the new product, idea, or practice is than the one it will replace
- **Compatibility:** Perception of the innovation's consistency with the values, past experiences, and needs of potential adopters
- **Complexity:** Perception of the degree of difficulty in understanding and using the new idea, practice, or product
- **Demonstrability:** The degree to which an innovation may be experimented with on a limited basis
- **Clarity of results:** The degree to which outcomes of an innovation are clearly visible
- **Costs:** The tangible and intangible expenses incurred in the adoption of a new idea, practice, or product
- **Reversibility:** The ability and degree to which the status quo can be reinstated by ceasing to use the innovation
- **Pervasiveness:** The degree to which an innovation requires changes or adjustments by other elements in the social system
- **Reinvention:** The degree to which a potential adopter can adapt, refine, or modify the innovation to suit his or her needs

These characteristics of innovations usually serve as independent variables in studies on this theory (Wolfe, 1994).

The second construct of the diffusion of innovations theory is **communication channels** (Rogers, 2003). These are the links between those who possess know-how regarding the innovation and those who have not yet adopted that innovation. They

TABLE 9.1   Key Attributes of Innovations

Attribute	Definition	How to Modify?
Perceived relative advantage	The perception regarding how much better the new product, idea, or practice is than the one it will replace	Increase the perception that the innovation is advantageous in monetary terms, social terms, or other respects.
Compatibility	The perception of the innovation's consistency with the values, past experiences, and needs of potential adopters	Make the idea consistent with the prevalent norms and values.
Complexity	The perception of the degree of difficulty in understanding and using the new idea, practice, or product.	Simplify the idea, practice, or product.
Demonstrability	The degree to which an innovation may be experimented with on a limited basis	Provide an opportunity to try the idea, practice, or product either in small units or in total.
Clarity of results	The degree to which outcomes of an innovation are clearly visible	Disseminate information on the results of the innovation and make it more visible.
Costs	The tangible and intangible expenses incurred in the adoption of a new idea, practice, or product	Minimize costs as far as possible.
Reversibility	The ability and degree to which the status quo can be reinstated by ceasing to use the innovation	Make innovations reversible.
Pervasiveness	The degree to which an innovation requires changes or adjustments by other elements in the social system	Minimize changes in other parts.
Reinvention	The degree to which a potential adopter can adapt, refine, or modify the innovation to suit his or her needs	Allow for modification(s) by the user.

are the means by which messages are transferred between individuals. Communication channels are of three kinds: (1) *mass-media channels*, such as television, radio, and newspapers; (2) *interpersonal channels*, which require face-to-face interaction between two or more individuals; and (3) *interactive communication channels*, such as the Internet. Mass media channels are the swiftest, reach a large number of people, and are especially advantageous in building awareness or knowledge about the innovation. Interpersonal channels are especially helpful in persuading a potential adopter. Therefore, in the initial stages of adoption one should use mass media channels, followed by interpersonal and interactive channels to reinforce the message and persuade the potential adopter.

The third construct of the diffusion of innovations theory is **time** (Rogers, 2003), which refers to the interval between becoming aware of an idea and adopting the idea. This can take from days to years, depending on the innovation. The time construct is involved with diffusion of innovations in three ways: (1) the innovation-decision process, (2) adopter categories, and (3) rate of adoption (Rogers, 2003). The *innovation-decision process* is a five-step process:

1. Gaining knowledge about the innovation
2. Being persuaded about the innovation
3. Deciding whether to adopt or reject the innovation
4. Implementing the innovation (putting it to use)
5. Confirming step: either reversing the decision or adopting the new innovation

Adopter categories are classifications of how people adopt an innovation, and fall into a bell-shaped distribution (Figure 9.1). The first category of adopters is the innovators

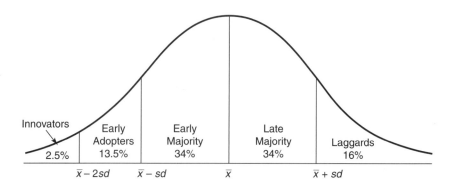

FIGURE 9.1   Adopter characterization on the basis of innovativenesss
Note: From Rogers, E. M. (2003). *Diffusion of innovations* (5th ed., p. 281). New York: Free Press. Reproduced with permission.

(2.5%), who adopt quickly. Innovators by nature are adventurous, cosmopolitan, have geographically dispersed contacts, are high risk takers, and have high tolerance of uncertainty and failure. The second category consists of the early adopters (13.5%). Early adopters are well-respected opinion leaders and well-integrated and judicious individuals. The early majority category (34%) consists of people who are deliberate, highly connected within a peer system, and are ahead of the average. These adopters are followed by the late majority (34%). Late-majority people are skeptical, responsive to economic necessity, responsive to social norms, have limited economic resources, and have low tolerance for uncertainty. The final group is that of laggards (16%). Laggards are more traditional in their disposition, are relatively isolated, have precarious economic situations, and are suspicious of change.

The *rate of adoption* refers to the speed with which an innovation is adopted. If we plot the cumulative frequency against time, an S-shaped curve is obtained, which is the rate of adoption (Figure 9.2). The diffusion rate usually serves as the dependent variable in studies with the diffusion of innovations theory (Wolfe, 1994).

The fourth construct of the diffusion of innovations theory is the social system (Berwick, 2003; Rogers, 2003). A **social system** implies people in a society connected by a common goal and is composed of individuals, groups, organizations, or communities. An important aspect of the social system is how similar the group members are. Similarity among group members is called **homophily**. Innovations spread faster among homophilous groups (Cain & Mitman, 2002; Rogers, 2003). Hence, to en-

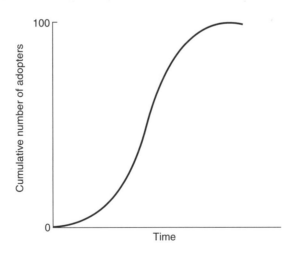

FIGURE 9.2   The S-shaped curve of diffusion

hance the rate of diffusion of an innovation, identify the degree of homophily in the target audience and use homophilous agents to spread the message.

Another aspect of the social system is the use of **social networks**, which are person-centered webs of social relationships (Heaney & Israel, 2002) that provide friendship, advice, communication, and support (Valente, 1996). Social networks can be physical or virtual (i.e., in the cyberworld). The configuration of social networks through which innovations diffuse governs the pace and extent of diffusion. For example, in the 1960s, studies showed that diffusion of the practice of tetracycline prescription occurred faster in physicians with denser social networks than in isolated physicians (Cain & Mitman, 2002). To hasten diffusion, identify and utilize physical and virtual networks and create new networks.

The third aspect of the social system is the **change agent**, an individual who influences a potential adopter's decision about innovation in a favorable way (Haider & Kreps, 2004). An example of a change agent might be a health educator at a health department. The change agent must be used to favorably influence the decision. The fourth aspect of social systems is **opinion leaders**, individuals who are influential in a community and sway the beliefs and actions of their colleagues in either a positive or negative direction (Locock, Dopson, Chambers, & Gabbay, 2001). These are individuals who have greater exposure to new ideas through the media, have greater social participation, have higher social status, and are more innovative (Rogers & Shoemaker, 1971). To hasten diffusion, identify true opinion leaders and involve them in the campaign. Opinion leaders have been used in heart health trials, such as the Stanford five-city project (Farquahar et al., 1990) and North Karelia project (Puska et al., 1986).

These characteristics of the social system usually serve as independent variables in studies on this theory (Wolfe, 1994). Table 9.2 summarizes the key constructs of the diffusion of innovations theory, along with ways to modify them.

To apply these constructs of the diffusion of innovations theory for health programming, Dearing (2004) has suggested a nine-step process. The first step is selecting the topic, in which the area of concern with high societal need and fewer previous programs is selected. Next is identifying the program population, in which the target population is selected. The third step is deriving a sample of best practices, in which the best existing products pertaining to the topic are identified. The fourth step is identifying intermediary networks. In this step potential adopters are identified; there must be existing communication within this network. The fifth step is identifying opinion leaders in the intermediary network. Opinion leaders, as we have seen, are individuals who are influential in a community. They can be identified by sociometric questionnaires (in which respondents characterize their relations with others in the

TABLE 9.2 Key Constructs of the Diffusion of Innovations Theory

Construct	Definition	How to Modify?
Innovation	An idea, practice, or product (including services) that is perceived as new by an individual or other unit of adoption	• Increase the perception that innovation is advantageous in monetary terms, social terms, or in other respects. • Make the idea consistent with the prevalent norms and values. • Simplify the idea, practice, or product. • Provide opportunity to try the idea, practice, or product either in small units or in total. • Disseminate information on results of the innovation and make it more visible. • Minimize costs as far as possible. • Make innovations reversible. • Minimize changes in other parts of the social system. • Allow for modification(s) by the user.
Communication channels	The link between those who have know-how regarding the innovation and those who have not yet adopted the innovation	• Use mass media for building awareness. • Use interpersonal channels for persuasion.
Time	The interval between becoming aware of an idea and adopting the idea	• Facilitate adoption over time.
Social system	People in a society connected by a common goal	• Facilitate adoption from person to person. • Use homophilous agents to spread the message. • Use social networks. • Use change agents. • Use opinion leaders.

network), participant observation, expert interviews, or self-reports. Opinion leaders typically consist of about 5% to 6% of the network membership. The sixth step is collecting pretest data, such as characteristics of members of the community and pretest opinions about the product. The next step is creation of a decision support tool, in which potential adopters can assess alternative best-practice products. The eighth step is to set up research design conditions, in which network members can be assigned to different conditions in which different variables are manipulated. The final step is post-test measurement, in which a post-test similar to the pretest can be administered and the rate of adoption in different conditions calculated. Table 9.3 summarizes these steps.

A similar model for the diffusion of innovations theory in public health organizations, FOMENT, has been suggested by Muhiuddin Haider of the George Washington University (Haider & Kreps, 2004). FOMENT is an acronym in which *F* stands for *focus* on a specific behavior change; *O* for *organization* of the behavior change program; *M* for *management*, which supports and approves the behavior change program; *E* for an *environment* that is conducive to behavior change; *N* for a *network* to diffuse innovations at the individual and organizational levels; and *T* for the *technology* available to diffuse innovations.

> *Improving the application of the Diffusion of Innovations model in the field of public health can lead to advances in health promotion and disease prevention on a global level.*
>
> —Haider and Kreps (2004, p. 3)

TABLE 9.3 Steps for Applying the Diffusion of Innovations Theory for Health Programming
1. Select the topic.
2. Identify the program population.
3. Derive a sample of best practices.
4. Identify intermediary networks.
5. Identify opinion leaders in the intermediary network.
6. Collect pretest data.
7. Create a decision support tool.
8. Set up research design conditions.
9. Measure the rate of adoption and participants' opinions post-test.

APPLICATIONS OF THE DIFFUSION OF INNOVATIONS THEORY

The diffusion of innovations theory has been used in a variety of applications in public health, health promotion, and health education. Most of the published studies on the diffusion of innovations theory use cross-sectional surveys of adopters done after they have adopted the innovation and pertain to a single innovation (Meyer, 2004). Some examples of the application of this theory for public health are adopting and implementing a picture archiving communication system (PACS) in hospitals (Pare & Trudel, 2006); adopting novel medication regimes for diabetes management (Pugh, Anderson, Pogach, & Berlowitz, 2003); adopting telemedicine in rural areas (Helitzer, Heath, Maltrud, Sullivan, & Alverson, 2003); designing Students Together Against Negative Decisions (STAND), a peer educator training curriculum for sexual risk reduction (Smith, Dane, Archer, Devereaux, & Katner, 2000; Smith & DiClemente, 2000); enriching a gerontology curriculum (Dorfman & Murty, 2005); implementing change strategy for primary care treatment of depression (Dietrich et al., 2004); implementing computerized provider order entry (CPOE) in the outpatient setting (Ash et al., 2006); implementing family planning in developing countries (Murphy, 2004; Sharma & Sharma, 1996; Vaughan & Rogers, 2000); implementing health counseling intervention in the cardiology outpatient clinic (Harting et al., 2005); implementing the National Quality Measurement and Reporting System (NQMRS) (McGlynn, 2003); implementing patient education in community pharmacies (Pronk, Blom, Jonkers, & Van Burg, 2001); implementing a sun protection program (Buller et al., 2005); implementing technology implementation systems to promote patient safety (Karsh, 2004); implementing telehomecare technology in community care (Hebert & Korabek, 2004); incorporating genomic medicine into primary care (Suther & Goodson, 2004); increasing Internet use by family physicians (Chew, Grant, & Tote, 2004); predicting radon testing (Peterson & Howland, 1996); predicting smoking cessation in Switzerland (Kuntsche & Gmel, 2005); reducing the spread of sexually transmitted diseases and HIV infection (Backer & Rogers, 1998; Bertrand, 2004; Valente & Fosados, 2006); translating research on diabetes self-management interventions into practice (Leeman, Jackson, & Sandelowski, 2006); using acetylcholinesterase inhibitors in Alzheimer's disease (Ruof, Mittendorf, Pirk, & von der Schulenburg, 2002); using patient-driven computers in primary care services (Shakeshaft & Frankish, 2003); and using voodoo practitioners in Haiti to educate people about HIV/AIDS (Barker, 2004). Table 9.4 summarizes these applications.

Examples of potentially constructive innovations in health care can be as simple as ensuring that an improved drug regimen published in a refereed journal article immediately becomes the norm in a practice group, or as complex as redesigning an entire scheduling system to better conform to sound principles from queuing theory.

—Berwick (2003, p. 1969)

TABLE 9.4   Examples of Applications of the Diffusion of Innovations Theory in Public Health

Adopting and implementing a picture archiving communication system (PACS) in hospitals

Adopting novel medication regimens for diabetes management

Adopting telemedicine in rural areas

Designing Students Together Against Negative Decisions (STAND), a peer educator training curriculum for sexual risk reduction

Enriching a gerontology curriculum

Implementing change strategy for primary care treatment of depression

Implementing computerized provider order entry (CPOE) in the outpatient setting

Implementing family planning in developing countries

Implementing health counseling intervention in the cardiology outpatient clinic

Implementing a National Quality Measurement and Reporting System (NQMRS)

Implementing patient education in community pharmacies

Implementing a sun protection program

Implementing technology implementation systems to promote patient safety

Implementing telehomecare technology in community care

Incorporating genomic medicine into primary care

Increasing Internet use by family physicians

Predicting radon testing

Predicting smoking cessation in Switzerland

Reducing the spread of sexually transmitted diseases and HIV infection

Translating research on diabetes self-management interventions into practice

Using acetylcholinesterase inhibitors in Alzheimer's disease

Using patient-driven computers in primary care services

Using voodoo practitioners in Haiti to educate people about HIV/AIDS

LIMITATIONS OF THE DIFFUSION OF INNOVATIONS THEORY _____

The diffusion of innovations theory has been in existence for quite some time and has been tested empirically and refined. It offers several advantages in guiding the adoption of something that is novel or new. However, like all other models and theories, there are some limitations of this approach. In health promotion and education, often there are no real innovations (Tornatzky & Fleischer, 1990). People are already knowledgeable about the issues and have often tried the behavior. For example, almost all smokers know that smoking is injurious to their health and have tried to quit. Thus, quitting is not an innovation for them. Use of the diffusion of innovations theory becomes challenging in these circumstances.

Public health interventions are preventive in nature, whereby the individual has to adopt the new idea today to avoid the likelihood of a negative consequence occurring at a later date. For example, a smoker would need to quit smoking today to prevent development of lung cancer 20 or so years later. Such a long interval poses special challenges, and diffusion occurs more slowly (Rogers, 2002). It needs to be kept in mind that diffusion of innovations in health is a complex process that occurs at multiple levels and across many different settings, and that utilizes different strategies (Oldenburg & Parcel, 2002; Parcel, Perry, & Taylor, 1990).

Oftentimes in health promotion and health education, the interventions have to be designed for lower socioeconomic groups, people with low literacy levels, and other vulnerable sections of the community. The adoption and diffusion process occurs easier and smoother in the wealthier and more highly educated sections, whereas in the vulnerable sections the process is not as smooth and offers a number of challenges and barriers. As a consequence, the gap between the haves and the have-nots widens even further.

Another issue with the diffusion of innovations theory is *pro-innovation bias* (Rogers, 2003). This refers to the preconception that an innovation should be diffused and adopted by all members of society in a rapid manner without rejection or reinvention. This is often not possible with many health promotion and education objectives. For example, it is virtually impossible at present to think that no one will smoke or that everyone will engage in 30 minutes of physical activity every day. Rogers (2003) suggests conducting research while the innovation is still being adopted rather than waiting for it to be completely adopted, studying unsuccessful innovations, and examining the broader context in which an innovation diffuses.

Finally, Nutley, Davies, and Walter (2002) have talked about the limitations of focusing on linear-stage models of decision making with the diffusion of innovations theory. Seldom does the adoption of innovation follow a linear path as suggested in the theory. Often the path is uneven, and fitting the innovation to the S-shaped curve is not possible (Chattoe & Gilbert, 1997; Mohr, 1987; Rosegger, 1996). Hence Nutley, Davies, and Walter (2002) advocate a nonlinear, dynamic process that pays more attention to systemic context and norms. In this regard, Westarp (2003) has suggested relational and structural models. Relational models analyze how direct contacts between participants in networks influence the decision to adopt or not adopt an innovation, whereas structural models focus on the pattern of all relationships and show how the structural characteristics of a social system determine the diffusion process.

> *D*iffusion is a multifaceted perspective about social change. Scholars dating at least to Georg Simmel and Gabriel Tarde 100 years ago theorized about imitative behavior at the level of small groups and within communities, and the relation between these micro-level processes to macro-level social change in which sectors, networks, and cities change.
>
> —Dearing (2004, p. 24)

SKILL-BUILDING ACTIVITY

Let us see how we can apply the diffusion of innovations theory in health education and health promotion. Currently in the profession of health education and health promotion, the National Commission for Health Education Credentialing (NCHEC) provides a certification system. Other professions, such as physicians, nurses, and dietitians, are registered practitioners. Let us assume we want to start the innovation of "registered health educators."

In applying the diffusion of innovations theory, we would first have to look at the construct of innovation and its attributes. The first attribute is perceived relative advantage. For all existing and prospective health educators, this innovation should seem advantageous. Employers could be convinced to give a nominal salary raise to those who become registered health educators, thus providing a monetary advantage. The social status that comes with being a registered member of the profession would need to be underscored. The ability to write the credential R.HEd. with one's name would need to be marketed. The second attribute is compatibility. This innovation is in direct synchrony with the previous innovation of Certified Health Education Specialist (CHES) and should build on that to be successful. The third attribute is that of complexity. The process should be similar to that of becoming a CHES, and thus not very complex. The simpler the process, the better its chances of adoption. The fourth attribute, demonstrability, would not be possible with this innovation. The fifth attribute is that of clarity of results. The results of several years of success with CHES and with registration in other disciplines could be shared. The sixth attribute is costs, which would have to be kept at a nominal rate similar to that involved with CHES. The seventh attribute of reversibility would be easy: a person who does not want to be registered would simply abstain from paying the annual dues. The eighth attribute is that of pervasiveness. To influence this attribute, employers would need to make adjustments by endorsing the idea of registered health educators and mandating that only such individuals be hired in health education jobs. The ninth attribute, reinvention, does not apply to this innovation.

The second construct is that of communication channels. Mass mailing of information about the innovation (registration for health educators) would need to be sent to existing CHESs, 258 institutions of higher education that award degrees in health education, and all major employers who hire health educators (e.g., county health departments, state health departments, major hospitals, major school systems, large companies with health and wellness units). Interpersonal communication using people who have adopted the innovation would also need to be done. A website detailing the innovation would need to be set up.

The third construct is that of time. The flow of time would involve the five-step process of providing knowledge about the innovation, persuading health educators about the innovation, helping health educators decide about the innovation, starting the first batch of registered health educators, and then confirming their continuation as registered health educators. A count of people adopting the innovation can be kept so that a rate of adoption curve can be plotted.

The fourth construct is that of the social system. The first aspect of the social system is homophily. Health educators comprise diverse groups. Thus, the first task would be to decrease the diversity and make the innovation appeal to the common attributes of all health educators. The second aspect is social networks. Health educators who have adopted the innovation can be used to spread the message to other health educators. The electronic network of health educators (HEDIR) can also be used in this process. The third aspect of social system is the change agent. The leadership at the National Commission for Health Education Credentialing should take up the task of coordinating and sending the necessary information and becoming change agents. The fourth aspect of the social system is opinion leaders, who would be composed of supervisors at workplaces and department chairs at the various institutions of higher education.

Using this approach, you can plan to work on spreading any innovation using the diffusion of innovations theory. Table 9.5 provides a set of questions to consider.

TABLE 9.5   Shaping Constructs of the Diffusion of Innovations Theory for Health Education Program Planning

1. What should be considered while developing the innovation?
   - Increase perceived relative advantage
   - Increase compatibility
   - Decrease complexity
   - Give opportunity for demonstrability
   - Show clarity of results
   - Minimize costs
   - Allow for reversibility
   - Work on factors affecting pervasiveness
   - Allow for reinvention

2. What should be considered while developing the communication channels?
   - Mass media
   - Interpersonal
   - Interactive

3. What should be considered while developing the time?
   - Innovation-decision process
   - Rate of adoption
   - Adopter categories

4. What should be considered while developing the social system?
   - Homophily
   - Social networks
   - Change agents
   - Opinion leaders

SUMMARY

The diffusion of innovations theory deals with adoption of a new idea, practice, or object over a period of time. The origins of this theory are almost 100 years old, but the first empirical study was done by Bryce Ryan and Neal Gross at Iowa State University with hybrid corn seed in the 1940s. They studied the adoption process and the characteristics of the farmers who adopted the hybrid corn seed. Their work had implications not only in agriculture but also for a variety of disciplines, including health promotion and health education.

The four main constructs of the diffusion of innovations theory are innovation, communication channels, time, and social system. Several attributes of innovation are as follows: perceived relative advantage (perception about how much better the new product, idea, or practice is than the one it will replace); compatibility (the perception regarding the innovation's consistency with the values, past experiences, and needs of potential adopters); complexity (the perception of the degree of difficulty in understanding and using the new idea, practice, or product); demonstrability (the degree to which an innovation may be experimented with on a limited basis); clarity of results (the degree to which the outcomes of an innovation are clearly visible); costs (the tangible and intangible expenses incurred in the adoption of a new idea, practice, or product); reversibility (the ability and degree to which the status quo can be reinstated by ceasing to use the innovation); pervasiveness (the degree to which an innovation requires changes or adjustments by other elements in the social system); and reinvention (the degree to which a potential adopter can adapt, refine, or modify the innovation to suit his or her needs).

The communication channels are of three kinds: (1) mass-media channels, such as television, radio, and newspapers; (2) interpersonal channels, which require face-to-face interaction between two or more individuals; and (3) interactive communication channels, such as the Internet.

The time construct is involved with the diffusion of innovations in three ways: (1) the innovation-decision process, (2) adopter categories, and (3) rate of adoption. The social system construct comprises homophily (similarity among group members), social networks (person-centered webs of social relationships), change agents (people who influence a potential adopter's decision about innovation in a favorable way), and opinion leaders (influential individuals in a community who sway the beliefs and actions of their colleagues in either a positive or negative direction). The diffusion of innovations theory has been widely applied in public health.

REVIEW QUESTIONS

1. Describe the historical genesis of the diffusion of innovations theory.
2. Discuss any five attributes of innovations.
3. What does the acronym FOMENT mean in the context of diffusion of innovations?
4. Describe the four constructs of the diffusion of innovations theory.
5. Discuss the limitations of the diffusion of innovations theory.
6. Apply the diffusion of innovations theory for spreading any innovation of your choice.

WEBSITE

Go to the Web component of *Theoretical Foundations of Health Education and Health Promotion* at http://health.jbpub.com/foundations for Web exercises, additional resources related to this chapter, and student review tools.

GLOSSARY TERMS

change agent

clarity of results

communication channels

compatibility

complexity

costs

demonstrability

diffusion

homophily

innovation

opinion leaders

perceived relative advantage

pervasiveness

reinvention

reversibility

social networks

social system

time

REFERENCES AND FURTHER READING

Ash, J. S., Sittig, D. F., Dykstra, R. H., Guappone, K., Carpenter, J. D., & Seshadri, V. (2006). Categorizing the unintended sociotechnical consequences of computerized provider order entry. *International Journal of Medical Informatics*, Epub PMID: 16793330.

Backer, T. E., & Rogers, E. M. (1998). Diffusion of innovations theory and work-site AIDS programs. *Journal of Health Communication*, 3(1), 17–28.

Barker, K. (2004). Diffusion of innovations: A world tour. *Journal of Health Communication*, 9(Suppl. 1), 131–137.

Bertrand, J. T. (2004). Diffusion of innovations and HIV/AIDS. *Journal of Health Communication*, 9(Suppl. 1), 113–121.

Berwick, D. M. (2003). Disseminating innovations in health care. *Journal of the American Medical Association*, 289, 1969–1975.

Buller, D. B., Andersen, P. A., Walkosz, B. J., Scott, M. D., Cutter, G. R., Dignan, M. B., et al. (2005). Randomized trial testing a worksite sun protection program in an outdoor recreation industry. *Health Education and Behavior*, 32(4), 514–535.

Cain, M., & Mitman, R. (2002). *Diffusion of innovation in health care*. Oakland, CA: California Health Care Foundation. Retrieved July 20, 2006, from http://www.iftf.org/docs/SR-778_Diffusion_of_Innovation_in_HC.pdf.

Chattoe, E., & Gilbert, N. (1997). Modelling the adoption of AEMs as an innovation diffusion process. Retrieved July 20, 2006, from http://wwwlisc.clermont.cemagref.fr/ImagesProject/Results/models/Diffusion%20Model/dolomieu.html.

Chew, F., Grant, W., & Tote, R. (2004). Doctors on-line: Using diffusion of innovations theory to understand Internet use. *Family Medicine, 36*(9), 645–650.

Dearing, J. W. (2004). Improving the state of health programming by using diffusion theory. *Journal of Health Communication, 9*, 21–36.

Dietrich, A. J., Oxman, T. E., Williams, J. W., Jr., Kroenke, K., Schulberg, H. C., Bruce, M., et al. (2004). Going to scale: Re-engineering systems for primary care treatment of depression. *Annals of Family Medicine, 2*(4), 301–304.

Dorfman, L. T., & Murty, S. A. (2005). A diffusion of innovations approach to gerontological curriculum enrichment: Institutionalizing and sustaining curricula change. *Gerontology and Geriatrics Education, 26*(2), 35–50.

Farquahar, J. W., Fortmann, S. P., Flora, J. A., Taylor, C. B., Haskell, W. L., Williams, P. T., et al. (1990). Effects of a communitywide education on cardiovascular disease risk factors: The Stanford five-city project. *Journal of the American Medical Association, 264*, 359–365.

Frerichs, G. R. (1994). The diffusion of innovations. In S. J. Levy, G. R. Frerichs, & H. L. Gordon (Eds.), *The Dartnell's marketing manager's handbook* (3rd ed., pp. 774–785). Chicago: Dartnell.

Gladwell, M. (2000). *The tipping point: How little things can make a big difference.* Boston: Little Brown.

Greenhalgh, T., Robert, G., Bate, P., Macfralane, F., & Kyriakidou, O. (2005). *Diffusion of innovations in health service organizations: A systematic literature review.* Malden, MA: Blackwell Publishing.

Haider, M., & Kreps, G. L. (2004). Forty years of diffusion of innovations: Utility and value in public health. *Journal of Health Communication, 9*, 3–11.

Harting, J., van Assema, P., Ruland, E., van Limpt, P., Gorgels, T., van Ree, J., et al. (2005). Implementation of an innovative health service: A "real-world" diffusion study. *American Journal of Preventive Medicine, 29*(2), 113–119.

Heaney, C. A., & Israel, B. A. (2002). Social networks and social support. In K. Glanz, B. K. Rimer, & F. M. Lewis (Eds.), *Health behavior and health education: Theory, research, and practice* (3rd ed., pp. 185–209). San Francisco: Jossey-Bass.

Hebert, M. A., & Korabek, B. (2004). Stakeholder readiness for telehomecare: Implications for implementation. *Telemedicine Journal and e-Health, 10*(1), 85–92.

Helitzer, D., Heath, D., Maltrud, K., Sullivan, E., & Alverson, D. (2003). Assessing or predicting adoption of telehealth using the diffusion of innovations theory: A practical example from a rural program in New Mexico. *Telemedicine Journal and e-Health, 9*(2), 179–187.

Karsh, B. T. (2004). Beyond usability: Designing effective technology implementation systems to promote patient safety. *Quality and Safety in Health Care, 13*(5), 388–394.

Kuntsche, S., & Gmel, G. (2005). The smoking epidemic in Switzerland: An empirical examination of the theory of diffusion of innovations. *Sozial und Praventivmedizin, 50*(6), 344–354.

Leeman, J., Jackson, B., & Sandelowski, M. (2006). An evaluation of how well research reports facilitate the use of findings in practice. *Journal of Nursing Scholarship, 38*(2), 171–177.

Locock, L., Dopson, S., Chambers, D., & Gabbay, J. (2001). Understanding the role of opinion leaders in improving clinical effectiveness. *Social Science and Medicine, 53*, 745–757.

McGlynn, E. A. (2003). An evidence-based national quality measurement and reporting system. *Medical Care, 41*(Suppl. 1), I8–I15.

Meyer, G. (2004). Diffusion methodology: Time to innovate. *Journal of Health Communication*, *9*, 59–69.

Mohr, L. B. (1987). Innovation theory. In J. M. Pennings & A. Buitendam (Eds.), *New technology as organizational innovation* (pp. 13–31). Cambridge, MA: Ballinger.

Murphy, E. (2004). Diffusion of innovations: Family planning in developing countries. *Journal of Health Communication*, *9*(Suppl. 1), 123–129.

Nutley, S., Davies, H., & Walter, I. (2002). Learning from the diffusion of innovations. Retrieved July 21, 2006, from http://www.st-andrews.ac.uk/~ruru/Learning%20from%20the%20Diffusion%20of%20Innovations.pdf.

Oldenburg, B., & Parcel, G. S. (2002). Diffusion of innovations. In K. Glanz, B. K. Rimer, & F. M. Lewis (Eds.), *Health behavior and health education: Theory, research, and practice* (3rd ed., pp. 312–334). San Francisco: Jossey-Bass.

Parcel, G. S., Perry, C. L., & Taylor, W. C. (1990). Beyond demonstration: Diffusion of health promotion interventions. In N. Bracht (Ed.), *Health promotion at the community level*. Thousand Oaks, CA: Sage Publishers.

Pare, G., & Trudel, M. C. (2006). Knowledge barriers to PACS adoption and implementation in hospitals. *International Journal of Medical Informatics*, Epub PMID: 16478675.

Peterson, E. W., & Howland, J. (1996). Predicting radon testing among university employees. *Journal of Air and Waste Management Association*, *46*(1), 2–11.

Pronk, M. C., Blom, A. T., Jonkers, R., & Van Burg, A. (2001). The diffusion process of patient education in Dutch community pharmacy: An exploration. *Patient Education and Counseling*, *42*(2), 115–121.

Pugh, M. J., Anderson, J., Pogach, L. M., & Berlowitz, D. R. (2003). Differential adoption of pharmacotherapy recommendations for type 2 diabetes by generalists and specialists. *Medical Care Research and Review*, *60*(2), 178–200.

Puska, P., Koskela, K., McAlister, A., Mayranen, H., Smolander, A., Moisio, S., et al. (1986). Use of lay opinion leaders to promote the diffusion of health innovations in a community programme: Lessons learned from the North Karelia Project. *Bulletin of the World Health Organization*, *64*(3), 437–446.

Rogers, E. M. (2002). Diffusion of preventive interventions. *Addictive Behaviors*, *27*, 989–993.

Rogers, E. M. (2003). *Diffusion of innovations* (5th ed.). New York: Free Press.

Rogers, E. M. (2004). A prospective and retrospective look at the diffusion model. *Journal of Health Communication*, *9*, 13–19.

Rogers, E. M., & Shefner-Rogers, C. L. (1999). Diffusion of innovations and HIV/AIDS prevention research. In W. N. Elwood (Ed.), *Power in the blood: A handbook on AIDS, politics, and communication* [electronic resource, pp. 405–414]. Mahwah, NJ: Erlbaum.

Rogers, E. M., & Shoemaker, F. F. (1971). *Communication of innovations: A cross cultural approach* (2nd ed.). New York: The Free Press.

Rogers, E. M., & Singhal, A. (1996). Diffusion of innovations. In M. B. Salwen & D. W. Stacks (Eds.), *An integrated approach to communication theory and research* (pp. 409–420). Mahwah, NJ: Lawrence Erlbaum Associates.

Rosegger, G. (1996). *The economics of production and innovation: An industrial perspective* (3rd ed.). Oxford, UK: Butterworth Heinemann.

Ruof, J., Mittendorf, T., Pirk, O., & von der Schulenburg, J. M. (2002). Diffusion of innovations: Treatment of Alzheimer's disease in Germany. *Health Policy, 60*(1), 59–66.

Ryan, B., & Gross, N. C. (1943). The diffusion of hybrid seed corn in two Iowa communities. *Rural Sociology, 8,* 15–24.

Schumann, P. A., Prestwood, D. C. L., Tong, A. H., & Vanston, J. H. (1994). *Innovate! Straight path to quality, customer delight, and competitive advantage.* New York: McGraw Hill.

Shakeshaft, A. P., & Frankish, C. J. (2003). Using patient-driven computers to provide cost-effective prevention in primary care: A conceptual framework. *Health Promotion International, 18*(1), 67–77.

Sharma, V., & Sharma, A. (1996). Training of opinion leaders in family planning in India: Does it serve any purpose? *Revue d'épidémiologie et de santé publique, 44*(2), 173–180.

Smith, M. U., Dane, F. C., Archer, M. E., Devereaux, R. S., & Katner, H. P. (2000). Students Together Against Negative Decisions (STAND): Evaluation of a school-based sexual risk reduction intervention in the rural South. *AIDS Education and Prevention, 12*(1), 49–70.

Smith, M. U., & DiClemente, R. J. (2000). STAND: A peer educator training curriculum for sexual risk reduction in the rural South. Students Together Against Negative Decisions. *Preventive Medicine, 30*(6), 441–449.

Suther, S. G., & Goodson, P. (2004). Texas physicians' perceptions of genomic medicine as an innovation. *Clinical Genetics, 65*(5), 368–377.

Tarde, G. (1969). *The laws of imitation* (E. C. Parsons, Trans.). New York: Dover. (Original work published 1903.)

Tornatzky, L. G., & Fleischer, M. (1990). *The process of technological innovation* (p. 122). Lexington, MA: Lexington Books.

Tornatzky, L. G., & Klein, K. J. (1982). Innovation characteristics and innovation adoption-implementation: A meta analysis of findings. *IEEE Transactions on Engineering Management, 29,* 28–45.

Valente, T. W. (1996). Social network thresholds in the diffusion of innovations. *Social Networks, 18,* 69–89.

Valente, T. W., & Fosados, R. (2006). Diffusion of innovations and network segmentation: The part played by people in promoting health. *Sexually Transmitted Diseases, 33*(Suppl. 7), S23–S31.

Valente, T. W., & Rogers, E. M. (1995). The origins and development of the diffusion of innovations paradigm as an example of scientific growth. *Science Communication, 16,* 242–273.

Vaughan, P. W., & Rogers, E. M. (2000). A staged model of communication effects: Evidence from an entertainment-education radio soap opera in Tanzania. *Journal of Health Communication, 5*(3), 203–227.

Westarp, F. V. (2003). *Modeling software markets: Empirical analysis, network simulations, and marketing implications.* New York: Physica-Verlag.

Wissler, C. (1923). *Man and culture.* New York: Thomas Y. Crowell.

Wolfe, R. A. (1994). Organizational innovation: Review, critique, and suggested research directions. *Journal of Management Studies, 31,* 407–431.

CHAPTER 10

Freire's Model of Adult Education

KEY CONCEPTS

- Codification
- Conscientization
- Critical consciousness
- Dialogue
- Informal education
- Popular education

- Praxis
- Problematization or problem posing
- SHOWED model
- Social reality
- Transformation

AFTER READING THIS CHAPTER YOU SHOULD BE ABLE TO

- Describe Paulo Freire's contribution to adult education
- List five constructs from Freire's adult education model
- Explain the application of Freire's model in health education
- Identify educational methods and match these to modify each construct from Freire's model to influence a health behavior
- Apply Freire's model to design an intervention to change a health behavior of your choice

Paulo Freire (1921–1997) was a Brazilian educator, philosopher, and political activist who worked in the area of adult literacy. His book *Pedagogy of the Oppressed* (Freire, 1970b) is currently one of the most cited books in education in Asia, Africa, and South America (Smith, 2005). His model is also popular in the United States, where, besides adult education, it has been used for community organization, health education, and social work. His work is commonly used by those who work with oppressed people and use informal education or popular education. **Informal education** is based on experiential learning (learning from one's experiences), uses simple conversation, and can take place in any setting. **Popular education** is similar to informal education; it is need based, does not have a hierarchical relationship between learners and facilitators, builds on community knowledge, and aims at political action (Hamilton & Cunningham, 1989). Therefore, Freire's model is also sometimes called the *theory of liberation education* (Freire, 1985).

Freire believed that education was a means of freeing people from the "culture of silence" that is widely prevalent among the masses, especially in nonindustrialized countries (Freire, 1970b). The essence of Freire's teaching is **dialogue**, or becoming adept at two-way communication. He believed that the individual deprived of dialogue was oppressed. He looked at dialogue as the process and practice of liberation. Since dialogue is the essence of the Freirean approach, the latter is also called *participatory research* (Cornwall & Jewkes, 1995). The second hallmark of Freirean methodology is the fundamental technique of **problematizing**, or **problem posing**. This approach is essentially the opposite of traditional education (which Freire labeled "banking education") (Freire, 1970b). Banking education, or traditional education, provides ready-made answers or solutions to one's problems and does not allow people to think for themselves. The emphasis of the problem-posing approach lies in raising questions without providing any predetermined answers. The students reflect and arrive at the answers themselves.

> *Paulo Freire was a Brazilian educator whose book* Pedagogy of the Oppressed *is one of the most cited books in education in Asia, Africa, and South America.*

HISTORICAL PERSPECTIVES

Paulo Freire was born in 1921 in northeast Brazil in a well-to-do middle-class family that was severely affected by the Great Depression (1929–1939), during which his father died when Paulo was only 13 years old. He underwent great difficulties during that period. With great efforts he attended the Recifé University and studied law, philosophy, and linguistics. Thereafter, he worked as a legal assessor in trade unions for a number of years but gradually drifted toward the field of education. In 1963, he became the director of the National Literacy Program in Brazil. The program created great political upheaval in its time because it overturned the electoral base (in Brazil at the time, only the literate could vote).

Freire's work is considered an important example of education being used to bring about social change. In the 1970s his book *Pedagogy of the Oppressed* (Freire, 1970b) and its reviews in Harvard publications established Freire as a radical, revolutionary pedagogue. He became a consultant in the Office of Education of the World Council of Churches. Through this position he became active in the struggles of several nonindustrialized countries, mostly in Africa. In the 1980s he returned to Brazil; in 1989, with the help of the mayor of São Paulo, he started a literacy program based on his theory of education that combined the church and the university. He was scheduled to teach at Harvard in September of 1997, but he died of a heart attack in May of that year at the age of 76.

Paulo Freire's work in literacy enabled illiterate people in Brazil to gain the right to vote, which is a great example of using education for political action.

Some of Freire's other well-known books are *Cultural Action for Freedom* (1970a), *Education for Critical Consciousness* (1973), *Education: The Practice of Freedom* (1976), *The Politics of Education: Culture, Power and Liberation* (1985), *Pedagogy of Hope: Reviving Pedagogy of the Oppressed* (1995), and *Pedagogy of the Heart* (1997).

APPROACH OF FREIRE'S MODEL

The Freirean model uses a three-phase process that is summarized in Table 10.1. Although this approach appears to be simple, it is often difficult in practice because helping people reflect on their experiences requires a high degree of facilitation. The first phase in this approach is the *naming phase*, in which the facilitators and learners reflect on the question "What is the problem?" or "What is the question under discussion?" This has also been called the *listening stage*. It is conducted in equal partnership with the community members to identify problems and determine priorities (Gugushe, 1996). For example, when applying this theory with a group of overweight high school students, the group may identify their problem as that of being overweight or may identify the problem as that of spending too much time using computers and other media.

The second phase is the *reflection phase*, in which the facilitator poses the question "How do we explain this situation?" or "Why is this the case?" This phase is also called the *dialogue stage*. The discussion objects in this stage are often called **codes**, and the process itself **codification**. The codes are created to structure a discussion or problem-posing dialogue around the main issue or issues. A code is a physical representation of an identified community issue in any form. It could be a case study, role play, story, slide show, photograph, song, or so on. An effective code exemplifies a problematic situation with many facets so that participants can express their emo-

TABLE 10.1   Three Phases of the Freirean Model

Phase	Main Question for Reflection
Phase 1: Naming phase (listening stage)	What is the problem?
Phase 2: Reflection phase (dialogue stage)	How do we explain this situation?
Phase 3: Action phase	What can be done to change this situation?

tional and social responses to it. The emphasis is on bringing out the inner emotions of participants as much as possible.

In some training programs, facilitators help in this reflection by using a five-step questioning strategy (debriefing) in which participants, after undergoing the codification process, are asked to (1) describe what they see and feel, (2) as a group define the many levels of the problem, (3) share similar experiences from their lives, (4) question why this problem exists, and (5) develop action plans to address the problem (Gugushe, 1996). For example, in a group of overweight high school students, the facilitators might implement a role play in which the various problems, such as being teased by fellow classmates, inability to participate in some activities in which they would like to participate, and not being comfortable with their body appearance, could be brought out and stir emotions in the participants. These emotions would then be used by the facilitator to initiate learning and moving to the next step of action.

The third phase is the *action phase*, characterized by the question "What can be done to change this situation?" or "What options do we have?" The unique feature of this pedagogical approach is that it is *process centered* as opposed to being outcome centered or product centered. It does not prescribe the attainment of any acceptable end product in the beginning; rather, it focuses on the approach that needs to be followed. In the example of working with a group of overweight high school students, the health educator needs to arrive at an action plan, but the specific content of that action plan is up to the group. The group might choose teasing about the problem of overweight as the most significant issue and might develop a strategy of peer education, or the group might see physical inactivity as the major issue and might develop an approach for becoming more physically active.

Another practical method for applying this model and remembering all the facilitation steps has been described by Wallerstein and Bernstein (1988). They applied

TABLE 10.2 SHOWED Model: A Practical Way to Apply the Freirean Model
What do we *see* here?
What is really *happening*?
How does the story relate to *our* lives?
Why did the person acquire the problem?
How is it possible for this person to become *empowered*?
What can we *do* about it?

Freire's ideas to alcohol and substance abuse prevention programs in youth and coined the acronym SHOWED. Their **SHOWED model** is depicted in Table 10.2.

CONSTRUCTS OF FREIRE'S MODEL

As discussed in earlier chapters, when using theories to design health education and health promotion programs it is very important to organize the ideas from the theory into discrete constructs or building blocks that can be distinctly identified. However, this aspect is particularly challenging with Freire's model. No source clearly identifies the constructs from his model. Still, this chapter identifies five main concepts of Freire's theory that can be used by health education programs and presents these as key constructs (Table 10.3).

TABLE 10.3	Key Constructs of Freire's Model	
Construct	**Definition**	**How to modify?**
Dialogue	Two-way exchange between the learners and educators	• Opportunity for two-way communication (e.g., open group discussion)
Conscientization	Identification of underlying systemic forces of oppression	• Identification of oppressive sources (e.g., brainstorming on root causes) • Working together as change agents (e.g., team-building activities) • Personalizing the issue (e.g., using role plays to generate emotions)
Praxis	Reflective action or active reflection	• Working on a specific project (e.g., a pilot project assignment)
Transformation	Relationship that identifies one as a political and social being	• Discussion on political and social implications of chosen issues (e.g., use of case studies)
Critical consciousness	Political organization of those adversely affected	• Political organization of those adversely affected (e.g., creation of a not-for-profit group)

The first construct of Freire's model is *dialogue*, described as an authentic exchange between the learners and educators (or, for health education, between health educators and the persons needing behavior change or their families). Dialogue entails real, concrete awareness of the context of facts (**social reality**). This reality or context must be from the perspective of the clients. This construct can be applied in health education settings by providing opportunities to have a two-way discussion between health educators and the persons needing behavior change or their families. The discussion must explore the root causes of their behaviors. The techniques of brainstorming, small group discussion, large group discussion, and online discussion forums can be employed in this regard.

Evaluation of health education programs using the Freirean model is mostly done qualitatively (Sharma, 2001). However, quantitative measurement is also possible. To quantitatively evaluate the construct of dialogue, some of the dimensions that can be measured are the extent of two-way communication through self-reports, the extent of problem posing through an objective evaluation of the transcript or video of the discussions, and the extent of joint discovery of the social reality as measured by either self-reports or analysis of the end products of dialogue. Table 10.4 summarizes the quantitative indicators for different constructs of the Freirean model and their methods of measurement.

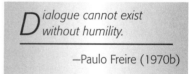

Dialogue cannot exist without humility.

—Paulo Freire (1970b)

The second construct is **conscientization**, or efforts to identify and address the underlying systemic forces of oppression and inequality. Freire (1970b) calls conscientization a process of "humanization" or an effort to enlighten people about the obstacles preventing them from a clear perception of reality. For health education, it refers to identification of the root causes of unhealthy behaviors, which can be done by techniques such as brainstorming or reflecting on case studies. The second component of this construct is working together as change agents. This can be achieved by using team-building activities such as the broken squares game, team juggling game, and so on (Business Fundamentals, 2005). Finally, to influence this construct, the health educator needs to personalize the issue for the participants as much as possible. This can be done by using techniques such as role plays or simulations to generate emotions.

After implementation of this construct in community-based rehabilitation programs, the extent of identification of oppressive sources can be measured by self-report or by checking the transcripts or video recordings. The extent of working together as change agents can also be evaluated by self-report or gauged by the products generated and tasks completed. Finally, the extent to which the key issue influences each participant at a personal level can be ascertained by a self-report questionnaire.

TABLE 10.4   Quantitative Indicators for Different Constructs of the Freirean Model and Their Methods of Measurement

Construct	Quantitative Indicators	Method of Measurement
Dialogue	• Extent of two-way communication • Extent of problem posing • Extent of joint discovery of social reality	• Self-reports • Evaluation of the transcript or video • Self-reports or analysis of the end products of dialogue
Conscientization	• Extent of identification of oppressive sources • Extent of working together as change agents • Extent to which the key issue influences each person at a personal level	• Self-reports or evaluation of transcript or video • Self-reports or evaluation of products generated and tasks completed • Self-reports
Praxis	• Extent of participation and reflection in project planning, implementation, and evaluation • Extent of perceived utility of the project	• Self-reports or assessment of actual products • Self-reports
Transformation	• Extent of focus on issue from the perspective of the people with the unhealthy behavior • Extent of unison on a collective viewpoint	• Self-reports • Self-reports
Critical consciousness	• Extent of cooperation among members; joint identification with the articulated issues, mission, and vision of the group • Extent of communication within the group • Extent of political organization of the group	• Self-reports • Self-reports or evaluation of video • Self-reports or analysis of the tasks completed

The third construct of Freire's model is **praxis**, which refers to what Freire (1985) calls "reflective action" or "active reflection." It is the method of tying together theory and practice. Often we find that there is a gap between preaching (theory) and practice. The purpose of this construct is to narrow that gap and possibly eliminate it. In technical terms, praxis is the linkage between epistemology (source of knowledge) and ontology (reality). In health education interventions, it can be used when the participants work on a specific project and accomplish some tasks. An example could be joint creation of an action plan for behavior change and collective evaluation of it. Some of the researchable aspects that process and impact evaluation can assess for this construct include extent of participation in project planning, extent of reflection in project planning, extent of participation in project implementation, extent of reflection in project implementation, extent of participation in project evaluation, extent of reflection in project evaluation, and extent of perceived utility of the project. All of these can be gauged by self-reports or assessment of actual products.

The fourth construct of the Freirean model is **transformation**. Freire (1976) describes this as the process of changing *objects* (who have a naive consciousness of reality) into *subjects* (who see the theory behind the reality). It connotes independence, status, and integrity. It implies possession of "social consciousness," or being in a relationship that identifies one as a political and social being. In transformation, the solution is not to "integrate" people into the structure of oppression but to transform the structure so that they can become "beings for themselves" (Freire, 1970b). In simple terms, it means making people more aware of the political aspects of any issue.

This construct can be applied in health education by providing the participants opportunity for self-reflection followed by discussion. Educational techniques such as case studies would be quite useful in influencing this construct. For example, a group of high school smokers could start to understand the profit-making motive of the tobacco industry through a case study in which they learn how the industry buys advertising on various media and lobbies legislators to get its products sanction, visibility, and coverage. Finally, they can become cognizant as to how these issues influence smoking behaviors. Evaluators of health education programs can measure the extent of focus on the issue from the perspective of the people negatively affected by the unhealthy behavior, and the extent of unison on a collective viewpoint. These dimensions can be measured by self-reports.

> *Education is never neutral ... either it conforms or it transforms.*
>
> —Paulo Freire (1985)

The final construct of the Freirean model is **critical consciousness**. In essence, this refers to the political organization of those adversely affected. This can be applied in health education by building cooperation between health educators and persons with disabilities, fostering unity on issues, developing effective communication, and augmenting the process of political organization to change policies and legislations. In health education programs, it may often lead to formation of a not-for-profit group. Evaluators of health education programs can measure the extent of cooperation among members; the extent of joint identification with the articulated issues, mission, and vision of the group; the extent of communication within the group; and the extent of political organization of the group. These dimensions can be measured by self-reports.

Table 10.4 summarizes the quantitative indicators for different constructs of the Freirean model and their methods of measurement.

APPLICATIONS OF FREIRE'S MODEL IN HEALTH EDUCATION

The first application of Paulo Freire's work in health education and health promotion in the United States began in the 1980s in a study by Wallerstein and Bernstein (1988). They developed a youth-centered, intergenerational, experiential prevention program called the Adolescent Social Action Program (ASAP) in New Mexico. The program aimed at preventing substance abuse, particularly alcohol, in youth. The program was found to be useful in influencing several process variables, such as empathy, critical thinking, and belief in group action, and some impact variables, such as extent of participation in social action among the participants (Wallerstein & Sanchez-Merki, 1994). Over the years, the program, which started in one school, was successfully extended to several other schools utilizing the peer-to-peer model (Wallerstein, Sanchez-Merki, & Dow, 1997).

Since the initial application in the 1980s, the model has been used in a variety of applications in health education and promotion, both for individual-level behavior change as well as community-level changes. Table 10.5 summarizes these applications in health education and promotion. Freire's model has been used in breast cancer control (Mishra et al., 1998), breast-feeding promotion (Daghio, Vezzani, & Ciardullo, 2003), building health literacy (Kickbusch, 2001; Nutbeam, 2000; Schillinger, 2001; Wang, 2000), community organization (Flick, Reese, Rogers, Fletcher, & Sonn, 1994; Minkler & Wallerstein, 1997), evaluation of coalitions (Sharma, 2002), evaluation of worker safety programs (Cole, 2002; McQuiston,

TABLE 10.5   Applications of Freire's Model in Health Education and Health Promotion

Breast cancer control

Breast-feeding promotion

Community organization

Evaluation of coalitions

Evaluation of worker safety programs

HIV/AIDS prevention

Improving decision making

Informing policy makers of the status of community health through community-taken photographs

Intercultural health promotion

Oral health promotion

Nutrition education

Participatory development of health education materials

Participatory program planning

Participatory evaluation

Patient education

Peer-to-peer approach for reproductive health

People with mental illness

Preparation of health educators

Preparation of nurse educators

Reducing nutritional inequities

Self-care education

Sexually transmitted diseases (STD) education

Training of health functionaries

Work with abused women

2000; Weinger & Lyons, 1992), HIV/AIDS prevention (Campbell, 2004; Gil, 1998), improving decision making (Wittmann-Price, 2004), informing policy makers of the health situation in the community through community-taken photographs (Wang & Burris, 1994), intercultural health promotion (Ditton, 2005), oral health promotion (Gugushe, 1996; Watt, 2002), nutrition education (Krawinkel, Mahr, Wuestefeld, & ten Haaf, 2005), participatory development of health education materials (Rudd & Comings, 1994), participatory program planning (Campbell & Jovchelovitch, 2000; Laverack & Labonte, 2000), participatory evaluation (Sharma & Deepak, 2001), patient education (Fahrenfort, 1987; Roter, 2000; Waters, 2000), a peer-to-peer approach for reproductive health (United Nations Educational, Scientific, and Cultural Organization, 2003), people with mental illness (Bellamy & Mowbray, 1998; Caragata, 2000; Rindner, 2004; Wells, Miranda, Bruce, Alegria, & Wallerstein, 2004), preparation of health educators (Helitzer & Wallerstein, 1999), preparation of nurse educators (Chalmers & Bramadat, 1996; Hartrick, Lindsey, & Hills, 1994; Liimatainen, Poskiparta, Karhila, & Sjögren, 2001; Rush, 1997), reducing nutritional inequities (Travers, 1997), self-care education (Levin, 1999), education about sexually transmitted diseases (Dal Sasso,

> *Education must begin with the solution of the teacher-student contradiction, by reconciling the poles of the contradiction so that both are simultaneously teachers and students.*
>
> —Freire (1970b, p. 53)

Pedrini, & Branco, 2004), training of health functionaries (Fonn & Xaba, 2001; Labonte, Feather, & Hills, 1999), and work with abused women (Mann, 1987).

The model has been applied with different racial and ethnic subgroups. For example, it has been used with African Americans (Waters, 2000), Native Americans (Davis & Reid, 1999), rural Chinese women (Wang & Burris, 1994), Hispanic girls (Gil, 1998), and South African health workers (Fonn & Xaba, 2001).

LIMITATIONS OF FREIRE'S MODEL

Like all the models and theories discussed in this book, the Freirean model has some limitations. Freire has often been criticized for his contorted manner of writing and his obscurantism, which makes interpretation of concepts difficult and measurement complex. The terminology that has been used in this chapter is evidence that Freire's writing style is not very easy and lends itself to multiple interpretations.

Freire's viewpoints are often considered too utopian or ideal. There is excessive idealism in the descriptions of knowing and of learners and educators participating as equals. Such participation is seldom achieved in real-world settings. It is often very difficult for a more educated person (educator) to shed his or her ego and begin to learn from the participants.

Freire presents a circular logic and demonstrates confusing repetitiveness in his writing style. As a consequence, it is difficult to differentiate the constructs of this model so that they are mutually exclusive. To use a theory, educators need all the ideas to be separate from each other so that they can be measured and evaluated distinctly.

The model has also been criticized for requiring social manipulation, which can often be used to domesticate people instead of liberating them. Finally, the choice of codes (such as words, songs, etc.) in the dialogue step is purposively done so that there are no neutral words; instead, the codes challenge the social reality. This adds a bias to the scientific inquiry. In a way, the model is making people think and react in a predetermined fashion. Therefore, the political and social purpose inherent in the model can be challenged as being manipulative.

SKILL-BUILDING ACTIVITY

Let us see how we can apply Freire's model to the issue of unhealthy eating behaviors in high school students. Figure 10.1 depicts each of the constructs from the Freirean

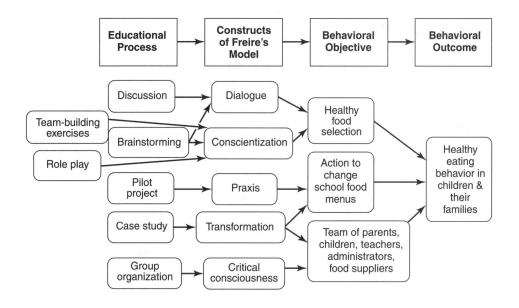

FIGURE 10.1   How Freire's model can be used to modify healthy eating behavior

model and links these with the educational processes and behavioral objectives in this example to modify the eating behavior of the students.

The health education intervention would start by modifying the construct of dialogue, which can be done through a discussion among students, their parents, school teachers, and administrators. The discussion could be organized outside of school hours, and the facilitator would need to ensure that it is conducted in an egalitarian manner. One or more sessions might be used to build initial rapport and then to identify problems regarding eating behaviors.

Brainstorming can be used to build conscientization and explore the root causes of eating problems and their consequences. Role plays on these aspects and team-building exercises can be used to further modify this construct. The construct of praxis can be modified by having participants implement a pilot project related to healthy eating. The specific nature of the pilot project needs to be decided by the participants, but an example could be reading food labels and researching the caloric information of all food products used in the school and finding low-fat alternatives for each high-fat product. To modify the transformation construct, political and social awareness needs to be increased, which can be done by a case study. For example, the reasons why certain food products are included in school menus and others are excluded can be explored. Finally, to raise critical consciousness, the action group of students, teachers, administrators, parents, food providers, and service personnel can form themselves into a regular unit to monitor healthy food products in the school.

Using this approach, you can plan to work on a health behavior issue for a target group of your choice using Freire's model. Table 10.6 provides a set of questions to assist you in choosing an educational method that corresponds to different constructs.

SUMMARY

Paulo Freire (1921–1997), a Brazilian educator, is well known for his work using popular education to build adult literacy. Besides adult education, his model has been used in community organization, development fields, social work, and health education. The three phases in his method are the naming phase, reflection phase, and action phase.

The constructs of his theory are dialogue (two-way communication), conscientization (exploration of root causes of the problem), praxis (action and reflection), trans-

TABLE 10.6	Choosing the Educational Methods for Health Education Program Planning Using Freire's Model

1. What will be the best educational method to facilitate dialogue?
   - Small group discussion
   - Large group discussion
   - Online discussion
   - Other

2. What will be the best educational method to facilitate conscientization?
   - Discussion
   - Brainstorming
   - Role play
   - Simulation
   - Team-building exercises
   - Other

3. What will be the best educational method to facilitate praxis?
   - Pilot project
   - Other

4. What will be the best educational method to facilitate transformation?
   - Case study
   - Field visit
   - Other

5. What will be the best educational method to facilitate critical consciousness?
   - Group formation
   - Coalition building
   - Registration of not-for-profit organization
   - Other

formation (comprehension of political and social causes), and critical consciousness (formation of an organization). Dialogue can be facilitated through small group discussion, large group discussion, or online discussion. Conscientization can be facilitated by brainstorming, discussion, role play, simulation, and team-building exercises. Praxis can be facilitated by providing opportunities to develop action plans or implement pilot projects. Transformation can be facilitated by case studies, field visits, and so on. Critical consciousness can be developed by forming groups, building coalitions, and forming organizations.

REVIEW QUESTIONS

1. Discuss the three-phase approach of the Freirean model.
2. What does the acronym SHOWED mean in the context of the Freirean model?
3. Briefly describe the five constructs of Freire's model.
4. Differentiate between praxis and transformation.
5. How can critical consciousness be modified?
6. Using Freire's model, work to modify a health behavior issue for a target group of your choice.

WEBSITE

Go to the Web component of *Theoretical Foundations of Health Education and Health Promotion* at http://health.jbpub.com/foundations for Web exercises, additional resources related to this chapter, and student review tools.

GLOSSARY TERMS

codes
codification
conscientization
critical consciousness
dialogue
informal education

popular education
praxis
problematization (problem posing)
SHOWED model
social reality
transformation

REFERENCES AND FURTHER READING

Bellamy, C. D., & Mowbray, C. T. (1998). Supported education as an empowerment intervention for people with mental illness. *Journal of Community Psychology, 26*, 401–413.

Business Fundamentals. (2005). Team building activities. Retrieved January 1, 2006, from http://www.businessfundamentals.com/TeamBuilding.htm.

Campbell, C. (2004). Creating environments that support peer education: Experiences from HIV/AIDS prevention in South Africa. *Health Education, 104*, 197–200.

Campbell, C., & Jovchelovitch, S. (2000). Health, community and development: Towards a social psychology of participation. *Journal of Community and Applied Social Psychology, 10*, 255–270.

Caragata, L. (2000). Using popular education groups: Can we develop a health promotions strategy for psychiatric consumers/survivors? *Canadian Journal of Community Mental Health, 19*, 5–20.

Chalmers, K. I., & Bramadat, I. J. (1996). Community development: Theoretical and practical issues for community health nursing in Canada. *Journal of Advanced Nursing, 24*, 719–726.

Cole, H. P. (2002). Cognitive-behavioral approaches to farm community safety education: A conceptual analysis. *Journal of Agricultural Safety and Health*, *8*, 145–159.

Cornwall, A., & Jewkes, R. (1995). What is participatory research? *Social Science and Medicine*, *41*, 1667–1676.

Daghio, M. M., Vezzani, M. D., & Ciardullo, A. V. (2003). Impact of an educational intervention on breastfeeding. *Birth*, *30*, 214–215.

Dal Sasso, G. T. M., Pedrini, D., & Branco, I. (2004). Interactive media of health education in sexually transmitted diseases (STDs). Retrieved December 31, 2005, from http://cmbi.bjmu.edu.cn/news/report/2004/medinfo2004/pdffiles/papers/348_d040005155.pdf.

Davis, S. M., & Reid, R. (1999). Practicing participatory research in American Indian communities. *American Journal of Clinical Nutrition*, *69*, 755S–759S.

Ditton, M. (2005). Research plan for intercultural health promotion education. Retrieved December 31, 2005, from http://conference.herdsa.org.au/2005/pdf/non_refereed/075.pdf.

Fahrenfort, M. (1987). Patient emancipation by health education: An impossible goal? *Patient Education and Counseling*, *10*, 25–37.

Flick, L. H., Reese, C. G., Rogers, G., Fletcher, P., & Sonn, J. (1994). Building community for health: Lessons from a seven-year-old neighborhood/university partnership. *Health Education Quarterly*, *21*, 369–380.

Fonn, S., & Xaba, M. (2001). Health workers for change: Developing the initiative. *Health Policy and Planning*, *16*(Suppl. 1), 13–18.

Freire, P. (1970a). *Cultural action for freedom*. Cambridge, MA: Harvard Educational Review and Center for the Study of Development and Social Change.

Freire, P. (1970b). *Pedagogy of the oppressed*. New York: Continuum.

Freire, P. (1973). *Education for critical consciousness*. New York: Continuum.

Freire, P. (1976). *Education: The practice of freedom*. London: Writers and Readers Cooperative.

Freire, P. (1985). *The politics of education: Culture, power and liberation*. South Hadley, MA: Bergin and Garvey.

Freire, P. (1995). *Pedagogy of hope: Reviving pedagogy of the oppressed*. New York: Continuum.

Freire, P. (1997). *Pedagogy of the heart*. New York: Continuum.

Gil, V. E. (1998). Empowerment rhetoric, sexual negotiation, and Latinas' AIDS risk: Research implications for prevention health education. *International Quarterly of Community Health Education*, *18*, 9–27.

Gugushe, T. S. (1996). An overview of Paulo Freire's perspective on health education. *Journal of the Dental Association of South Africa*, *51*, 734–736.

Hamilton, E., & Cunningham, P. M. (1989). Community-based adult education. In S. B. Merriam & P. M. Cunningham (Eds.), *Handbook of adult and continuing education*. San Francisco: Jossey Bass.

Hartrick, G., Lindsey, E., & Hills, M. (1994). Family nursing assessment: Meeting the challenge of health promotion. *Journal of Advanced Nursing*, *20*, 85–91.

Helitzer, D., & Wallerstein, N. (1999). A proposal for a graduate curriculum integrating theory and practice in public health. *Health Education Research*, *14*, 697–706.

Kickbusch, I. S. (2001). Health literacy: Addressing the health and education divide. *Health Promotion International*, *16*, 289–297.

Krawinkel, M. B., Mahr, J., Wuestefeld, M., & ten Haaf, J. (2005). Nutrition education for illiterate children in southern Madagascar: Addressing their needs, perceptions and capabilities. *Public Health Nutrition, 8,* 366–372.

Labonte, R. Feather, J., & Hills, M. (1999). A story/dialogue method for health promotion knowledge development and evaluation. *Health Education Research, 14,* 39–50.

Laverack, G., & Labonte, R. (2000). A planning framework for community empowerment within health promotion. *Health Policy and Planning, 15,* 255–262.

Levin, L. S. (1999). Patient education and self-care. *International Journal of Self Help and Self Care, 1,* 21–31.

Liimatainen, L., Poskiparta, M., Karhila, P., & Sjögren, A. (2001). The development of reflective learning in the context of health counselling and health promotion during nurse education. *Journal of Advanced Nursing, 34,* 648–658.

Mann, B. (1987).Working with battered women: Radical education or therapy? In E. Pence (Ed.), *In our best interest: A process for personal and social change* (pp. 104–116). Duluth: Minnesota Program Development.

McQuiston, T. H. (2000). Empowerment evaluation of worker safety and health education programs. *American Journal of Industrial Medicine, 38,* 584–597.

Minkler, M., & Wallerstein, N. (1997). Improving health through community organizing and community building: A health education perspective. In M. Minkler (Ed.), *Community organizing and community building for health* (pp. 30–52). New Brunswick, NJ: Rutgers University Press.

Mishra, S. I., Chavez, L. R., Magana, J. R., Nava, P., Burciaga, V. R., and Hubbell, F. A. (1998). Improving breast cancer control among Latinas: Evaluation of a theory-based educational program. *Health Education and Behavior, 25,* 653–670.

Nutbeam, D. (2000). Health literacy as a public health goal: A challenge for contemporary health education and communication strategies into the 21st century. *Health Promotion International, 15,* 259–267.

Rindner, E. C. (2004). Using Freirean empowerment for health education with adolescents in primary, secondary, and tertiary psychiatric settings. *Journal of Child and Adolescent Psychiatric Nursing, 17,* 78–84.

Roter, D. (2000). The medical visit context of treatment decision-making and the therapeutic relationship. *Health Expectations, 3,* 17–25.

Rudd, R. E., & Comings, J. P. (1994). Learner developed materials: An empowering product. *Health Education Quarterly, 21,* 313–327.

Rush, K. L. (1997). Health promotion ideology and nursing education. *Journal of Advanced Nursing, 25,* 1292–1298.

Schillinger, D. (2001). Improving the quality of chronic disease management for populations with low functional health literacy: A call to action. *Disease Management, 4,* 103–109.

Sharma, M. (2001). Freire's adult education model: An underutilized model in alcohol and drug education? [Editorial]. *Journal of Alcohol and Drug Education, 47*(1), 1–3.

Sharma, M. (2002, July). *Using Freire's model for impact evaluation of coalitions in health and human services.* Paper presented at the summer residency of Walden University at Indiana University, Bloomington, IN.

Sharma, M., & Deepak, S. (2001). A participatory evaluation of community-based rehabilitation program in North Central Vietnam. *Disability and Rehabilitation, 23,* 352–358.

Smith, M. K. (2005). Paulo Freire. Retrieved December 29, 2005, from http://www.infed.org/thinkers/et-freir.htm.

Travers, K. D. (1997). Reducing inequities through participatory research and community empowerment. *Health Education and Behavior, 24,* 344–356.

United Nations Educational, Scientific, and Cultural Organization. (2003). *Peer approach in adolescent reproductive health education: Some lessons learned.* Bangkok, Thailand: Author.

Wallerstein, N., & Bernstein, E. (1988). Empowerment education: Freire's ideas adapted to health education. *Health Education Quarterly, 15,* 379–394.

Wallerstein, N., & Sanchez-Merki, V. (1994). Freirian praxis in health education: Research results from an adolescent prevention program. *Health Education Research, 9,* 105–118.

Wallerstein, N., Sanchez-Merki, V., & Dow, L. (1997). Freirian praxis in health education and community organizing. A case study of an adolescent prevention program. In M. Minkler (Ed.), *Community organizing and community building for health* (pp. 195–211). New Brunswick, NJ: Rutgers University Press.

Wang, R. (2000). Critical health literacy: A case study from China in schistosomiasis control. *Health Promotion International, 15,* 269–274.

Wang, C., & Burris, M. A. (1994). Empowerment through photo novella: Portraits of participation. *Health Education Quarterly, 21,* 171–186.

Waters, C. M. (2000). End-of-life care directives among African Americans: Lessons learned—a need for community-centered discussion and education. *Journal of Community Health Nursing, 17,* 25–37.

Watt, R. G. (2002). Emerging theories into the social determinants of health: Implications for oral health promotion. *Community Dentistry and Oral Epidemiology, 30,* 241–247.

Weinger, M., & Lyons, M. (1992). Problem-solving in the fields: An action-oriented approach to farmworker education about pesticides. *American Journal of Industrial Medicine, 22,* 667–690.

Wells, K., Miranda, J., Bruce, M. L., Alegria, M., & Wallerstein, N. (2004). Bridging community intervention and mental health services research. *American Journal of Psychiatry, 161,* 955–963.

Wittmann-Price, R. A. (2004). Emancipation in decision-making in women's health care. *Journal of Advanced Nursing, 47,* 437–445.

action stage: Stage of change in which a person has made meaningful change in the past six months with regard to adopting a healthy behavior or quitting an unhealthy behavior.

advocacy: In health, advocacy is about creating a shift in the public opinion and mobilizing the essential resources to support any issue or policy that affects the health of a community or constituency.

analytical epidemiology: Study of the determinants of health, such as behaviors and environments.

Assessment Protocol for Excellence in Public Health (APEXPH) model: A public health planning model suitable for local levels that consists of three parts: organizational capacity assessment, community process, and completing the cycle.

attitude toward the behavior: A person's overall feeling of like or dislike toward any given behavior.

attitudes: Relatively constant feelings, predispositions, or set of beliefs directed toward an idea, object, person, or situation.

audience segmentation: Identifying distinct groups of people who are similar to each other in particular characteristics and thus likely to respond to messages in a similar way.

awareness: Becoming conscious of an action, idea, object, person, or situation.

behavior: Any overt action, conscious or unconscious, performed by an individual that has a measurable frequency, intensity, and duration; a category of actions with a specification of target, action, context, and time (TACT).

behavioral beliefs: Beliefs that performing a given behavior will lead to certain outcomes.

behavioral intention: The thought to perform the behavior, which is an immediate determinant of the given behavior.

beliefs: Statements of perceived facts or impressions about the world.

CDCynergy: A multimedia health communication planning model developed by the Centers for Disease Control and Prevention, based on a CD-ROM with tailored versions, that comprises six phases: problem definition and description, problem analysis, communication program planning, program and evaluation development, program implementation and management, and feedback.

certified health education specialist (CHES): An individual who meets the required health education training qualifications, has successfully passed the certification exam, and meets continuing education requirements.

challenge: A component of hardiness that refers to a willingness to undertake change and confront new activities and obtain opportunities for growth.

change agent: An individual who influences a potential adopter's decision about an innovation in a favorable way.

chronic strains: Chronic stressors that result from the responses of one social group to another, such as overt or covert, intentional or unintentional discriminatory behavior due to race, ethnicity, or so forth.

chronic stressors: Type of stressors that are ongoing and last for a sustained period of time. These include persistent life difficulties, role strains, chronic strains, community-wide strains, and daily hassles.

clarity of results: The degree to which outcomes of an innovation are clearly visible.

coalition: Grouping of separate organizations in a community united to pursue a common goal related to health or other matters affecting a large number of people.

code: A physical representation of an identified community issue in a form such as a case study, role play, story, slide show, photograph, song, or so on.

code of ethics for health educators: Written document for professional conduct of health educators that delineates responsibilities to the public, profession, and employers and responsibilities regarding the delivery of health education, research and evaluation, and professional preparation.

codification: The process of creating codes to structure a discussion that highlights problems.

commitment: A component of hardiness that refers to the tendency to involve oneself in whatever one encounters, or a feeling of deep involvement in the activities of life.

communication channels: The links between those who have know-how regarding an innovation and those who have not yet adopted that innovation; the means by which messages are transferred between individuals.

community: A collection of people identified by a set of shared values.

community development: A stage in which local initiative and leadership in a community has been organized and stimulated to a level at which change in health or other matters is occurring.

community empowerment: Process whereby individuals gain mastery over their lives in the context of changing their social and political environments.

community mobilization: Persuading community members to attend or participate in any activity planned by the health educator. Its purpose is to enhance awareness of a given issue at the community level.

community organization: Process in which community members identify needs, set objectives, prioritize issues, develop plans, and implement projects for community improvement in health and related matters.

community participation: When community members actively participate in planning or implementing projects.

community-wide strains: Chronic stressors that operate at an ecological level, such as residing in a high-crime neighborhood.

compatibility: The perception of an innovation's consistency with the values, past experiences, and needs of potential adopters.

complexity: The perception regarding the degree of difficulty in understanding and using a new idea, practice, or product.

comprehensibility: A component of the theory of sense of coherence that refers to the extent to which one perceives that the stressors that confront one make cognitive sense, implying that there is some set structure, consistency, order, clarity, and predictability.

Comprehensive Health Education Model (CHEM): An older model of health education that consists of six steps: involving people, setting goals, defining problems, designing plans, conducting activities, and evaluating results.

conscientization: A term coined by Paulo Freire and a distinct construct of his ideology. It refers to the process of identification of the root causes of any problem.

consciousness raising: An experiential process of change in the transtheoretical model that entails raising awareness of the causes, consequences, and cures for a particular problem.

contemplation stage: Stage of change in which a person is considering change in the foreseeable future but not immediately, usually defined as between one and six months.

contingency management: *See* reinforcement management.

control: A component of hardiness that refers to the belief that one causes the events of one's life and can influence the environment.

control beliefs: Beliefs about internal and external factors that may inhibit or facilitate the performance of a behavior.

coping: Purposive, psychological mechanisms of dealing with stressors.

costs: In diffusion of innovations theory, the tangible and intangible expenses incurred in the adoption of a new idea, practice, or product.

counterconditioning: A behavioral process of change in the transtheoretical model that requires learning of new, healthier behavior instead of the old, unhealthy behavior.

critical consciousness: A construct of the Freirean model that refers to the development of the political organization of those adversely affected by the problem.

cues to action: Precipitating forces that make a person feel the need to take action.

daily hassles: Chronic stressors that include everyday problems, such as getting stuck in traffic.

decisional balance: The construct of the transtheoretical model that addresses the relative importance placed by an individual on the advantages (pros) of behavior change as opposed to the disadvantages (cons).

defense mechanisms: The devices that the mind uses to alter an individual's perception of situations that disturb the internal milieu or mental balance.

demonstrability: The degree to which an innovation may be experimented with on a limited basis.

descriptive epidemiology: Study of the time, place, and population attributes of a health problem through the collection of data such as mortality (death), morbidity (illness), and disability rates.

development of social norms: Creating social acceptance for a practice, behavior, condition, policy, law, or environment that may affect health in a community.

dialogue: A construct of the Freirean model that refers to two-way communication between learners and educators.

diffusion: The process by which a new idea, object, or practice filters through various channels in a community over time.

dramatic relief: An experiential process of change in the transtheoretical model that enhances emotional arousal about one's behavior and emphasizes the relief that can come from changing it.

emotional coping: Techniques employed by a person to control the emotional and physiological states associated with acquisition of a new behavior.

emotion-focused coping: Method of dealing with a stressor in which the focus is inward, namely, on altering the way one thinks or feels about a situation or an event.

enabling factors: Antecedents to behavioral or environmental change that allow a motivation or environmental policy to be realized (e.g., availability of resources, accessibility, laws, or skills).

environment: Physical or social circumstances or conditions that surround a person.

environmental reevaluation: An experiential process of change in the transtheoretical model that involves both affective and cognitive components regarding how the behavior affects one's environment and how changing the behavior would influence the environment.

exchange theory: Marketing theory of voluntary transfer or transaction of something valuable between two individuals or groups.

event-based models: Models of stress that underscore the role of life events in the causation of stress.

forethought capability: The proposition that most behavior is purposive and regulated by prior thoughts.

formative research: In social marketing, collecting quantitative and qualitative data about a problem, its context, the attitudes and behaviors of the target audience, ways to reach the target audience, and existing messages and materials.

general adaptation syndrome: The three-stage physiological response (alarm reaction, resistance, and exhaustion) of any organism that encounters nonspecific stimuli.

goal setting: A determinant of behavior composed of setting goals and developing plans to accomplish chosen behaviors.

hardiness: A personality trait that is found to predict better coping with stressors; it consists of three components: commitment, control, and challenge.

health: A means to achieve desirable goals in life while maintaining a multidimensional (physical, mental, social, political, economic, and spiritual) equilibrium that is operationalized for individuals as well as for communities.

health behavior: Actions with a potentially measurable frequency, intensity, and duration performed at the individual, interpersonal, organizational, community, or public policy level for primary, secondary, or tertiary prevention. *See also* preventive behaviors.

health belief model (HBM): Theory designed to exclusively predict health behaviors based on the constructs of perceived susceptibility, perceived severity, perceived benefits, perceived costs, cues to action, and self-efficacy.

health education: Systematic application of a set of techniques to voluntarily and positively influence health through changing the antecedents of behavior (awareness, information, knowledge, skills, beliefs, attitudes, and values) in individuals, groups, or communities.

health literacy: The capacity of an individual to obtain, interpret, and understand basic health information and services and the competence to use such information and services in ways that are health enhancing.

health promotion: Process of empowering people to improve their health by providing educational, political, legislative, organizational, social, and community supports.

helping relationships: A behavioral process of change in the transtheoretical model that entails developing caring, open, trusting, and accepting relationships that help in adherence to the healthy behavior.

homophily: The degree of similarity among group members.

illness behaviors: Actions taken by a person who feels sick and indulges in the behavior for the purpose of defining the state of his or her health and for discovering suitable remedies.

informal education: Type of education that uses experiential learning (i.e., learning from one's experiences) and simple conversation and can take place in any setting.

information: The collection of facts related to an action, idea, object, person, or situation.

innovation: A new idea, object, or practice that is to be adopted.

intervention mapping: A health promotion and education planning model that comprises six steps: needs assessment or problem analysis; creating matrices of change objectives; selecting theory-based intervention methods and practical strategies; developing an organized program; planning for adoption, implementation, and sustainability of the program; and generating an evaluation plan.

knowledge: Learning of facts and gaining insights related to an action, idea, object, person, or situation.

legislation: A law passed by elected officials at the local, state, or federal level.

levels of change: Five distinct but interrelated levels of psychological problems that can be addressed in psychotherapy: symptom/situational problems, maladaptive cognitions, current interpersonal conflicts, family/system conflicts, and intrapersonal conflicts.

life change events: *See* life events.

life events: A distinct category of stressors that are discrete, major happenings affecting or having the potential to influence one's body, mind, family, or community (e.g., death of a family member). Also known as life change events.

lobbying: Working with and influencing policy makers to develop an issue or policy that affects the health of a given community.

manageability: A component of the sense of coherence that refers to the extent to which one feels that the resources under one's control are adequate to meet the demands posed by the stressors.

marketing mix: The combination of product, price, place, and promotion.

meaningfulness: A component of the sense of coherence that refers to the extent to which one feels that life makes sense emotionally and that at least some of the stressors in life are worth investing energy in and are worthy of commitment and engagement.

model: An eclectic, creative, simplified, and miniaturized application of concepts for addressing problems.

Model for Health Education Planning (MHEP): One of the older models of health education planning; it comprises six phases: program initiation, needs assessment, goal setting, planning/programming, implementation, and evaluation.

Model for Health Education Planning and Resource Development (MHEPRD): A five-phase model of health education planning developed in the 1980s that consists of the following phases: health education plans, demonstration programs, operational programs, research programs, and information and statistics.

motivation to comply: Degree to which a person wants to act in accordance with the perceived wishes of those significant in his or her life.

Multilevel Approach to Community Health (MATCH) model: A health education planning model that consists of five phases, namely, goals selection, intervention planning, program development, implementation preparations, and evaluation.

networking: Creating interdependent relationships with individuals, groups, and organizations to accomplish mutually set objectives in health or other matters.

nonevents: Absence of events that have the potential of causing stress; these include desired or anticipated events that do not occur, desired events that do not occur even though their occurrence is normative for people of a certain group, and situations in which a person has nothing to do.

normative beliefs: A person's beliefs about how other people who are significant in his or her life would like him or her to behave.

opinion leaders: Influential individuals in a community who sway the beliefs and actions of their colleagues in either a positive or negative direction.

optimism: A personality disposition that refers to the tendency to expect the best possible outcome or think about the most hopeful aspects of any situation.

outcome expectancies: Value a person places on the probable outcomes that result from performing a behavior.

outcome expectations: Anticipation of the probable outcomes that would ensue as a result of engaging in the behavior under discussion.

outcome evaluations: Value a person places on each outcome resulting from performance of a given behavior.

partnership: Establishment of collaboration with multiple partners who will work on the same issue.

PEN-3 model: A culturally appropriate planning model that is composed of three interrelated and interdependent dimensions, each with an acronym of PEN: (1) health education (person, extended family, and neighborhood); (2) educational diagnosis of health behavior (perceptions, enablers, nurturers); and (3) cultural appropriateness of health behavior (positive, exotic, and negative).

perceived barriers: Beliefs concerning the actual and imagined costs of following a new behavior.

perceived behavioral control: How much a person feels he or she is in command of enacting the given behavior.

perceived benefits: Beliefs in the advantages of the methods suggested for reducing the risk or seriousness of the disease or harmful state resulting from a particular behavior.

perceived power: A person's perception about how easy or difficult it is to perform the behavior in each condition identified in his or her control beliefs.

perceived relative advantage: The perception regarding how much better a new product, idea, or practice is than the one it will replace.

perceived severity: Subjective belief in the extent of harm that can result from an acquired disease or harmful state as a result of a particular behavior.

perceived susceptibility: Subjective belief regarding a person's likelihood of acquiring a disease or reaching a harmful state as a result of indulging in a particular behavior.

perceived threat: The combination of perceived susceptibility and perceived severity.

persistent life difficulties: Chronic stressors that include life events lasting longer than 6 months, such as long-term disability.

pervasiveness: The degree to which an innovation requires changes or adjustments by other elements in the social system.

place: The distribution channels, or where and how customers are going to get the product.

Planned Approach to Community Health (PATCH) model: A health planning model developed by the Centers for Disease Control and Prevention that comprises five phases: mobilizing the community, collecting and organizing data, choosing health priorities, developing a comprehensive intervention plan, and evaluating results.

policy: Creating the environmental supports needed to sustain a behavior change.

policy development: The process of developing a policy with ramifications for affecting the health of communities.

popular education: Type of education that is based on community needs, fosters equal relationship between learners and teachers, builds on a community's experience, and aims at social change.

praxis: A construct of the Freirean model that refers to the method of tying together theory and practice; also known as active reflection or reflective action.

PRECEDE-PROCEED model: A health promotion and health education model that is composed of eight phases: social assessment and situational analysis, epidemiological assessment, educational and ecological assessment, administrative and policy assessment and intervention alignment, implementation, process evaluation, impact evaluation, and outcome evaluation. The acronym PRECEDE stands for predisposing, reinforcing, and enabling constructs in educational/environmental diagnosis and evaluation. The acronym PROCEED stands for policy, regulatory, and organizational constructs in educational and environmental development.

precontemplation stage: Stage of change in which a person is not considering change in the foreseeable future, usually defined as the next six months.

predisposing factors: Factors that are antecedents to behavioral change and that provide motivation for the behavior (e.g., knowledge, beliefs, attitudes, values, perceptions).

preparation stage: Stage of change in which a person is planning for change in the immediate future, usually defined as in the next month.

preventive behaviors: Actions taken by a person who believes himself or herself to be healthy for the purpose of preventing disease or detecting disease in an asymptomatic phase. Also known as health behaviors.

price: The tangible and intangible things that the target audience has to give up in order to adopt the new idea (product).

primary appraisal: A process in which a person determines the severity of the stressor and makes an assessment regarding whether he or she is in trouble; one of the constructs of theories of stress and coping.

primary prevention: Preventive actions that are taken prior to the onset of disease or an injury with a view to removing the possibility of their ever occurring.

problem posing: *See* problematization.

problematization: The essence of Freirean methodology; it includes emphasis on raising questions without providing any predetermined answers. The participants have to reflect and arrive at answers themselves. Also known as problem posing.

problem-focused coping: Method of dealing with a given stressor by one's ability to think and to alter the environmental event or situation.

product: In social marketing, the behavior or offering that is intended for the target audience to adopt.

promotion: The mechanism by which one gets a message across to a target audience.

publics: The primary and secondary audiences involved in a social marketing program.

purse strings: The amount of money available at one's disposal for a social marketing campaign.

reappraisal: The feedback loop by which a person determines whether the effects of the stressor have been effectively negated; one of the constructs of theories of stress and coping.

recent life events: Discrete major life happenings that have occurred within the past year.

reciprocal determinism: The triadic reciprocity of causation among personal factors, environment, and behavior.

reinforcement management: A behavioral process of change in the transtheoretical model that utilizes reinforcements and punishments for taking steps in a particular direction.

reinforcing factors: Factors that follow a behavior and provide continuing rewards for sustenance of the behavior (e.g., family, peers, teachers, employers, health providers, community leaders, decision makers).

reinvention: The degree to which potential adopters of an innovation can adapt, refine, or modify the innovation to suit their needs.

remote life events: Discrete major life happenings that have occurred in the distant past, beyond one year.

response-based model: Model of stress that underscores the role of responses arising out of stress.

reversibility: In the diffusion of innovations theory, the ability and degree to which the status quo can be reinstated by ceasing to use the innovation.

role strains: Chronic stressors that include either strain from performing specific roles (such as parenting, working, being in a relationship, etc.) or performing a multiplicity of roles at the same time.

secondary appraisal: A process in theories of stress and coping in which a person determines how much control he or she has over the stressor. If control is high, then no stress develops; if control is low, then stress develops.

secondary prevention: Actions that block the progression of an injury or disease at its incipient stage.

self-control: *See* goal setting.

self-efficacy: The confidence that a person has in his or her ability to pursue a behavior.

self-efficacy in overcoming impediments: Confidence that a person has in overcoming barriers while performing a given behavior.

self-liberation: A behavioral process of change in the transtheoretical model that entails belief that one can change and a commitment and recommitment to act on that change.

self-reevaluation: An experiential process of change in the transtheoretical theory that involves both affective and cognitive components and includes a person's assessment of his or her self-image with the new behavior.

self-reflective capability: Human attribute that entails analysis of experiences and thinking about one's own thought processes.

self-regulatory capability: Human attribute that entails the setting of internal standards and self-evaluative reaction's for one's behavior.

sense of coherence: A theory that purports that comprehensibility, manageability, and meaningfulness in life improve coping with stress.

SHOWED model: A mnemonic acronym of the phases of Freirean methodology for facilitating a discussion. The steps are as follows: What do we *see* here? What is really *happening*? How does the story relates to *our* lives? *Why* does the person have the problem? How is it possible for the person to become *empowered*? What can we *do* about it?

sick role behaviors: Actions taken for the purpose of getting well by people who are sick.

situational perception: How one perceives and interprets the environment around oneself.

skill: Act involving physical movement, coordination, and use of the motor function.

social cognitive theory (SCT): Theory that posits a triadic reciprocity among behavior, environment, and cognitive personal factors.

social learning theory: Theory that posits that learning takes place from imitation, reinforcements, and self-control.

social liberation: An experiential process of change in the transtheoretical theory that refers to an increase in social opportunities or alternatives.

social marketing: The use of commercial marketing techniques to help in acquisition of a behavior that is beneficial for the health of a target population.

social networks: Person-centered webs of social relationships.

social reality: Awareness of the context of facts. This context must be from the perspective of the participants or clients.

social support: The help obtained through social relationships and interpersonal exchanges.

social system: People in a society connected by a common goal.

stages of change: Discrete phases in the transtheoretical model through which a person transits when undergoing change of a behavior. The stages consist of precontemplation, contemplation, action, and maintenance.

stimulus control: A behavioral process of change in the transtheoretical model that involves modifying the environment to increase cues for healthy behavior and decrease cues for unhealthy behavior.

stress: The response of the body and mind, including behaviors, as a result of encountering stressors, interpreting them, and making judgments about controlling or influencing the outcomes of these events.

stressors: Various external events that pose actual or perceived threats to the body or mind.

subjective norm: One's belief that most of the significant others in one's life think one should or should not perform a particular behavior.

symbolizing capability: Human attribute that entails the use of symbols in attributing meaning to experiences.

temptation: The urge to engage in unhealthy behavior when confronted with a difficult situation.

termination: The point in the transtheoretical model at which the person has completely quit the habit, has no temptation to relapse, and is fully self-efficacious to continue with the change.

tertiary prevention: Those actions taken after the onset of disease or an injury with a view to assisting diseased or disabled people.

theory of planned behavior (TPB): A theory of behavior that posits that intention precedes behavior and is determined by attitude toward the behavior, subjective norm, and perceived behavioral control.

theory of reasoned action (TRA): A theory of behavior that posits that intention precedes behavior and is determined by attitude toward the behavior and subjective norm.

time: In the diffusion of innovations theory, the interval between becoming aware of an idea and adopting it.

transactional model: Model of stress and coping that is characterized by the interaction of a person with the environment in four stages: primary appraisal, secondary appraisal, coping, and reappraisal.

transformation: A construct of the Freirean methodology that implies comprehension of the political and social causes of any given problem.

transtheoretical model (TTM): A model of behavior change that posits that people move through five stages of change, from precontemplation (not thinking about change) to maintenance (acquisition of the healthy behavior), in which they are aided through ten processes of change and the constructs of decisional balance, self-efficacy, and overcoming temptation.

type A personality: Personality type that is characterized by a hurrying nature, exercising control over people and things, sense of urgency, and challenging nature.

type B personality: Personality type that is characterized by a more laid back lifestyle and a more relaxed disposition than a type A personality.

value expectancy theories: Theories that postulate that a behavior depends on the importance placed by an individual on an outcome (value) and the individual's estimate of the likelihood that a given action will result in that outcome (expectancy).

values: Enduring beliefs or systems of beliefs that a specific mode of conduct or end state of behavior is personally or socially preferable.

vicarious capability: Human attribute that entails the ability to learn from observing other people's behavior and the consequences that they face.

PHOTO CREDITS

INDEX

Action stage, 94, 95
Adler, Alfred, 141
Adopter categories, 215–216
Advocacy, defined, 27
Ajzen, Icek, 117, 118
Allport, Gordon, 165
American Academy of Health Behavior
   (AAHB), 14, 15
American Association for Health Education
   (AAHE), 10, 11, 14, 15–16
American College Health Association (ACHA),
   14, 16–17
American Public Health Association (APHA)
   Public Health Education and Health
      Promotion (PHEHP), 14, 17
   School Health Education and Services
      (SHES), 14, 18
American School Health Association (ASHA),
   14, 18–19
Analytical epidemiology, 43
Andreasen, Alan, 190, 192
Antonovsky, Aaron, 142
Appraisal
   primary, 143, 145
   secondary, 144, 145
Assessment Protocol for Excellence in Public
   Health (APEXPH), 40, 52–53
Atkinson, J. W., 71
Attitudes, defined, 24
Attitude toward the behavior, 120, 123
Attribution theories, 118
Audience segmentation, 193
Awareness, defined, 21–22
Bandura, Albert, 28, 29, 165–167, 168
Behavior
   as a construct, 118–120, 123
   defined, 4–5
   health-directed, 6
   health-related, 6
   risk, 6

Behavioral beliefs, 120, 123
Behavioral intention, 120, 123
Behavioral research
   health belief model and, 78, 79
   social cognitive theory and, 173–174
   transtheoretical model and, 100–101
*Belief, Attitude, Intention and Behavior: An
   Introduction to Theory and Research* (Fishbein
   and Ajzen), 117
Beliefs, defined, 24

Cannon, Walter, 139
Capabilities, social cognitive theory, 167–168
CDCynergy, 41, 57–58
Centers for Disease Control and Prevention
   CDCynergy, 41, 57–58
   Planned Approach to Community Health
      (PATCH), 40, 46–49
Certification, 10–12
Certified health education specialist (CHES),
   10–11
Challenge, 146
Change agent, 217
Change theories, 28
Chronic strains, 143
Chronic stressors, 143
Clarity of results, 213, 214
Coalition building, defined, 26–27
Code of Ethics, 14–15
Codes, 234
Codification, 234
Commercial marketing, differences between
   social marketing and, 190–192
Commitment, 146
Communication channels, 213, 215, 218
Community, defined, 25
Community development, 26
Community empowerment, 26
Community mobilization, 25
Community organization, 25

Community participation, 25–26
Community-wide strains, 143
Compatibility, 213, 214
Competency-Based Framework for Graduate Level health Educators, A, 11
Complexity, 213, 214
Comprehensibility, 146, 147
Comprehensive Health Education Model (CHEM), 40, 53–54
Conscientization, 236, 237, 238
Consciousness raising, 95, 96
Consistency theories, 117–118
Constructs, 29
    of diffusion of innovations, 212–219, 223–225
    of Freire's model, 236–240
    of health belief model, 72–77
    of social cognitive theory, 168–173
    of social marketing, 192–197, 202, 203–204
    of stress and coping theories, 142–148
    of theory of planned behavior, 118–122, 124
    of theory of reasoned action, 118–123
    of transtheoretical model, 94–100
Contemplation stage, 94, 95
Contingency management, 98
Control, 144, 146
Control beliefs, 122, 124
Coping
    See also Stress and coping, theories of
    use of term, 140, 141
Costs, 213, 214
Counterconditioning, 96, 98
Critical consciousness, 236, 238, 240
Cues to action, 74, 77

Daily hassles, 143
Decisional balance, 99
Decision making under uncertainty model, 71
Defense mechanisms, 141
Demonstrability, 213, 214
Descriptive epidemiology, 43
Descriptive theories, 28
Development of social norms, 28
Dialogue, 233, 236, 237, 238
DiClemente, Carlo, 93
Diffusion, defined, 210

Diffusion of innovations
    applications of, 219, 220–221
    choosing educational methods for, 225
    constructs of, 212–219, 223–225
    defined, 210–211
    development of, 211–212
    limitations of, 222–223
    skill-building activity, shaping constructs, 223–225
Diffusion of Innovations (Rogers), 212
Directors of Health Promotion and Education (DHPE), 14
Dramatic relief, 96, 97

Education
    informal, 232
    popular, 232–233
Edwards, W., 71
Effectiveness-based model, 58
Emotional coping, 170, 173
Emotion-focused coping, 144, 145
EMPOWER, 45
Enabling factors, 43
Environment, 169, 171–172
Environmental reevaluation, 96, 97
Epidemiology, descriptive versus analytical, 43
Eta Sigma Gamma, 14, 19–20
Ethics, code of, 14–15
Event-based models, 140, 153
Evidence-based/risk factor analysis model, 58
Exchange theory, 192
Explanatory theories, 28

Feather, N. T., 71
Fishbein, Martin, 117, 118
FOMENT, 219
Forethought capability, 168
Formative research, 193
Framework for the Development of Competency-Based Curricula for Entry-Level Health Educators, 10
Freire, Paulo, 232
    background of, 233–234
Freire's model of adult education
    applications of, 240–242
    approach of, 234–236
    choosing educational methods for, 245

constructs of, 236–240
development of, 233–234
limitations of, 242–243
methodology, 232–233
phases of, 234
skill-building activity, unhealthy eating behaviors, 243–244
Freud, Anna, 141
Freud, Sigmund, 141, 165
Future of Public Health, 13
Future of the Public's Health in the 21st Century, 13–14

General adaptation syndrome, 28, 139–140
Gladwell, Malcolm, 212
Goal setting, 170, 173
Gross, Neal, 211

Haan, Norma, 141
Hardiness, 142, 148–150
Health
definitions of, 2–4
political dimensions of, 3
spiritual dimensions of, 3
Health behavior, defined, 5
Health belief model (HBM)
applications of, 78–80, 81, 82–83
choosing educational methods for, 84
constructs of, 72–77
development of, 70, 71–72
limitations of, 80–82
skill building activity, safer sex practices and use of, 82–83
Health-directed behaviors, 6
Health education
defined, 6–7
Freire's model and, 240–242
social marketing and, 197–198
theory of hardiness and, 148–150
theory of planned behavior and, 126, 127
theory of reasoned action and, 124–125
theory of sense of coherence and, 150–151
theory of stress and coping and, 148, 149
Health educators, responsibilities of, 10–14
Health literacy, defined, 23–24
Healthy People: The Surgeon General's Report on Health Promotion and Disease Prevention, 7

Healthy People 2000, 7
Healthy People 2010, 7
focus areas in, 8
leading health indicators, 8
Health programming, diffusion of innovations theory and, 219, 220
Health promotion
defined, 7, 9–10
Freire's model and, 240–242
social marketing and, 197–198
theory of hardiness and, 148–150
theory of planned behavior and, 126, 127
theory of reasoned action and, 124–125
theory of sense of coherence and, 150–151
theory of stress and coping and, 148, 149
Health-related behaviors, 6
Helping relationships, 97, 98
Hochbaum, Godfrey, 71
Holmes, Thomas, 140–141
Homophily, 216–217
Hygienic Laboratory, 3

Illness behaviors, 72
Indicators, 29
Informal education, 232
Information, defined, 22
Innovations
See also Diffusion of Innovations
attributes of, 213, 214
defined, 210, 218
types of, 213
Institute of Medicine, 13
International Conference on Health Promotion (1986), 4
Intervention mapping model, 40, 51–52

Jakarta Declaration on Leading Health Promotion into the 21st Century, 9
Joint Committee for the Development of Graduate-Level Preparation, 11
Joint Committee on Health Education and Promotion Terminology, 6, 9, 23

Kegels, Stephen, 71
Knowledge, 22, 168, 169, 170
Kobasa, Suzanne, 142
Kotler, Philip, 189

Laws of Imitation, The (Tarde), 211
Lazarus, Richard, 141
Learned Optimism (Seligman), 148
Learning theories, 117, 118, 165
Legislation, defined, 27
Levels of change, 99–100
Lewin, Kurt, 71
Life events (life change events), 143
Lobbying, defined, 27

Macro theories, 28
Maintenance stage, 94, 95
Manageability, 147
Marketing mix, 193
Meaningfulness, 147
Middle-range theories, 28
Model for Health Education Planning
    (MHEP), 40, 54
Model for Health Education Planning and
    Resource Development (MHEPRD), 40,
    55
Models
    Assessment Protocol for Excellence in Public
        Health (APEXPH), 40, 52–53
    CDCynergy, 41, 57–58
    Comprehensive Health Education Model
        (CHEM), 40, 53–54
    defined, 39
    differences between theories and, 39–41
    intervention mapping, 40, 51–52
    Model for Health Education Planning
        (MHEP), 40, 54
    Model for Health Education Planning and
        Resource Development (MHEPRD), 40,
        55
    Multilevel Approach to Community Health
        (MATCH), 40, 49–50
    other, 58
    PEN-3, 41, 55–57
    Planned Approach to Community Health
        (PATCH), 40, 46–49
    PRECEDE-PROCEED, 39, 40, 41–46,
        58–61
Motivation to comply, 121–122, 123
Multilevel Approach to Community Health
    (MATCH), 40, 49–50

National Association of County and City
    Health Officials (NACCHO)
    Assessment Protocol for Excellence in
    Public Health (APEXPH), 40,
    52–53
National Commission for Health Education
    Credentialing (NCHEC), 10
National Health Educator Competencies
    Update Project (CUP), 12, 40
National Institutes of Health, 3
Networking, defined, 26
Nonevents, 143
Normative beliefs, 121, 123

Opinion leaders, 217, 219
Optimism, 148
Organizations, 15–21
Ottawa Charter for Health Promotion, 4, 9
Outcome evaluations, 120–121, 123
Outcome expectancies, 169, 171
Outcome expectations, 169, 170–171

Partnership, 194, 197
Parsons, Talcott, 28
Pedagogy of the Oppressed (Freire), 232,
    233
PEN-3 model, 41, 55–57
Perceived barriers, 74, 76
Perceived behavioral control, 122, 124
Perceived benefits, 74, 76
Perceived power, 122, 124
Perceived relative advantage, 213, 214
Perceived severity, 73–74, 76
Perceived susceptibility, 73, 74, 76
Perceived threat, 74
Performance behavior theory, 72
Persistent life difficulties, 143
Pervasiveness, 213, 214
Place, 194, 196
Planned Approach to Community Health
    (PATCH), 40, 46–49
Policy, 194–195, 197
Policy development, defined, 27
Political dimensions of health, 3
Popular education, 232–233
Praxis, 236, 238, 239

PRECEDE-PROCEED model
  description of, 39, 40, 41–46
  example of using, 58–61
Precontemplation stage, 94, 95
Predisposing factors, 43
Preparation stage, 94, 95
Prevention
  See also under type of
  primary, 5
  secondary, 5
  tertiary, 5–6
Preventive (or health) behaviors, 72
Price, 193, 196
Primary appraisal, 143, 145
Primary prevention
  defined, 5
  health belief model and, 78–79, 80
  social cognitive theory and, 174–175
  transtheoretical model and, 101–102
Principles of Behavior Modification (Bandura), 166
Problematizing, 233
Problem-focused coping, 144, 145
Problem posing, 233
Prochaska, James, 93
Product, 193, 196
Professionalism, development of, 10–14
Promotion, 194, 196
Psychodynamic theory, 165
Public health, diffusion of innovations theory
  and, 220–221
Public Health Functions Steering Committee,
  13
Publics, 194, 196
Purse strings, 195, 197

Rahe, Richard, 140–141
Readiness to Change Questionnaire (RCQ), 94
Reappraisal, 144, 145
Recent life events, 143
Reciprocal determinism, 165
Reinforcement management, 96, 98
Reinforcement model, 71–72
Reinforcing factors, 43
Reinvention, 213, 214
Remote life events, 143
Response-based models of stress, 139, 153

Reversibility, 213, 214
Risk behaviors, defined, 6
Risk-taking model, 71
Rogers, Everett, 212
Role Delineation Project, 10
Role strains, 143
Rosenstock, Irwin, 71
Rotter, J. B., 71–72
Ryan, Bryce, 211

Secondary appraisal, 144, 145
Secondary prevention
  defined, 5
  health belief model and, 79–80, 81
  social cognitive theory and, 176–177
  transtheoretical model and, 102–103
Self-control, 170, 173
Self-efficacy
  health belief model and, 75, 77
  social cognitive theory and, 169–170, 172
  transtheoretical model and, 99
Self-Efficacy in Changing Societies (Bandura), 167
Self-efficacy in overcoming impediments, 170,
  172–173
Self-liberation, 96, 98
Self-reevaluation, 96, 97–98
Self-reflective capability, 168
Self-regulatory capability, 168
Seligman, Martin, 148
Selye, Hans, 28, 139–140
Sense of coherence, 142, 150–151
SHOWED model, 235, 236
Sick role behaviors, 72
Simmel, Georg, 211
Situational perception, 169, 171
Skills, defined, 23
SMART, 30–31, 58
Social cognitive theory (SCT), 28, 29
  applications of, 173–177
  choosing educational methods for, 179–180
  constructs of, 168–173
  development of, 164–167
  features of, 167–168
  limitations of, 177
  self-building activity, problem-solving skills
    and use of, 177–179

Social Foundations of Thought and Action (Bandura), 167
Social functioning theory, 28
Social learning theory (SLT). *See* Social cognitive theory
Social Learning Theory (Bandura), 167
Social liberation, 97, 99
Social marketing
    applications of, 197–198
    choosing educational methods for, 203–204
    constructs of, 192–197, 202, 203–204
    defined, 188
    development of, 189–190
    differences between commercial marketing and, 190–192
    limitations of, 199–200
    planning for, 192–193
    skill-building activity, physical activity promotion, 200–202
    stages of, 192
Social Marketing Assessment and Response Tool. *See* SMART
Social Marketing Institute, 190
Social Marketing in the 21st Century (Andreasen), 190
Social Marketing Quarterly, 190
Social networks, 217
Social norms, development of, 28
Social Readjustment Rating Scale, 140–141
Social reality, 237
Social support, 147–148
Social system, 216–217, 218
Society for Public Health Education (SOPHE), 10, 11, 14, 20
    CDCynergy, 41, 57–58
Society of State Directors of Health, Physical Education and Recreation (SSDHPER), 14–15, 20–21
Spiritual dimensions of health, 3
Stages of change, 94–95
Stages of Change Readiness and Treatment Eagerness Scale (SOCRATES), 94
Stages of change (SOC) model. See Transtheoretical model (TTM)
Stimulus control, 97, 98
Stress, defined, 139

Stress and coping, theories of
    applications of, 148–151
    choosing educational methods for, 155–156
    constructs of, 142–148
    development of, 139–142
    limitations of, 152
    skill-building activity, college students and use of, 152, 154
Stressors, 142, 145
Subjective expected utility model, 71
Subjective norm, 121, 123
Symbolizing capability, 167

Tarde, Gabriel, 211
Temptation, 99
Termination, 95
Tertiary prevention
    defined, 5–6
    transtheoretical model and, 102–103
Theories
    differences between models and, 39–41
    role of, 28–30
    value expectancy, 71–72
Theory of liberation education. *See* Freire's model of adult education
Theory of planned behavior (TPB)
    applications of, 126, 127
    choosing educational methods for, 130
    constructs of, 118–122, 124
    development of, 117–118
    limitations of, 126, 128
    role of, 116–117
    skill-building activity, condom use and use of, 128–131
Theory of reasoned action (TRA)
    applications of, 124–125
    choosing educational methods for, 130
    constructs of, 118–123
    development of, 117–118
    limitations of, 126, 128
    role of, 116–117
    skill-building activity, condom use and use of, 128–131
Time, 215, 218

Tipping Point: How Little Things Can Make a Big Difference, The (Gladwell), 212
Tolman, E. C., 72
Total quality improvement (TQI), 58
Trait theory, 165
Transactional model, 141–142, 153–154
Transformation, 236, 238, 239
Transtheoretical model (TTM)
  applications of, 100–103
  choosing educational methods for, 106–108
  constructs of, 94–100
  development of, 92–94
  limitations of, 103–104
  other name for, 93
  phases of interventions based on, 100
  skill building activity, smoking cessation and use of, 104–105
Type A personality, 142
Type B personality, 142

Understanding Attitudes and Predicting Social Behavior (Ajzen and Fishbein), 118
University of Rhode Island Change Assessment (URICA), 93

Value expectancy theories, 71–72, 117, 118
Values, defined, 25
Variables, 29
Vicarious capability, 167–168

Walters, Richard, 165–166
What You Can Change and What You Can't (Seligman), 148
Wiebe, G. D., 189
Wissler, Clark, 211
World Health Organization (WHO), definitions of
  health, 3–4
  health behavior 5
  health education, 6–7
  risk behaviors, 6